THE CLOUDED VISION

THE CLOUDED VISION
The Student Movement
in the United States
in the 1960s

DAVID L. WESTBY

Lewisburg
Bucknell University Press
London: Associated University Presses

378.198
W523

© 1976 by Associated University Presses, Inc.

Associated University Presses, Inc.
Cranbury, New Jersey 08512

Associated University Presses
108 New Bond Street
London W1Y OQX, England

Library of Congress Cataloging in Publication Data

Westby, David L 1929-
    The clouded vision.

    Bibliography: p.
    Includes index.
    1. Student movements—United States. 2. College students—United
States—Political activity. 3. United States—Social conditions—
1960-   I. Title.
LA229.W44   322.4'4'0973   74-4845
ISBN 0-8387-1521-4

PRINTED IN THE UNITED STATES OF AMERICA

for my children

CONTENTS

FOREWORD

This book deals with the student activism during the
1960s in American universities and colleges. But it is not
a mere description of demonstrations, seizure of dor-
mitories or administration buildings, sit-ins or mass ral-
lies. A merely descriptive account of these events now
would be just another addition to the already long list of
such publications.

David Westby's analysis is more than that. He presents
the essential facts and immediate chain of happenings.
But his main concern is to go beyond them and beyond
the immediate triggers for agitation, disturbances, and
other manifestations of activism. Westby's mode of
analysis leads him into search for underlying causes that
are not peculiar to this particular unrest alone, but are
endemic to the rise and development of such movements
in general. As such, what is presented in this book is not
dated, but is of lasting significance.

During the days of student rebellion, the public was
shocked by what was happening at the university campuses. The outburst overflowed to the streets, to national conventions of political parties in violent confrontation, to the national capital, resulting in mass arrests of
students. The torchbearers of these activities in once-
genteel institutions of higher learning were not academic

failures nor social misfits. They were, as Westby points out, academically among the cream of the crop and youth from reasonably prosperous "good" families. In almost unbelieving puzzlement, people were apprehensive. They wanted to know how and why such unheard-of outburst could be committed by youth in the envied citadels of learning, of all places—not just in one or two, but in institutions spread across the land. Parents apprehensive about the upbringing of their own growing offspring attributed the source of trouble to the "permissive" upbringing given the current college generation. Dr. Benjamin Spock, for example, reports receiving torn copies of his child-care book in the mail from parents, accompanied by angry expressions of protest for his "permissive" approach.

Educators, psychologists, and psychiatrists, as well as social scientists, responded to the outburst by their own respective diagnoses and antidotes. A host of articles and interviews appeared in professional journals and newspapers and on television screens. In view of general interest and apprehension, scholars in various fields of social science published more than the usual harvest of books on the topic.

Westby's aim in this book is to place the problem of student unrest in its broad perspective and to proceed to the analysis of the particulars within it. For the author, the basic underlying causes of social movements are the contradictions, inequities, imbalances in the social system, creating gaps between haves and have-nots, exploiter and exploited, privileged and underprivileged. These, in turn, give rise to strainful differentials in income, education, and civil rights. The problems that become focal issues in given times are related to these contradictions and imbalances.

The central issues that gave rise to student activism in the sixties were the civil rights of black people and the

Vietnam war, with the associated draft issue that engulfed the whole generation of young people. Of course, there were also local issues of peculiar interest on the campuses themselves, such as a student voice in running the university, greater freedom of expression, dormitory regulations—all of which can be subsumed under the demand for "participatory democracy." These issues undoubtedly had special appeal value to draw occasional participation from the main bulk of students who, as a general rule, are lacking in political consciousness and tradition.

Proceeding from a broad perspective, the author considers specific aspects of the movement. These include discussions of the social origins of the radical and humanist activists who served as spearheads; the tremendous rise in the size of the college population from a mere two percent before World War I to 40 percent of that age bracket in the 60s; a discussion and evaluation of confrontations between the activists and authorities. In the final chapter, Westby pulls together and extends the themes running through the book into a theory of the student movement.

In my opinion, a high point of the book is the chapter on the theories of the student movement, expounding and critically evaluating the major lines of thought offered in the way of explanation for the dynamics of radical student activism. Heretofore lacking, and therefore needed today more than just amassing additional data, is a conceptualization of student unrest free of the common shortcomings. Such a conceptualization should (a) put the problem first, as Westby does, within its proper societal setting (for such movements are not self-contained entities), and (b) free itself of the time-honored analogy between societal systems and bodily equilibrium (homeostasis). No matter in what disguised terminology and sophistication it is garbed, the equilibrium analogy is bound to view as "dysfunctional" any movement aiming to bring about structural changes that are considered deviant at the time.

This book lends support to the healthy current trend that decidedly turns away from considering social movements mainly in terms of mobs and crowds indulging in irrational, impulsive outbursts of violence and destruction. As long as the treatment of social movements was cast in terms of irresponsible collective actions, in the tradition of Gustave Le Bon, it was impossible to see their invariably patterned sequence. The patterned sequence of a movement has a beginning in its formation, prompted by common deprivation, frustration, and aspiration of a large number of human beings, which impel them to rally around specific issues to bring about the longed-for changes under a deliberate leadership committed to an ideology. It is in terms of the particular ideology (a system of guiding ideas) that the causes of ills and unrest are diagnosed. It is in terms of the particular ideology that the broad orientation of action is charted, that the modes of tactics (violent or nonviolent) and their timing are selected, and that the specifics of "consciousness raising" of participants and potential recruits from target people are studiously programmed. The effective leaders of great social movements, we learn from history, were not only instigators of collective actions, but at the same time the ones who knew how to put restraints on naked action when naked action was premature or suicidal. In short, collective actions are only so many episodes in a social movement, and not the whole of it, no matter how decisive they prove to be in the final outcome.

Miles Wolff's well-documented book on the Greensboro sit-ins gives a description that is relevant. As is well known, it was that sit-in at the Woolworth lunch counter on February 1, 1960, that started a whole wave of sit-ins within a few weeks and then spread like a prairie fire throughout the country—black and white. The first sit-in, staged by four black freshmen from Greensboro Agricultural and Technical College of North Carolina, was not an impulsive act undertaken on the spur of the moment. It was carefully premeditated, discussed for weeks beforehand. Their conduct at the sit-in and how they would respond to provocations were decided in detail. Far from being cocky, forward, and irresponsible during the actual sit-in, the freshmen were apprehensive and even scared. As one of them later said: "Sure we were scared. I suppose, if anyone had come behind me and yelled 'Boo,' I would have fallen off my seat." Similarly, we learn from Howard Zinn's book on SNCC that, before getting into action, the participants of early sit-ins were learning and practicing the tactics of nonviolence in the face of insults or arrest. For example, in Nashville, the instructions to sit-in demonstrators were: "Do show yourself friendly on the counter at all times . . . . Don't strike or curse back if attached. . . . Don't block entrances." In Orangeburg, South Carolina, "students held classes in nonviolence" in preparation for their participation in sit-ins and demonstrations.

A similar critique is applicable to the psychoanalytic account of collective action that is part of a social movement. The psychoanalytic account has special fascination in many circles. Its grip is still widespread in the psychiatric profession and among writers on social issues of our times. However, when a social movement is considered mainly as a problem of collective actions that serve for catharsis of pent-up frustrations or discharge of aggressive impulses inherent in original human nature (under circumstances when external authority breaks down for the internal censorship of super-ego is lifted), one loses sight altogether of the formation, mobilization, and planning sequence in a social movement.

The appeal of psychoanalytic accounts stems largely

from the motivational dynamics that they furnish for collective interaction. However, that appeal is made at the
expense of ignoring the motivational base for the participants in the social movement. A motivational base
(consisting, for example, of deprivation of food, shelter,
and means of livelihood; frustration caused by denial of
equal social rights or equal opportunity; passion toward
actualization of human aspirations) is the *necessary*
condition for the rise and development of a social
movement. But it is not in itself the *sufficient* condition.
The motivational base for interaction has to be supplemented by a conceptual base, which is an appropriate
ideology. The conceptual base provides short dictums,
slogans, and guidelines for rallying the participants, for
drawing lines of identification (self-consciousness), for
defining values and strategies to be accepted, and for rejection of notions and kinds of people to be excluded. In
short, leadership and organizing activities are involved.

A social movement is not simply a series of discon-
nected, sporadic, transitory, collective interactions comparable to hitting back at an aggressor in anger. In
many places, there have been sporadic bursts of peasant
violence and rebellion instigated by hunger and oppression. Of course, these may be harbingers of the shape of
things to come in the rise of a social movement. But by
themselves, they are not sufficient for the consolidation
of a movement. An appropriate conceptual base (ideology) is needed, which is the test and responsibility of
leadership.

Even when commentators on the student activism of
the 60s saw that there was more to be understood than
the outbreaks themselves, many had great difficulty in
comprehending what the motivational base of the activism could be. After all, on the whole, were not these
the more fortunate of our youth? What on earth
bothered them?

In order to understand the motivations, the psychology of social judgment is helpful. Westby touches such issues in discussing the income gap between different strata of the population. Whenever members of a politically and economically disadvantaged human group manage to actualize some improvement in income or opportunity, they become more determined to push their gains to their logical extension. At such persistence in their dissatisfaction in what seems an improvement, the more privileged strata above them respond in a typical way: "Why are they so pushy, so aggressive? We have given them a big helping hand. Where were they before? Now look where they have reached!" Such perspective reflects their own ethnocentric judgment, made with obvious condescension from their "superior" reference group, with all that it implies.

A convenient factual illustration is that of income differentials and the experience they are bound to arouse in groups at the lower end of the scale. The U.S. Bureau of Census reports that, since the end of World War II there has been a rise in the income level of both whites and nonwhites in absolute terms, but the big gap between the two has not narrowed. The income gap between whites and nonwhites remains constant. Westby calls attention to this fact that ". . .relative shares of income and wealth remained almost constant for vertically ordered strata." It is that gap which leads to dissatisfaction.

The stubborn gap in income levels and reactions to it are not unique to money matters. In fact, the generality of such gaps and reactions to them led social scientists to introduce the concept of "relative deprivation." "Relative deprivation" is a convenient label for a general phenomenon in social judgment that is related to one's choice of standards for comparison. It occurs in judgments of many dimensions important in society where gaps or differentials between human groups prevail.

In judging what we are, what we have, what our

standing is, what our rights are, what is the worth of our accomplishment, whether or not we feel satisfied with them, whether we should feel elated or frustrated with them, we do not use fixed absolute standards. Nor do we invariably choose the standard of those most like ourselves. True, we measure our standing in these respects relatively to others in our reference groups. But the general standing of our reference group in comparison to others is also at issue. If we find a gap between ourselves and others, we *could* attribute it to our own inferiority, which is indeed the typical explanation for the status of our group by "superior" groups and which they want to instill for perpetuation of practices as usual. However, if we see the gap instead as attributable to a more privileged group that is denying our equality in opportunity or hypocritically affirming our rights while witholding them, we will feel, not inferior, but angry and deprived. Therefore, it is altogether erroneous, for example, to expect a black person to settle for whatever improvement he may attain within the scale to which his reference group is restricted when the same society does not consider the ultimate sacrifice in war too great for him to make.

Likewise, when the black person in America saw one African nation after another achieving full national liberation in rapid succession, it became intolerable for him or her to acquiesce to any restrictions at home. The social comparisons made by people between their own reference group and other groups within their own country and on an international scope may be utilized by the social scientist as convenient indicators of underlying contradictions, imbalances, and gaps which, after a period of smoldering, emerge to the surface as a developing social movement, triggered by precipitating events and circumstances.

Muzafer Sherif

PREFACE

The decade of the 60s lies in the past, but the issues raised have demanded new perspectives on society, new analyses, new urgencies for self-examination. Among the shock waves that intruded on the complacency of the Eisenhower years, the sturdy reform-mindedness of the Kennedy interlude, and the heady early days of Lyndon Johnson was the revolt of the students. Scarcely anything, save perhaps the war itself and the black liberation struggle, so exercised the moral sense of Americans.

This volume is an attempt to pull together and analyze the materials dealing with the student movement in the U.S. The reader may well ask, "Still more on students?" There is reason, in my judgment, for yet another book on the subject, for the understanding revealed through these analyses is scarcely what one would expect if the state of public belief and sentiment, or of official pronouncement, is taken as a guide. Nor is the situation much different among academics themselves, whose treatises have often borne a heavy load of condemnation and denunciation.

Largely because of the intense ideological climate within which discussions of the American student movement have proceeded, it is important that exceptional care in the selection of materials be exercised. Accordingly, only those analyses that in my judgment are relatively free from ideological taint have been utilized. I hasten to add at once that saying this by no means implies acceptance of the positivist doctrine of ethical neutrality in the sense that research can be carried out in some "value-free" or "ethically neutral" way. I mean only that I rely primarily on materials that are empirical, in the sense of presenting and interpreting data of some sort, rather than being merely impressionistic or polemical. In other words, this work is based almost entirely on materials that satisfy relatively stringent criteria of evidence. This most decidedly does not mean that analyses I have found insightful have been eliminated from consideration. Facts never "speak for themselves"; rather, they always demand an interpretation.

It is, I think, particularly important for academics engaged in political analysis to make clear their location within the political mosaic. This is so because valuational undercurrents and subtle ideological identifications always suffuse political analyses (other than, perhaps, the sheerest factual or descriptive reporting). As the son of a working-class father who was a member (and in some ways a victim) of a labor union, I early acquired the values of the labor movement during its days of struggle, then watched the corruption and incorporation of much of it into the ideological mainstream during the Cold War years.

Despite the conservatism of sociology, during my student days in the 50s our discipline served to give depth to and reinforce these feelings rather than causing me to suppress or relinquish them. In some important measure this was due to my good fortune in having such teachers as Hans Gerth at Wisconsin, Don Martindale at Minnesota, and Bill Form at Michigan State, all critical and independent minds to whom I stand in heavy intellectual debt.

During the ferment of the 1960s I was in different ways involved with students who were becoming increasingly political, as academic adviser to student organizations and in various political organizations. Concurrently, in my work with graduate students, in graduate courses in sociological theory and political sociology, in directing master's theses and doctoral dissertations, and in a myriad of informal ways, it was increasingly obvious that major shifts in student expectations of and conceptions of sociology were occurring. This tendency, an aspect of the movement toward a new sociology (variously characterized as "radical" sociology, "reflexive" sociology, "humanistic" sociology, etc.), has been resisted at all levels of professional life and organization.

Beginning in the middle 60s, I had also conducted some sociological studies of political students, studies that became part of a burgeoning literature on the student movement. Not only my own research, but that of many others as well, seemed both to confirm my sense of where the center of gravity of student protest was and to challenge significantly the image of radical students that was emerging in the public media after the Berkeley affair. This volume thus represents a convergence of concerns and experiences both personal and professional. I can only hope that it will help illuminate the meaning of what has been an important political event in American society.

ACKNOWLEDGMENTS

I would like to thank the following for their permission to reprint copyrighted material:

American Psychological Association for one extract and two tables from Norma Haan, M. Brewster Smith and Jeanne Block, "Moral Reasoning of Young Adults: Political-Social Behavior, Family Background, and Personality .Correlates," *Journal of Personality and Social Psychology* 10, no. 3 (1968). Copyright 1968 by the American Psychological Association. Reprinted by permission.

Basic Books, Inc., for permission to quote from *Confrontation,* edited by Daniel Bell and Irving Kristol. Copyright © by National Affairs, Inc., 1969.

The Journal of Social Issues for excerpt from Armand L. Mauss, "The Lost Promise of Reconciliation: New Left vs. Old Left," *Journal of Social Issues* 27, no. 1 (1971).

Dr. Armand L. Mauss for his permission to quote from "The Lost Promise of Reconciliation: New Left vs. Old Left," *Journal of Social Issues* 27, no. 1 (1971).

Much of this volume was written in Europe, during which time my neglect of my family went, I am sure, beyond all bounds of reason. I take this opportunity to express my deep regrets, and promise that the next time around will be different.

I am especially indebted to Dave Gottleib of the University of Houston, Bob O'Conner of Penn State University, Jim Petras of the State University of New York at Binghampton, and Norb Wiley of the University of Illinois for their extremely useful criticisms and comments on earlier drafts of the manuscript, and to my friend and colleague Muzafer Sherif for his trenchant observations on a later one. Any errors of fact, judgment, or omission, of course, are mine alone.

In addition to the friends I have named above, I want to note that I have benefited from discussion of many of the issues dealt with herein with Howard Ehrlich, Frank Sim, George Theodorson, Alex Simirenko, Wells Keddie, Tony Pollitt, Al Sack, Kevin Mulcahy, Gary Sykes, Dick Braungart, Diane Herman, Greg Giebel, Paul Müller, Micheal Bauer, Janpeter Kob, Tore Lindbeck, Erik Allardt, Ulf Himmelstrand, Paavo Seppanen, Bob Rath, Joachim Isreal, and Marvin Hunt.

Special thanks go, as usual, to Blanch Thomson, whose patience in typing several drafts of the manuscript defies comprehension. For general facilities and encouragement I remain, as always, in the debt of Bob Mowitz and the Institute of Public Administration. Finally, thanks go to Tom Magner for supporting the typing of the final draft, and to Patricia Kidder, who did the job with such speed and competence.

THE CLOUDED VISION

1
SOCIAL MOVEMENTS
AND STUDENT REVOLT

The subject of this volume is the student movement as it
has been known in the United States in recent years. I
refer to the "student movement," not the "New Left,"
because I construe this analysis to encompass a broader
range of phenomena that what has ordinarily been
meant by "New Left." If the New Left was the relatively
organized sector of the student movement as represented by such groups as the Students for a Democratic Society (SDS) or, later on, its fragments, the student
movement encompasses a considerably broader category.
Quite a few of those who in one way or another either
participated in protest activities or identified with Left
principles or goals, could not reasonably be said to be of
the New Left. Indeed, many would explictly reject such
an identification. Many protest activities have had nothing to do with New Left organizations. In fact, the organized student Left has sometimes found itself clutch-
ing the coattails of spontaneously generated protest,
scampering after its own constituency, so to speak, in
order to catch up with it. The student movement, as I
conceive of it here, extended beyond New Left circles to

broader spheres of student life, milieux rooted in a rejection of American life that cannot be identified exclusively with the New Left.

Not only is student protest broader than the New Left; the New Left has itself by no means been confined to student circles, but from its earliest period embraced a number of radical or revolutionary groups that have had little or nothing to do with the campus, such as The Student Non-Violent Coordinating Committee and the Black Panthers. For this reason as well, the analysis of this volume cannot be correctly construed as being concerned strictly with the New Left. We should note, however, that insofar as the student Left has produced an *analysis* of American society, of education, of imperialism, or of itself, this has emanated from New Left circles. Indeed, one sense of "New Left" is its identification with a certain kind of analysis that, more than anything else, distinguishes it from the "Old Left."[1]

1. The matter of differences between Old and New Left is somewhat peripheral to the immediate *foci* of analyses of this volume, but I would nevertheless indicate the essentials that set them apart. A recent statement by Armand L. Mauss suits this purpose nicely:

By "Old Left" we shall mean a somewhat heterogeneous radical political movement which started early in the century but had its chief impact during the depression years of the 1930s and the war years of the 1940s. It included a number of small parties of Marxist, Fabian, and other left-wing persuasions, some militant labor organizations, and a number of outstanding intellectuals, many of whom are still very active (e.g., Irving Howe, Sidney Hook, Murray Kempton). The various segments of this movement seem to have had in common a commitment to a radical revision of the capitalist system (or even for some its complete overthrow), the establishment of some kind of socialist (or at least welfare) state, and a tendency to sympathize with new foreign political systems, such as that in Soviet Russia, which seemed to exemplify some of these ideals. Some of the participants in this movement looked to the Communist party for leadership, or even joined the party for a while. Many others affiliated with various socialist parties, and still others gave their support (and their pressure) to the Democratic party, seeing in the emerging New Deal a chance for the ultimate realization of many of their hopes. Class conflict and the acquisition of political power by the workers were key themes in

The place of protest within the larger complex of student political orientation is illustrated in Figure 1. In the nucleus are found members of organizations such as the Students for a Democratic Society. Highly ideological and even revolutionary, these students did indeed constitute a small part of the total student body. But they can be distinguished from the first ring not by their activism, but by the fact that they were organized. The first ring embraces sometime participants not so highly committed and generally not revolutionary, although they have been strongly opposed to the system. The line between

this older movement, but its Marxism became latent (or even anathema) as it developed a strong anti-Communist tendency, especially after World War II. Organizational expressions of the Old Left might range from the scarcely radical ADA, the NAACP, or the old CIO, to the somewhat more radical League for Industrial Democracy and the Socialist party (of Norman Thomas), all the way to at least the American Communist party (and its youthful affiliates mentioned above), though there are those Old Leftists who would wince at the inclusion of the Communists in their movement.

To the New Left, this older variety of radicalism has died out, sold out, or become irrelevant, and those perceived as the contemporary spokesmen for the Old Left are regarded impatiently as mere "meliorists" and "tired old liberals." Having had its birth and infancy in the civil rights movement of the late 1950s, the New Left began to take form as a much more broadly committed youth movement in the early 1960s, stressing not only civil rights and racial justice, but also militant opposition to the war in Vietnam. The new watchwords in foreign policy were to be "peace" instead of anti-communism, and the new domestic policy called not only for the elimination of poverty and suffering, but for the radical redistribution of political power and changes in the quality of life. At times, campus issues were especially important to the New Left, beginning with the Berkeley free speech movement several years ago, but the composition and programs of the New Left have gone far beyond students, student activism, and campus conflicts. Students have constituted a very important element in the New Left, but also important have been young political organizers who were non-students or ex-students, militant blacks, segments of the urban poor, and a great many young and not-so-young intellectuals. The chief organizational expressions of the New Left (also called The New Radicals, The Movement, etc.) have been the Students for a Democratic Society (SDS), the Student Non-Violent Coordinating Committee (now practically extinct), together with more ephemeral ad hoc organizations like the Vietnam Day Committee (VDC) and the Free Speech Movement (FSM). See Armand L. Mauss, "The Lost Promise of Reconciliation: New Left vs. Old Left," *The Journal of Social Issues* 27, no. 1 (1971): 4-5.

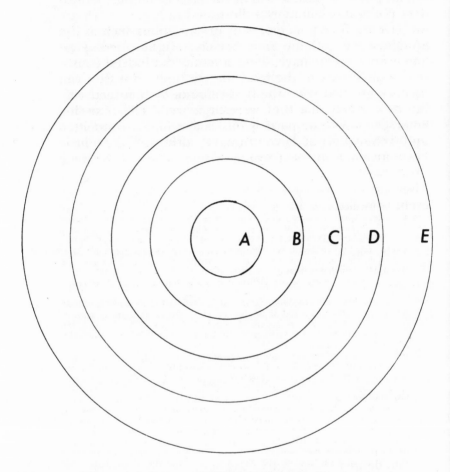

FIGURE 1

A. Organized Participants — Many New Left
B. Unorganized and Occasional Participants
C. Sympathetic Nonparticipants
D. Indifferent, Nonpolitical, Nonparticipants
E. Conservatives

the nucleus and the first ring is not a clear one. Many have moved into the nucleus and out again.

The second ring represents those sympathetic to the movement who for the most part have been opposed to the system or the way it is being run, but whose activities have been sporadic, periodic, or relatively unorganized. This category includes a wide spectrum of students ranging from those harboring sentiments of a rather traditional liberal sort to many with the most radical and uncompromising *ideas* about American society. The empirical composition of this category over time has fluctuated enormously.

Beyond ring two are those who are essentially indifferent to political matters.

The analysis presented in this volume is focused mainly on the participants—those falling in the core and the first ring—although I will have some things to say about the others by way of comparison. It is this group—core and first ring—that will be defined as the student movement. The ideologically sympathetic and indifferent have not been part of the movement; rather, they have constituted its potential constituency within academia.

What do we mean by a social movement? A recent textbook concludes an extensive discussion with the following definition:

> social movements are emergent ideological realities given social significance during periods of a consciousness of dysfunction, which provide referents for mobilization to bring about desired change within and/or of the social system.[2]

2. Gary B. Rush and R. Serge Denisoff, *Social and Political Movements* (New York: Appleton-Century-Crofts, 1971), p. 252.

Student protest in the 60s qualifies as a movement because it is an "ideological reality" with "social significance," acting during a period of "consciousness of dysfunction" and providing "referents for mobilization to bring about desired change." It has defined and attempted to analyze the nature of society and its own significance within society in ideal terms, has been socially recognized as a force, has proposed models of society as alternatives, and has attempted to change the system radically. Although there are many definitional complexities that could occupy us at length, I will deliberately avoid these and move forward to a delineation of those aspects of the student movement which will occupy our attention throughout the book. For more extensive treatment, the reader may refer to the many standard works on social movements.[3] Students of social movements have approached them from many different standpoints. A fruitful, if not completely comprehensive, analysis of the American student movement is possible within the rubric of the following four dimensions: (1) the social origins of movement participants; (2) the structural situation within which political consciousness arises and mobilization occurs; (3) the dynamics of confrontation; and (4) the societal drift of the movement. Beyond these particular facets of the movement lies a fifth problem, the master issue of propounding a satisfactory *theory* of the student movement that incorporates and unifies the empirical materials that define the movement dimensions indicated above.

The social origins of movement participants have always been considered fundamental to understanding the movements themselves. David Donald's analysis of the social backgrounds of participants in the abolitionist movement for instance, showed that their high-status old family Presbyterianism and Congregationalism, their

3. An extensive discussion utilizing much empirical material can be found in *ibid.*, chapters 4 and 5.

high levels of education, along with their economic conservatism, went a long way to explain their abolitionist
activities.[4] Studies of the composition of the Nationalist
Socialist Party in Germany prior to the election seem to
demonstrate that its membership was disproportionately
lower middle class and small town.[5] The social origins of
movement participants are particularly important under
conditions of high geographic and social mobility. Thus,
participants in the urban rebellions of the late 60s were
largely the young "second-generation" descendents of
migrants from the South.

The social origins of movement participants are important because of the way particular experiences are
communicated or made meaningful through family, class,
religious, or other milieux. Such "socialization" often
works in rather complex ways in creating predispositions
for participation in a social movement. Family and related experiences are probably especially important in
the case of youth movements, because they constitute a
relatively large part of the totality of experience of the
members. Unlike those involved in labor, feminist, race,
and other types of social movements, the young as a
whole have relatively little experience in societal institutions other than their families, the schools, and quite
possibly the churches. Economic, occupational, and political institutions, at least in capitalist societies, tend to be
somewhat beyond the immediate experience of the
young, as is much of the dense associational structure of
middle-class American life. I will address this question in
chapter 2.

The social origins of movement participants are not
usually sufficient grounds for an explanation of the
movement itself. Movements develop out of structural

4. See David Donald, "Abolitionism," in *Protest, Reform and Revolt*, ed. Joseph
Gusfield (New York: John Wiley & Sons, Inc., 1970).
5. See, for instance, Theodore Abel, *The Nazi Movement* (New York:
Prentice-Hall, Inc., 1938).

situations that may seem to bear little relation to the origins of those who create and participate in them. This is especially true of the student movement, located as it is within the academic setting and clearly standing in some relation to that setting. But the specific nature of this relationship (as well as the manner in which it relates to the social origins of participants) is in some doubt. Any casual perusal of the writings on the first question reveals that various aspects of the academic setting—bad teaching, paternalism, bureaucratization, the quality of the institution, and so on—have been frequently advanced as among the causes of student protest. In chapter 3 we will examine the various conditions within the university under which the mobilization of protest has occurred.

Much of the literature about any social movement deals with its politics, a rubric under which I include all questions of political strategy and tactics. The student movement has often expressed itself in tactics of "confrontation," a style of direct action that by-passes whatever existing channels of communication and influence exist or seem to exist. Confrontation has been the context of much of the violence and, more important, violent imagery associated with the movement in the public mind. Closely related to this is the question of the relation between the capacity to achieve movement goals and the employment of tactics inside or outside existing structures of law, administrative hierarchies, or normative constraints. Movements usually must deal with the problem of violence in two senses: as a tactic in achieving their goals, and as repression—means employed by those in power to quell the growth of the movement itself. In chapter 4 I will focus on the political process as it has unfolded within the campus milieu.

In a larger historical sense, the politics of a movement must be understood in terms of its growth and the relation of that growth to shifts in issues and styles of action.

The student movement progressed from its early period, when it was organized mainly around civil rights issues central to the black liberation movement, through opposition to the war and confrontation within the universities, and then began to decline organizationally. It is in this context that the question of movement ideology and its relationship to mobilization is best treated. These questions of development and change will occupy us in chapter 5.

The social origins of the movement, the academic situation in which it flourished, the nature of its politics, and its societal drift, then, are the dimensions upon which this analysis will focus. It should be understood that any such paradigm of analysis is selective in its way of viewing a movement; other paradigms are possible and, in the view of some, undoubtedly preferable.

In chapters 6 and 7 I will turn from the assembling of empirical evidence to the problem of theory. To what kinds of interpretations has the student movement given rise? To what extent are these interpretations consistent with the empirical evidence? Theory is the way in which we try to make ultimate sense of the body of evidence about the movement, the manner in which we will attempt to parsimoniously grasp what is essential about the movement in terms of themes that resonate within its several aspects.

Theoretical concerns, however, cannot be entirely deferred until later. Although detailed explication and criticism of the various theories that have been propounded to explain student revolt will not be presented here (rather, in chapter 6), it is of some importance to at least adumbrate for the reader the basic paradigm that will be advanced as an explanatory scheme.

In these chapters I will attempt to demonstrate that the several dimensions of the student movement in the 60s are explicable in terms of a descriptive characterization of industrial society that, from a structural standpoint, distinguishes between its generating core and responding periphery, and, from an underlying dynamic standpoint, identifies as a master (but by no means linear) trend the "disaccumulationist" tendencies of "post-industrial" capitalism. Disaccumulation, a neo-Marxian conception, focuses our attention on the consequences of an expansion of the productive system at a rate faster than that at which the market is able to absorb workers. This will be discussed in more detail later. At this point it will serve my purpose to confine discussion to the core-periphery paradigm.

In capitalist societies there is little doubt that the functioning of economic and political systems at the societal or national level is highly determinant of what goes on in other institutional spheres—family, church, education, leisure, and the like. This idea is basic not only to Marxism, but to much of more conventional social science as well. In fact, it lies at the core of our conception of industrial society generally, even though it requires some important modifications when applied to socialist societies. One may speak, in this sense, of a societal generating core, as against the periphery. By this I mean three interrelated things. First, the institutions of the generating core are generally determinant of the character or forms of other aspects of society, although reciprocal influences are present. This is surely true of corporation and state in the contemporary United States. Second, the activities within the generating core institutions, as well as the principles in accordance with which they are conducted, are the more highly valued ones. This is true of economic activity generally, and of profit-seeking economic activity in particular. Disciplined and systematic productive work, as Weber was among the earliest to understand, became during the late nineteenth and early twentieth centuries, the master value of large-scale economic enterprise. Noneconomic activities—religious, educational, aesthetic, etcetera —came increasingly to be relegated to second-rate status, less highly valued and less well rewarded. Third, the values appropriate to the generating core—"core values"—are more strongly institutionalized, that is to say, believed in and enforced, within the core than at the periphery. At the periphery, core values are more casually held; they penetrate to only a limited extent. This is in varying degrees true of welfare, medicine, education, and many professional worlds. Of course, there are substantial differences between capitalist societies. For example, medical practice is conducted in a much more businesslike manner in the U.S. than in any of the European capitalist societies. Here, the norm of profit competes powerfully with those of humanitarianism, service, and strictly professional dedication.

This point has been well stated by Parkin in his excellent study of participation in the British Campaign for Nuclear Disarmament (CND):

> Whilst it is true to say that the notion of capitalism generally implies not merely a particular type of economy but an entire social system, it is nevertheless within the framework of economic relationships that the defining characteristics of the system are at their most intrusive. The fields of commerce and private industrial enterprise are almost synonymous with capitalism in a way that teaching, medical and social work, scientific research and the like are not. The political radical's involvement in one of these latter occupations would therefore be a way of escaping direct implication in capitalist economic relations.[6]

To paraphrase, we might say that the values that so totally suffuse the core institutions of economy and state are significantly less salient in these other occupational spheres. One implication of this is that oppositional values are more likely to arise within the periphery than within the generating core. And this has indeed been true not only of the student movement, but of other contemporary movements as well.

6. Frank Parkin, *Middle-Class Radicalism* (New York: Praeger Publishers, Inc., 1968), p. 187.

More specifically, in the following chapters I will show that: (1) in terms of social origins, movement participants have stemmed from families organized about values that diverge sharply from those of the economic and political center; (2) in terms of facilitating conditions of mobilization in the colleges and universities, those institutions and curricula intellectually and ideologically most remote from the instrumental and "practical" concerns of the core have provided the most fertile conditions for student activism; (3) in terms of the actual dynamics of confrontation, student protest and violence have ironically grown out of alienating conditions of nonparticipation in precisely those spheres structurally closest to, but ideologically most "deviant" from, the core, where the *perceived* or *felt* powerlessness of students has been, accordingly, the greatest; and (4) the growth and decline of the movement is comprehensible only in terms of the variability of both cultural and organizational bases of mobilization, factors best formulated in terms of the relation between periphery and core.

The last point made above reflects the importance of rooting analysis of social movements historically, and this stricture will be implemented, particularly in later chapters. At this point, however, it is worth noting that questions having to do with historical continuities of American student protest can have little currency, since there has been little *direct* continuity between the period of the 30s and that of the 60s. Compared with many other countries, American students have developed little or no sense of political tradition, and during no period of American history can they be characterized as having exhibited any degree of collective will to power. This is so despite the fact that large numbers of students were mobilized during the depression as well as during the 60s.

The absence of political continuity between the 30s and 60s is most evident if one reflects on the fact that almost all of the organizations prominent during the 60s were new ones. Of 38 politically oriented organizations that have constituted the organizational universe of student protest activities in the twentieth century, only two, the Young Socialist Alliance (YSA) and the Students for a Democratic Society (SDS) were in existence continuously from the 30s into the 60s;[7] and the SDS, originally the student affiliate of the League for Industrial Democracy (LID) known as the Student League for Industrial Democracy (SLID), in effect repudiated the Old Left connections when it assumed its new designation. Insofar as any continuities may be said to have been present, they were for the most part mediated generationally. The offspring of old college radicals of the 30s acquired political identities that became activated on the campuses in the 60s and were particularly important during the vanguard phase of the movement (as we shall see in chapter 2). Continuity has been recognized most prominently in the so-called Red Diaper baby theory of the student movement, an interpretation that had some currency during the earlier days of the movement.

The absence of organizational continuity does not mean, however, that there have not been commonalities. Apparently unlike earlier periods during which campus conditions were the main targets of protest, the 30s and 60s were both times during which student *radicalism* developed and was mobilized mainly against high government policy, especially the issue of American involvement in foreign wars[8]. A second important issue focus during both periods had to do with civil rights

7. Philip G. Altbach, *Student Politics in America: A Historical Analysis* (New York: McGraw Hill, Inc., 1974), pp. 235-36.
8. See the discussion by S. M. Lipset and Everett Carll Ladd, Jr., "the Political Future of Activist Generations," in *The New Pilgrims: Youth Protest in Transition*, Philip G. Altbach and Robert S. Laufer (New York: David McKay Company, Inc., 1972), pp. 63-84. The authors cite the extensive *Literary Digest* survey of 1934-35, which indicated that 82 percent of those students polled would not bear arms if the U.S. were to invade another country, that 63 percent rejected a proposition holding that a superior military establishment in being was insurance against becoming involved in another war, and that 91 percent favored control of the armaments industry by the government. See pp. 68-69.

questions, a concern that has never, at least in the last four decades, been found absent from the campus, as the stormy controversy over the House Unamerican Activities Committee hearings in the Bay area in the early fifties and later protests against atmospheric nuclear testing demonstrate.

It may also be the case that the scope of the organized Left during the 30s and the 60s was roughly comparable. Lipset and Ladd, in fact, have suggested that the proportionate organizational involvement may well have been greater, or at least as great, during the earlier period.[9]

There exists a further parallel in the connections of students to the great underclass struggles that dominated the two epochs. Just as the students of the 60s took up the cause of the Black Liberation struggle, and in considerable degree learned their trade and earned their radical spurs in that crucible, their earlier counterparts were involved in the labor organizing efforts of the 30s.

It is my belief, however, that the salience of these commonalities is outweighed by the differences. First, the student groups of the 30s were all linked to adult organizations, and to a considerable extent their positions on issues and political activities were controlled, even dominated, by the latter. Related to this was the practical absence of profound feelings of generational alienation. Partly in consequence of these differences, the student movement of the 30s never developed along countercultural lines and never became oriented to activism in the ways that became so commonplace and to most, so uncomfortable, in the 60s. On all these points I think that the movement of the 60s has differed profoundly, and it is therefore a mistake to propose easy identification of the two.

9. Lipset and Ladd, p. 70.

A final comment. Except for certain specific matters, the protest of black students will not be subjected to independent analysis. This is not because black student protest has been unimportant; indeed, it assuredly has been, in terms of both its thrust in opening up the system of higher education, and serving as a tactical model and legitimizing agency for white radicals. For the most part black campus protest has developed independently—as an extension or outreach of the ghetto revolts—to open up opportunities specifically for blacks, and to a lesser extent for other minorities. This has given the campus politics of blacks *qua* blacks a very different cast from student protest generally. For example, it has been able to garner considerable faculty support, largely because, despite the rhetoric and confrontations, it has been a demand for social justice in harmony at least with received American abstract values, if not practices.

Black students have, of course, participated in the movement generally, although on a relatively small scale. Insofar as this has been the case, there seems to be no reason to separate them out for special treatment. Beyond this, white student radicals have sometimes attempted to legitimize themselves by becoming aligned with black campus insurgents, commonly with an outstanding lack of success. The latter, realizing this, and the dangers to their typically limited, reformist goals that such accommodations have represented, have ordinarily maintained an independent stance.

2
SOCIAL ORIGINS

In all societies the class structure is crucial for an understanding of social movements, especially in their early stages. This is so in the United States as elsewhere, but in some contrast to working-class movements, the effects of class structure on the student movement have been mediated in very important ways through the family. It is therefore in terms of the microcosm of the family that this analysis will begin. In this chapter I shall first show how the experiences of the early student activists, in particular, have differed from those of their peers with respect to (1) class and the class-related factors of (2) politics, (3) values, and (4) primary relationships, as these are mediated through the family. Following this I shall construct a portrait of the more or less modal character of the activists themselves.[1] The reader should keep in mind that this analysis applies primarily to the origins and early phases of the movement, the period of its

1. Unless otherwise indicated, I will employ the terms "radical," "activist," and "protester" interchangeably to refer to students on the Left who in one degree or another have been involved in the student movement. Wherever specific distinctions of meaning are necessary they are spelled out. Unless otherwise indicated, I will also use "student movement" and "movement" interchangeably.

genesis and growth, and less to its later stages. The decline of the movement after 1969 was coterminous with a shift in base and directions, matters to be considered in a later chapter.

Family and Social Class

It has never been a secret that student rebels have come overwhelmingly from middle-class backgrounds. In an important early study at the University of Chicago, Richard Flacks found that participants in a sit-in protesting release by the University to their draft boards of information regarding their class standing, were primarily from upper-status backgrounds.

> When compared with students who did not sit in, and with students who signed the anti-sit-in petition, the sit-in participants reported higher family incomes, higher levels of education for both fathers and mothers, overwhelmingly perceived themselves to be "upper-middle class."[2]

Similarly, Watts and Whittaker showed that participants in the Berkeley Free Speech Movement (FSM) in 1964, when compared with a cross-section of the student body, were much more likely to have come from homes where both mother and father had academic degrees.[3] And at Penn State University, Braungart and I found that participants in a Left-wing peace organization were overwhelmingly from upper-middle-class circumstances, quite in contrast to the members of the conservative Young Americans for Freedom (YAF) chapter at the same institution.[4]

2. Richard Flacks, "The Liberated Generation: An Exploration of the Root of Student Protest," *Journal of Social Issues* 23, no. 3 (1967): 65.
3. William Watts and David Whittaker, "Free Speech Advocates at Berkeley," *Journal of Applied Behavioral Science* 2 (January 1966): 53.
4. David Westby and Richard Braungart, "Class and Politics in the Family Backgrounds of Student Political Activists," *American Sociological Review* 31 (October 1965): 691.

All those who have approached the issue systematically agree on this point.[5] Keniston maintained that "a disproportionate number are drawn from professional and intellectual families of upper middle-class status."[6] And after an exhaustive review, Braungart concluded that

> left-wing student activists do not come from working-class radical homes, but instead from predominantly upper-middle-class homes where the father is highly educated and generally employed in a professional occupation, while...right-wing activists tend to be drawn from lower-middle and working-class homes.[7]

Braungart's analysis is particularly important because in it he compared an array of campus political organizations on ten campuses, thus circumventing the possible biases of single campus studies. Furthermore, he analyzed data taken not only from the Students for a Democratic Society (SDS) but from the Young Americans for Freedom and two traditional campus political organizations as well, the Young Democrats (YD) and Young Republicans (YR).[8] Because it was comprised of data systematically collected and analyzed for a range of campus political organizations, the Braungart study permits us to isolate social backgrounds specific to Left-wing radicals from those of politically involved students in general.

First, as the reader can see from Table 1, the conservative YAF members score consistently low on all class indicators, closely approximating the proportions found

5. See for example, Richard E. Peterson, "The Student Left in American Higher Education," *Daedalus* 97 (1968): 304, and Roger M. Kahn and William J. Bowers, "The Social Context of the Rank-and-File Student Activists: A Test of Four Hypotheses," *Sociology of Education* 43, no. 1 (Winter, 1970): 40-45.
6. Kenneth Keniston, "The Sources of Student Dissent," *Journal of Social Issues* 23, no. 3 (1967): 117.
7. Richard Braungart, *Family Status, Socialization and Student Politics,* (doctoral dissertation, Penn State University, 1969), p. 241.
8. Braungart, chap. 4.

to exist in the control group. Second, the two Left-wing organizations are seen to be very close with respect to all the indicators. Of particular interest is the fact that parents of Young Republicans are distributed in ways roughly similar to those of the Left groups, although their fathers' *educational achievements* are somewhat lower than, and their incomes substantially higher than, those of the SDS fathers.

This suggests that the membership of the YR is drawn from more or less traditional bastions of Republican strength—the upper-middle and upper classes, particularly the segments of these strata that depend less on educational achievement as such for attaining their level of affluence. For while the total proportion of YR members stemming from homes where the father holds a baccalaureate degree (46.9%) is about the same as for SDS and YD (49.2 and 45.4% respectively), the number holding advanced professional or other degrees is substantially smaller. To a considerable extent then, incomes of these YR families seem not to be dependent on the achievement of higher levels of education. Very likely they represent the more or less moderate conservatism of main-line Republicanism—what C. W. Mills years ago called "practical conservatism."

In this fashion the status situation of the YR's contrasts sharply with that of the ultra-conservative YAF, whose members are drawn from substantially lower class levels, as all three class indicators make clear. We may say that while SDS, YD, and YR members diverge greatly from the general pattern displayed by the student bodies as a whole, the YAFers are rather clearly representative of it. So, while early student radicals have been strongly middle-class in origin, this fact alone does not differentiate them very well from other politically oriented student groups of either liberal or conservative bent. Merely to establish the predominantly upper-middle-class origins of Left-wing student protesters does not,

Table 1

Class Factors in the Social Backgrounds of Members of Left and
Right-Wing Student Political Organizations (in percents)

Education

Father's Education	SDS	YD	Cont. Group	YR	YAF
	(230)	(99)	(452)	(105)	(201)
Grad. or Prof. degree	31.4	28.5	12.3	17.7	16.8
College Grad.	17.8	17.0	12.7	29.2	13.0
High School Grad., incl. partial coll.	36.4	35.5	50.9	36.3	44.7
less than H.S. Grad.	14.4	18.8	24.1	16.8	25.5

Occuption

Father's Occupation					
Higher white-collar	56.8	44.1	25.7	50.5	27.6
Lower white-collar	35.7	48.0	50.4	40.5	49.3
Blue-collar	7.5	7.9	23.9	8.8	23.1

Income

Father's Income					
over $20,000	16.5	15.2	12.8	28.6	15.9
$10,000-$20,000	41.3	39.3	43.4	40.0	28.8
$6,000-$10,000	31.3	31.3	31.9	30.9	38.3
under $6,000	10.9	14.2	11.9	10.5	17.0
Mean	$12,528	$12,668	$12,674	$14,981	$11,233

SOURCE: Adapted from Richard G. Braungart, *Family Status, Socialization, and Student Politics* dissertation, Penn State University, 1969), pp.
326 and 336. Data for the political groups were drawn from the total
memberships of each group at ten Eastern U.S. universities and col-

leges. Control group data were taken from general class attendance
at four of the ten.

therefore, greatly advance our understanding. It is, in
fact, only the starting point of serious analysis. For one
thing, at least some other student political activists of
quite different bent share these general class origins.
And for another, to speak of the upper middle class is to
invoke a vast stratum embracing millions of families,
thousands of occupations, and significant variations in
values.

Politics

Of particular importance for an understanding of
early student protest are the political backgrounds and
experience of youth. In this instance the popular view is
quite at variance with the facts. The view that student
protesters have been in revolt against their parents is
widespread, and has had its academic promulgators as
well. Whatever else the "generation gap" may mean, it
does not apply very well to the parental relations of radical students. Particularly insofar as this view applies
specifically to the *politics* of one's parents, it must for the
most part be held false. Many analyses have shown that
radicals share their parents' general political orientations, especially their fathers'.[9]

In the study mentioned above, Braungart and I found
that the solid majority of the parents of Left-wing students were politically to the Left—over 58 percent were
identified as either Democrats or Socialists. Furthermore, 29 percent were identified as Independents, and

9. Reasons for the general unlikelihood of politics as a vehicle for youth rebellion are discussed in Robert E. Lane, "Fathers and Sons: Foundations
of Political Belief," *American Sociological Review* (August 1959).

it must be inferred that many, if not most, of these were on the Left. The same situation holds for the Right-wing student activists, where 56 percent identified their fathers as either radical Right or as Republicans. Again, many of the 27 percent reported as Independents must be assumed to be on the Right. Thus, at least some degree of generational continuity is exhibited by perhaps 70 percent or more of student activists on both Left and Right, a fact that confounds at least one interpretation of the generation-in-revolt thesis.[10]

The conclusions of other studies are consistent with this. Flacks found that 60 percent of the Chicago activists who sat in reported their fathers to be either "highly liberal" or "Socialist."[11] Virtually identical findings have been presented by Lubell,[12] Keniston,[13] and Braungart.[14] And many Left-wing activists further report that this continuity of political values underlies the actual support for their radicalism they have received from their parents.[15]

These continuities are more than superficialities, as Flacks demonstrated in a direct analysis of the politics of the parents of Left-wing activists. His data showed that parental attitudes on a series of contemporary political issues were skewed very strongly in the direction of those of their children. For example, only 27 percent of the activists' fathers approved the bombing of Vietnam (in 1967), as against 80 percent of the fathers of nonactivists. Eighty percent approved of student participation in demonstrations, compared with 37 percent for those of nonactivists, and 57 percent approved of civil dis-

10. That of Lewis Feuer, in his *The Conflict of Generations* (New York: Basic Books, 1969).
11. Flacks, pp. 66-68.
12. Samuel Lubell, "That Generation Gap," *The Public Interest* (Fall 1968). Reprinted in *Confrontation: The Student Rebellion and the Universities*, ed. Daniel Bell and Irving Kristol, pp. 58-66.
13. Kenneth Keniston, *The Young Radicals* (New York: Harcourt Brace, 1968).
14. Braungart, chap. 7.
15. Frederick Soloman and Jacob Fishman, "Youth and Peace: A Psychological Study of Student Peace Demonstrators in Washington, D.C.," *Journal of Social Issues* 23, no. 3 (1967).

obedience in civil rights protests as against 23 percent of the nonactivist fathers. Only seven percent approved of congressional investigations of "unamerican activities," as against 20 percent of the nonactivist fathers.[16] Clearly, in terms of a range of significant issues, the politics of the fathers of activists have been both in the same direction as those of their children and quite distinct from those of adults in general.

All this should not, of course, be interpreted to mean that the political standards of the students are *identical* with those of their parents. When student activists have accused their parents of being "sell-outs," this has resulted not from significant differences in political beliefs, but because the parents have not *acted* on these beliefs.[17]

> The major conclusion to be drawn from a large number of studies in the United States and other countries is that *left-wing students are largely the children of left-wing or liberal parents.* The activists are more radical than their parents; but both parents and children are located on the same side of the spectrum. Conversely, studies of those active in conservative groupings, such as the Goldwaterite Young Americans for Freedom (YAF), indicate that they are largely from right-wing backgrounds. Students are more "idealistic" and "committed" than their parents—but generally in the same direction.[18]

Finally, we should note that all this is generally consistent with our knowledge of the form in which political beliefs and values are transmitted intergenerationally. Voluminous evidence demonstrates conclusively that children generally adopt the politics of their parents. In fact, it can be said that, at least for large aggregates, parental political orientations are the single best predictor of the politics of their children.[19] This is not to say that this general relationship cannot be modified by a variety

16. Flacks, "The Liberated Generation. . .," p. 67.
17. The case for this has been best put by Keniston. See *The Young Radicals.*
18. S. M. Lipset, "The Activists: A Profile," in Bell and Kristol, pp. 51-52.
19. See Fred Greenstein, *Children and Politics* (New Haven, Conn.: Yale University Press, 1965).

of other processes that complicate the "simple" experience of receiving the values of one's parents. Thus, upward social mobility tends to decrease the liberalism of
young adults, just as direct experiences of blatant and
especially *violent* injustices may move the conservatism of
some in a Leftward direction. But the general relationship is the most important; other modifying experiences
are probably best understood in its context.

The kind of middle-class families that are especially
conducive to activism can now be delineated more precisely: those that are educated and politically liberal or
radical. From a political standpoint it is a minority subtype within the middle class—a middle class that as a
whole is not politically liberal, but rather tends toward
conservatism, votes overwhelmingly Republican, and at
all crucial points stands in defense of the established
order. But the fact that such a "deviant" subtype can be
identified only piques our interest further. What do we
know about the values of these families that can help
advance our understanding of student protest?

Values

A highly disproportionate number of student activists
have come from homes that placed great emphasis on
cultural, aesthetic, and intellectual values. This has been
most convincingly demonstrated by Flacks,[20] who
showed that the families of student political activists
were overwhelmingly "humanist," by which he meant (1)
"a sincere concern for the social condition of others. . .,"
and (2) "a basic concern with individual development
and self-expression, with a spontaneous response to the
world."[21] Humanitarianism "is grounded in a compas-

20. Flacks, "Student Activists: Result, Not Revolt," *Psychology Today* 11, no. 1
(1967): 18-61.
21. *Ibid.*, p. 20.

sion and sympathy for the suffering of others, and outrage at institutions which deprive individuals or groups
at any level."[22] Concern with spontaneous self-
development leads to a stress on experimentation and
creativity, and often involves high degrees of involvement in intellectual activities.[23]

Humanist families consistently encourage appreciation
and understanding of art, literature, and music, and systematically expose their children to aesthetic
experiences—in museums, libraries, and concert halls as
well as at home. The activist students in Flacks's study
identified themselves as humanists much more frequently than did nonactivists.

A humanistic style of life represents not only an alternative to the dominant middle-class family but, to some
degree at least, stands in opposition to it. In contrast to
the humanistic variant, most middle-class families are
oriented to more conventional achievement values having to do mainly with success in occupational life, and in
particular in those occupations crucial to the functioning
of the instrumentally oriented institutions—business, industry, certain learned professions, government. Still,
humanist families stand opposed to dominant middle-
class values not so much because career conceptions and
the value of success are involved (in fact Flacks notes a
low association between activism-nonactivism and acceptance of success defined in occupational career terms),
but because of the specific conditions and assumptions
thought to be required for "normal" occupational
achievement. It is indeed a commonplace that the big
bureaucracies of business and government exact high
degrees of conformity as a condition of getting ahead,
and it is precisely this externally imposed (and in activists' terms, often irrational, in the sense of the ends
served and real consequences) control that is rejected by

22. *Ibid.*, p. 22.
23. *Ibid.*, pp. 20-21.

such humanist families. Such conditions of work—along with their increasing penetration into "private" spheres of life as well—are felt to deny the authenticity of individual expression. In fact, Flacks argued that this difference in life-orientation lies at the very core of the conflict between the dominant and humanistic variants of middle-class life. Other evidence supports these observations. Watts, Lynch, and Whittaker, in comparing a group of Berkeley activists to nonactivists, found much the same pattern.[24] And Keniston's discussion suggests strongly that the families of his "Vietnam Summer" (Summer 1967) radicals were clearly humanistic.[25]

Related to the humanistic value systems of these families is their general lack of involvement in organized religions. Although there has been an important minority segment of activists who have participated on religious grounds (particularly pacifists such as the Quakers, who have been mostly involved in the Peace Movement), the great majority of families are either nonreligious or practice a relatively secularized form of religion. The high proportion of Jewish students in the movement, in particular, has often been remarked upon, and a few observers have gone so far as actually to define it as basically a Jewish phenomena. Without going to such an extreme, one can readily assent to the argument that the traditional intellectualism of Judaist education, in conjunction with a traditional liberalism-radicalism associated with their social fate as a persecuted minority group in American life, is of great importance in understanding the disproportionate Jewish representation in political activity on the student Left.[26] And this high level of participation, I should add, is by no means

24. William A. Watts, Steve Lynch, and David Whittaker, "Alienation and Activism in Today's College-Age Youth," *Journal of Couns. Psychology* 16, no. 1 (1969): 1-7.
25. Keniston, *The Young Radicals.*
26. For a discussion see Nathan Glazer, "The Jewish Role in Student Activism," *Fortune* 79 (Jan.): 112-29.

merely a consequence of the fact that Jews are overrepresented in the American student population, for they have constituted a proportion of student activists far higher than would be expected on this basis alone.

This high proportion of Jewish youth in the movement seems even less problematic in the light of evidence that they differ hardly at all from non-Jewish participants. Block, Haan, and Smith tested Lipset's contention that the "permissive, maternally dominated movement is basically and uniquely Jewish," but were unable to find any supporting evidence.[27]

There is plenty of evidence supporting the contention that Left-wing political activists stem mostly from nonreligious homes. Braungart's and my analysis of the four campus political groups indicated strongly that about half of the SDS leadership in 1966 came from homes in which no religion whatever was practiced. This is based on the fact that fifty percent of this group reported that they did not attend church or synagogue during their high school years. At the same time this nonreligiosity characterized only 13 percent of the members of the YAF national leadership at the same time.[28] Although the relationship was weaker, essentially the same was suggested by Haan, Smith, and Block. Their analysis of FSM students showed that 32 percent came from Jewish homes and 24 percent from nonreligious ones, compared with figures of 19.3 and 16 percent, respectively, for their nonactivist control group.[29] The analyses of Watts, Lynch, and Whittaker lead to the same conclusion.[30] It seems clear that political activists have

27. Norma Haan, M. Brewster Smith, and Jeanne Block, "Moral Reasoning of Young Adults: Political-Social Behavior, Family Background, and Personality Correlates," *Journal of Pers. and Soc. Psych.* 10, no. 3 (1968): 183-201.
28. Westby and Braungart, "The Alienation of Generations and Status Politics: Alternative Explanations of Student Political Activism," in *Learning About Politics,* ed. Roberta Siegel (New York: Random House, Inc. 1970), pp. 476-89.
29. Haan, Smith, and Block, pp. 185-86.
30. Watts, Lynch, and Whittaker, pp. 3-4.

come disproportionately from nonreligious homes, and that a great many of those that have not, have experienced religious backgrounds of a relatively secularized nature.

This concludes the review of the roles of class, politics, and values in the backgrounds of activists. But these factors do not enter the consciousness and behavior of the young in any mechanical or automatic fashion. This occurs only through the everyday interactional drama within the family. We will next inquire into the manner in which the socialization of young radicals has occurred. How have these factors characterizing the upper-middle-class family, politically liberal or radical and humanistic in values, actually entered the experience of the young?

The Family

Americans have been greatly exercised over the matter of permissiveness versus discipline in child-rearing, a fact attested to by books like that of Dr. Spock. And this national preoccupation has been paralleled by a strong academic concern. Today, in a prevalent popular view, permissiveness and even Spock himself (especially since his trial) are assailed as responsible for the student radicals. How much truth is there in this?

Sociologists and others have for decades been studying family socialization patterns and, to some degree, the more recent research on student activists represents a continuation of this tradition. In a well-known paper, Arnold Green argued that a very important difference between middle-class and working-class ethnic (Polish-American) families lay in the form of discipline characteristic of each. The middle-class families, Green argued, used more verbal, manipulative techniques of gaining compliance, techniques typically incorporating a systematic offering and withdrawal of love as reward and punishment, while the working-class families resorted regularly to much more impulsive, physical punishments. In an even more famous treatment, Bronfenbrenner argued that there had been very strong trends away from direct physical punishment toward more "permissive" forms, and treated this development as a cultural movement accompanied by formation of various institutionalized agencies supportive of the trend. However, he also pointed out that great ambiguity and conflicting norms were often involved in actual socialization, with consequent high levels of inconsistency.[31] In general, the finding that middle-class and working-class norms of socialization differ in these respects has been supported by subsequent research.

The research literature dealing with the families of activists suggests that they cannot be understood simply in terms of permissiveness. Although there is a sense in which permissiveness is present in the life experience of the activists, it is one that cannot be grasped in the overly simple meaning that has often accompanied popular discussion. Typically, "permissiveness" connotes a strongly pejorative sense of an absence of "discipline" as a training principle. Most student activists, indeed, seem not to have been subjected to "discipline" in the sense of externally imposed rules enforced by sanctions or the threat of sanctions. Neither does it seem to be the case, on the other hand, that they have been raised independent of any guiding principles. In order to explain what is meant by this I will try to draw together the several elements that seem to constitute the unity of their experience. Fundamentally this is a pattern centering

31. Arnold Green, "The Middle-Class Male Child and Neurosis," in N. W. Bell and E. P. Vogel, *A Modern Introduction to the Family* (Glencoe, Illinois, Free Press, 1960), pp. 563-72; and Urie Bonfenbrenner, "Socialization and Social Class Through Time and Space," in E. E. Maccoby, T. M. Newcomb, and E. H. Hartley, eds. *Readings in Social Psychology* (New York: Holt, Rinehart and Co., 1958), pp. 400-425.

around the ideas of autonomy and independence training.

In the study mentioned earlier, Flacks analyzed the extent to which parents intervene in the affairs of their children. He asked the parents what they would do in two hypothetical situations—if their child dropped out of school, and if he or she were found to be living with a member of the opposite sex. In both cases the parents of the activist youth were much lower in their reported propensity to intervene than was true of parents of nonactivists.[32] Elsewhere, Flacks commented in a more general vein:

> Parents who scored high on this value (authenticity) viewed their children as autonomous individuals who must have the chance to realize their potentialities. Children of these parents always have been encouraged to make their own decisions, even if they violated parental standards of morality.[33]

An important aspect of autonomy is encouragement of open expression. In his Vietnam Summer study, Keniston found that the radicals' families had encouraged such openness:

> the dominant ethos of (activists') families is unusually equalitarian, permissive, "democratic," and highly individuated. More specifically, we might expect that these will be families where children talk back to their parents at the dinner table, where free dialogue and discussion of feelings is encouraged, and where "rational" solutions are sought to everyday family problems and conflicts. We would also expect that such families would place a high premium on self-expression and intellectual independence, encouraging their children to make up their own minds and to stand firm against group pressures.[34]

32. Flacks, "The Liberated Generation. . .," pp. 71-72.
33. Flacks, "Student Activists. . .," p. 22.
34. Keniston, *The Young Radicals*, p. 120.

A study of activists at Michigan State University revealed that Left-wing activists scored higher on independence from their families than either nonactivists or student government leaders.[35] And Braungart found that the same pattern characterized the families of the Left and Right campus groups. SDS members reported their homes to have been highly egalitarian, YAF members that theirs were much more authoritarian:

> our findings substantiated the plethora of empirical litera-
> ture that avers that leftist students tend to come from
> equalitarian or democratic upper-middle-class homes where
> argumentation or freedom of expression is permitted and
> encouraged.[36]

Interestingly, Braungart found also that student members of Young Democrats reported their parents to be permissive with regard to family *decision-making,* yet evidently experienced much less in the way of political argument with them.[37] Perhaps this is a factor of some importance in differentiating liberals from the radically predisposed. Quite possibly such routinized argumentation, expected and in a sense "required" in the home, encourages development of a toughness important for continuing radicalism, which must persist against strenuous opposition, threats, and repression.

It is interesting that in these families it is the role of the mother that has apparently been decisive. In his studies of alienated[38] and activist youth, Keniston found that in both situations the mother was more significant. In the case of alienated youth she was dominant and

35. George Paulus, *A Multivariate Analysis Study of Student Activist Leaders, Student Government Leaders, and Non-Activists* (Ph.D. dissertation, Michigan State University), p. 38.
36. Braungart, p. 239.
37. *Ibid.*
38. Keniston's earlier study of alienated youth is entitled *The Uncommitted* (New York: Harcourt Brace, 1965).

overprotective, and intruded regularly in the affairs of the developing child, tending to bind him to her in neurotic fashion. In the families of the activists, however, the mother was a force pressing him to greater autonomy and independence. Furthermore, these mothers themselves were often atypical, being much more frequently employed or otherwise involved in the world of social (not "social") or political affairs. And activists' mothers have very commonly worked in social service or humanitarian occupations such as education or social work. Thus, espousal of humanitarian values by these mothers occurred not in a rhetorical vacuum, but often in their work and activity.[39]

It is within the form of equalitarian and independence-oriented socialization that youth in humanistic families have assimilated the humanitarian values discussed earlier. The strength of these values—the stubbornness with which they are held, the depth to which they have clearly been implanted in some youth—is probably related to the intensity of this pattern of socialization. We do know from a variety of other studies that values come by through democratic process, through mutual problem-solving and equalitarian discussion, tend to become more firmly held than those inculcated by authority, which is to say, by order or exhortation.[40] The form in which humanitarian and

39. The place of the father in the lives of activists seems to be both more equivocal and somewhat peripheral. Many activists have apparently viewed their fathers as idealistic but rather ineffectual men who never really acted out their values. And the sons and daughters feel they must, at all costs, avoid this form of failure, which in its most intense form becomes hypocrisy. It may be that, although in these families relationships between parents tend to be quite equalitarian, the bourgeois pattern of radically distinct roles for husband and wife still makes itself felt to some degree. The bourgeois insistence on a radical separation of work and life tends to isolate the father from the "expressive" activities of the home and limit his role to the instrumental, occupational sphere.

40. See particularly the classic works of Lippitt and Piaget. Ronald Lippitt, "An Experimental Study of Authoritarian and Democratic Group Atmospheres: Studies in Topological and Vector Psychology," (Iowa City, Ia.: *University of Iowa Studies in Child Welfare* 16, no. 3 [1940]: 44-195; and Jean Piaget, *The Moral Judgment of the Child* [London: Routledge and Kegan Paul, 1932]).

democratic values have been introduced to youth in humanistic families seems to be consistent with the substance that is supposed to be learned. That is, these are *not* double-bind situations. The message that one desires to get across is not itself inherently contradicted by the manner of its presentation. This *would* be the case, for instance, where one *ordered* or insisted that a decision, or decisions in general, be arrived at by democratic discussion. Such situations are common, but apparently they have not been a very significant part of the learning experience of young radicals. For them, the process and the principles seem to have cohered and meshed in a way that avoided the frustrations ensuing from such a contradiction.

It has sometimes been claimed that relations between parents and children in these families have been characterized by high levels of intimacy.[41] By this is meant that the actual feelings and thoughts of both parents and children are, in principle and in fact, typically open, or "on the table"; it is the individual's capacity for self-disclosure that is involved. In consequence, there is presumably more valid knowledge of others as a working principle in the relationship. This is not, of course, to say that there are no conflicts, only that they tend to have been worked out openly rather than being suppressed (and perhaps, therefore, sublimated in different ways). Real knowledge of others is a condition of understanding them and, in the long run, of responding to them in authentic and meaningful ways.

So much for the theory. The extent to which we can generally characterize the families of student radicals in this fashion seems *prima facie* to be a matter of easy inference, given the other attributes already discussed. At least some of the evidence, however, suggests otherwise. For instance, Braungart's and my analysis of alienation among SDS and YAF members showed that on several

---

41. Keniston, *The Young Radicals,* and Flacks, "Student Activists. . ."

items YAF members reported somewhat greater closeness to their parents than did the SDSers. Fewer of the latter felt that they could "go and talk over. . .personal and emotional problems" with their parents. And fewer of them reported that their relationships with their fathers and mothers were "very close with much communication and mutual understanding."[42]

While such a sense of high alienation later is perhaps not necessarily inconsistent with independence training, it requires a rather tortuous explanation to make sense of it. One could argue that independence as a behavioral principle might in one way lead to greater alienation from parents, in the sense that it would not allow for intellectual or moral submission to one's parents. One consequence could, in some cases, be an enhanced sense of alienation—of distance or separation. But in this case the feeling of alienation might be expected to manifest itself later, after other influences had had an opportunity to exert themselves. Such an *ex post facto* argument, however, is not very convincing, at least in the absence of further confirming evidence.

Certain other findings having to do with differences *among* humanistically oriented families may help resolve this issue. Block and her colleagues compared "Activist" students with "Dissenters," the former being defined as those who not only protest actively but are also engaged in a variety of socially "constructive" activities, such as hospital volunteer work or tutoring, the "Dissenters" being uninvolved. Although the social and demographic characteristics of their backgrounds were virtually identical, Dissenters reported a lower affective quality in their relationships with their parents, and despite great emphasis on self-expression and individuality, a low valuation on their youthful privacy and secrecy needs. Those inconsistencies seemed to be the core of a relatively in-

42. Westby and Braungart, "The Alienation. . .," p. 482.

coherent pattern of socialization, resulting in greater rebellion against parents. Whereas

> the parents of Activists. . .see themselves and are seen by their children as functioning at more mature ego levels. . .than the parents of students with other political-social orientations [and] see their parents as preparing them to lead responsible, independent lives[;] this coherent set of expectations seems lacking in the Dissenters' perceptions of their parents.[43]

It is possible, although there is unfortunately no direct evidence, that variations in styles of protest have been linked to these differences in upbringing. More specifically, it may be that the incoherent, inconsistent pattern described by Block and her colleagues involves less intimacy and openness than the coherent one. The former type might more likely create alienated youth, the latter autonomous youth.

If this is correct, we may have at least the beginnings of an explanation of how emerging styles of protest have been related to early experiences. Although both patterns have occurred within humanist families, the distinction may make all the difference. Has this difference been reflected in tactical conflicts between those desiring confrontation and those wishing to avoid it? Between those who have become revolutionaries or counterculturists on the one hand, and those others who have elected to "work within the system" on the other? Who have been the creators of the participants in the violent fringe (especially the "Weathermen") that emerged following the Democratic National convention in 1968?

These considerations in general clearly suggest that many, possibly most activists have by no means been reared in a moral void, whether in the coherent or in-

---

43. Jeanne H. Block, Norma Haan, and M. Brewster Smith, "Socialization Correlates of Student Activism," *Journal of Soc. Issues* 25 (1969): 143-77. See also pp. 170-73.

coherent pattern. Development of independence in thought and action surely cannot be equated with the popular understanding of permissiveness.

The patterns I have been describing have, of course, often come early into conflict with the institutions of the world outside the family. Keniston relates how some of his subjects regularly had trouble with the schools over moral issues. Others have noted, in those families where some degree of religiosity was practiced, a common early disaffection. In any case, we should expect the youth reared in these circumstances would feel intensely alienated from the conventional practices of school, church, and other institutional repositories of conventionality. And, indeed, this is the case. Braungart and I found that about twice as many SDS (55%) as YAF members (27%) believed that most high school teachers were "more interested in their status and throwing their authority around than in actually relating to the students and trying to teach them something." And about the same proportions (46% versus 22%) agreed that their experiences in high school were generally frustrating and unpleasant. With respect to their capacity to relate to religious functionaries while in high school, only 16 percent of SDSers found in this relationship anything "meaningful, personal, or satisfying," as against 42 percent of YAF.[44] Accounts of high school students in revolt convey the flavor of these experiences in a most compelling and convincing way.[45]

It is probably the case that the sense of felt contradiction between the substantive values and democratic practices of the home on the one hand, and the experience of capricious, arbitrary, and sometimes violent authority in other spheres of experience, has been one important root of the radicalization process. The type of youth that these humanistic and democratic homes have tended to

44. Westby and Braungart, "The Alienation. . . ."
45. See, for instance, Marc Liberale and Tom Seligson, ed., *The High School Revolutionaries* (New York: Random House, Vintage Book, 1970).

produce is commonly the one that has the greatest difficulty in finding logical or psychological bases on which to adapt to or accept what seems to him or her unprincipled authority of institutions like the public schools. Individuals who learned to examine their own and others' behavior in terms of how it can or cannot be justified, and who continually question the basis of all sorts of practices and the authority that undergirds and enforces them, will find themselves involved in a myriad of conflicts and subject to all manner of formal and informal punishments. In this sense, the democratic humanistic home can be truly subversive of authority as it is exercised within schools, business, voluntary associations, churches, and other institutions. Such youth resist encroachments on their freedom because they have learned, and have had implanted in their basic behavioral expectations, the value of autonomy. To be the object of authority that seems unable to explain or justify itself grows intolerable. Those accustomed to discussing and arguing about the goodness or rightness of one's own and others' actions seem unbearably impertinent and threatening to the authorities they challenge, who tend to label them as chronic troublemakers or worse. Ultimately, such a challenge inevitably seems not only to challenge the operating principles of those in authority, but to mock the idealized abstractions of society on which they, their authority, and their organizations are held to rest.[46]

46. I emphasize here contradictions between the experience in the home and in other institutions. There is also evidence of strain within the families of activists themselves, often centering on the role of the father, as noted. Some fathers are rhetorically radical in principle, yet play the game on the terms of the system. Furthermore, these families are by no means immune either to the possibilities of a good life in material terms or to the importance of achievement in conventional terms. I suppose we might assume that, to the extent that these factors have been present in the families of activists-to-be, they have been sources of turmoil for the young. Specifically for activist youth, however, the literature does seem to show in a more definite, clear-cut way the sense of contradiction between the humanistic values of the home and the instrumental ones of the societal institutions.

But we are getting ahead of ourselves. We must now take a closer look at the activists themselves.

The Activists

All of these facts do not tell us a great deal about the character of student radicals themselves. Popular notions polarize at the extremes: those opposed have viewed radical students in terms of negative stereotypes —arrogant, violent, intolerant, and vicious—images reinforced by the media in both obvious and subtle ways, and even by presidential and vice-presidential rhetoric. The more or less liberal minority, on the other hand, has emphasized the idealism and humanitarianism of the students, though often condemning what are believed to be their methods.

The evidence having to do with the characters of radical students must be understood both apart from and in relation to their behavior: apart from it because it represents, in and of itself, a summation of their nature and of their view of themselves; related because their actions cannot be understood *in vacuo*. Under different conditions, characterological formations can be linked to many different sorts of action. Many an idealist has plundered and killed. But neither does this mean that we can make simple inferences from behavior back to character. And particularly because the media have often systematically distorted the meaning and intentions of activists in action by unrepresentative portrayals and other techniques, it is especially important to have empirically rounded and verified understanding of their characterological qualities. At least for the earlier activists, these qualities are about what we would expect, knowing what we do about the nature of their experience. Activists seem to have been set off from students in general by their personal sense of autonomy.

Personal autonomy means the capacity of the self to engage the world on its own terms through one's inner resources, without giving in to social pressures that compromise ideals, becoming narrowly or ideologically bound by dogmas, or becoming a prisoner of one's own conventionalized styles of action. In short, autonomy is the capacity to act freely. Paulus's study at Michigan State University revealed that the activists were more independent than the other two groups in terms of their susceptibility to influence from their parents or their peers.[47] Trent and Craise's comparison of FSM arrestees with a national sample of students and Berkeley seniors placed the FSM group considerably higher on a scale designed to determine the extent of their autonomy.[48] McCloskey's earlier study had already revealed greater self-confidence among liberals than among the other categories of his analysis.[49] Barron's instrument rated the Rhode Island SANE identifiers high on the achievement of independence and self-development,[50] and Baird's sample of over 5,000 students in 29 colleges and universities showed the activists to be more self-sufficient.[51] Keniston also emphasized the high degree of autonomy of the radicals he studied.[52]

A sense of autonomy among radicals is no more than one would expect, given the nature of their family experiences. Beyond this, however, student radicals have been rather clearly set off from students in general by their: (1) intellectualism, (2) system of moral values, (3) capacity for self-reflection, (4) expressiveness, and (5) re-

47. Paulus, *A Multivariate Analysis*. . . .
48. James W. Trent and Judith L. Craise, "Commitment and Conformity in the American College," *Journal of Social Issues* 23, no. 3 (1967).
49. Herbert McCloskey, "Conservatism and Personality" *Am. Pol. Sci. Rev.* 20.
50. Frank Barron, *Creativity and Psychological Health* (Princeton, N. J.: Van Nostrand, 1963).
51. Leonard L. Baird, "Who Protests: A Study of Student Activists," in Julian Foster and Durward Long, *Protest: Student Activism in America* (New York: William Morrow and Co., Inc., 1970), pp. 123-33.
52. Keniston, "The Sources . . . ."

lative lack of dogmation. All of these are more specific qualities related to the holistic idea of autonomy.

Intellectualism

Evidence dealing with intelligence and performance levels suggests that radicals have stood well above the student population in general.[53] This is so despite the fact that conventional measures of achievement may not represent their true capacity, since they often have not committed themselves to achievement within the conventional terms of the system, i.e., getting high grades. Furthermore, it seems also to be the case that Right-wing student activists have achieved relatively high grades (although perhaps somewhat lower than those on the Left).[54] It may be that their higher achievement results from their very *strong* commitment to the norms and practices of the university, and the articulation of these with the larger society. It has been shown, for example, that Right-wing students have exceptionally intense achievement motivations coupled with above-average achievement in conventional terms.[55] It may also be that the capacity to perform well has the effect, on both Left and Right, of freeing them from the academic grind to a greater extent than is possible for the average run of student, who must study harder and longer to keep up.

The sheer capacity for academic performance is in itself a rather narrow indicator of intellectualism. Yet, on other dimensions, the same pattern appears. Intellectualism as a value, contrary to the opinions of many, has had a high place in the radicals' scheme of things. For instance, in a study of activists at Boston University,

53. See, for instance, Braungart, Family. . .; Flacks, "The Liberated Generation. . .," and Frank Barron, *Creativity and Psychological Health.*
54. Braungart, p. 332.
55. Lawrence Shiff, "Dynamic Young Fogies: Rebels on the Right," *Transaction* (November 1966), pp. 31-36; and "The Obedient Rebels: Social Issues* 20, no. 4 (October 1964): 74-95.

Doress found that they scored highest in book ownership, in professing a personal search for truth, and in holding knowledge to be an end of life.[56]

In terms of specifically political knowledge, several analyses have shown radicals to be better informed than others. For example, this pattern appeared in Sack's analysis of a sample of Penn State students.[57] And some years ago McCloskey demonstrated the likelihood of a linear relationship between the degree of liberalism and political knowledge. In his analysis liberals, moderate liberals, moderate conservative, and conservatives scored in that order on a scale of political awareness.[58]

There is even some evidence that radicals may be more creative than students in general. In an analysis of students at the Rhode Island School of Design, Barron demonstrated that those favoring a "radical" position on nuclear testing scored much higher on a standarized test of creativity.[59] While this relationship is difficult to prove, it is certainly true that student radicals have tended to place a great *value* on creativity, and this is manifest in a variety of ways in aesthetics. Baird showed that the literary, artistic, and dramatic potentials of radicals were greater than those of others, that they displayed much greater competence in the arts, and that their level of interest in art was greater as well.[60] And in the analysis mentioned above, Doress found them to be more interested in music, modern art, the history of art, and art movies and least interested in Westerns and light entertainment in general.[61] The Vietnam Summer radicals in Keniston's study were deeply involved in the arts

56. Irvin Doress, *A Study of a Sampling of Boston Student Activists,* Doctoral Dissertation, Boston University, 1968, reported in Charles Hampden-Turner, *Radical Man* (Cambridge, Mass.: Shenkman, 1970), pp. 353.
57. Alan Sack, *General Support for Radical Student Politics* (Master's thesis, The Pennsylvania State University, 1970), p. 139.
58. McCloskey, "Conservatism and Personality."
59. Barron, *Creativity and Psychological Health.*
60. Baird, "Who Protests. . . ."
61. Doress, cited in Hampden-Turner, p. 353.

in various ways, and the same is maintained by Flacks for his Chicago demonstrators,[62] as measured by a scale tapping aestheticism from a more emotional perspective. In all, the evidence for a higher, more intense aesthetic competence and orientation of radical students is considerable.

Despite all this, it has been proposed that the evidence for the intellectual superiority of radical students is biased, a criticism based on the fact that many such analyses have relied on the self-reporting of grades. While this is a possibility, it remains unproved; virtually no evidence has been advanced in its support. Lipset, who raised the possibility in an 1968 essay, was able in 1970 to cite only one unpublished student paper in support.[63] And as I have emphasized, college grades indicate in any case only one dimension of intelligence or intellectual predisposition.

It is probably true, however, that the spread of radical sentiments among students (to be discussed later) has in later years had the effect of diluting the sharpness of the earlier relationship. If so, the significance would seem to lie not in the washing out of the relationship, but in the diffusion to other segments of the student body itself.

Moral Values

The place of ethical or moral systems in the lives of activists is especially important, in part because of frequent charges that radicals have been immoral and unethical in their manner of treating others, and fundamentally unprincipled in their attacks on the universities.[64] What, then, can be said of the ways in

62. Flacks, "The Liberated Generation. . . ."
63. Seymour M. Lipset, "Youth and Politics," in *Contemporary Social Problems*, 3d ed., ed. Robert K. Merton and Robert Nisbet (New York: Macmillan & Co., The Free Press, 1970), pp. 743-91.
64. Of course, evidence of the sort I am here presenting does not in itself necessarily imply that any particular kind or level of ethical or principled behavior must ensue: this would be to commit the crassest of sociological errors, that of assuming a 1:1 relationship between values and behavior.

which moral considerations enter into not only the plans and calculations of the radical young, but their thought and lives as well? A penetrating analysis of this question was carried out by Haan, Smith, and Block at Berkeley,[65] who analyzed the relationship between different types of moral judgment and other aspects of experience, utilizing the Kohlberg Moral Judgment Scale. This instrument specifies three general levels of moral judgment, each of which is further subdivided according to an age-developmental scheme, as given in Table 2. The pool of subjects used in the study consisted of San Francisco State and University of California students and Peace Corps Volunteers in training. Some of the University of California students were members of the Free Speech Movement who had been arrested in connection with events of the fall of 1964. The relationship between activism and moral judgment can be seen in Table 3. The reader will note that the University of California activists scored much higher, followed by the San Francisco State activists.

Haan, Smith, and Block then went on and performed a series of further analyses, finally concluding,

> Within these limitations and qualifications the results show strong associations between political protest, social action, and principled reasoning—qualified by the finding that pre-moral men also protest—and that young people of conventional moral reasoning are inactive.[66]

The three types displayed great differences in their basic orientations toward society. Those espousing a conventional morality reasoned from the standpoint of the maintainance of society, and perceived "the good" from *inside* society, as it were. Those whose mentality is one of "pre-moral reasoning," on the other hand, tend often to *reject* the status quo because it will often not be in line with their essentially instrumental view of relationships.

65. Hahn, Smith, and Block, "Moral Reasoning. . . ."
66. *Ibid,* p. 198.

However, pre-moralists differ from principled moralists, who also reject the existing order, in being unable to assume the standpoint of others—the condition underlying the fact that they evidently operate almost totally in instrumental ways. Principled reasoners are like the conventional ones in that they are capable of taking, and in fact do take, the standpoint of others. However, the authors argued that

Table 2

Classification of Moral Judgment Into
Levels and Stages of Development

Levels	Basis of Moral Judgment	Stages of Development
I	Premoral	Stage 1: Obedience and punishmen orientation. Egocentric deference t superior power or prestige, or trouble-avoiding set. Objective respons bility.
II	Moral value resides in external, quasi-physical happenings, in bad acts, or in quasi-physical needs rather than in persons and standards.	Stage 2: Instrumental Relativists (IR Naively egoistic orientation. Right actio is that instrumentally satisfying the self needs and occasionally others'. Aware ness of relativism of value to each actor needs and perspective. Naiv egalitarianism and orientation to ex change and reciprocity.
III	Conventional	Stage 3: Personal Concordance (PC Good-boy orientation. Orientation t approval and to pleasing and helpin others. Conformity to stereotypical im ages or majority of natural role be havior, and judgment by intentions.
	Moral value resides in performing good or right roles in maintaining the conventional order and	Stage 4: Law and Order (LO). Authorit and social-order maintaining orienta tion. Orientation to "doing duty" and t showing respect for authority and mair

the expectancies of others.

taining the given social order for its own sake. Regard for earned expectations of others.

Principled

Stage 5: Social Contract (SC). Contractual legalistic orientation. Recognition of an arbitrary element or starting point in rules or expectations for the sake of agreement. Duty defined in terms of contract, general avoidance of violations of the will or rights of others, and majority will and welfare.

Moral value resides in conformity by the self to shared or shareable standards, rights, or duties.

Stage 6: Individual Principles (IP). Conscience or principle orientation. Orientation not only to actually ordained social rules but to principles of choice involving appeal to logical universality and consistency. Orientation to conscience as a directing agent and to mutual respect and trust.

SOURCE: Hahn, Smith and Block, "Moral Reasoning of Young Adults." Political-Social Behavior, Family Background and Personality Correlation; *Journal of Personality and Social Psychology* 10, no. 3 (1968): 184.

TABLE 3

Distribution of Moral Types by Student Type*

Student Type	Pre-moral N	percent	Conventional N	percent	Principled N	percent	Total
Univ. of Cal. random	6	5	96	81	16	14	118
FSM Arrestees	1	13	15	28	31	59	59
Other Univ. of Cal.	0	0	34	79	9	21	43
San Fran. St. random	2	1	116	83	22	16	140
San Fran. St. Activist	2	5	24	60	114	35	40
Peace Corps	6	5	85	74	25	21	116

*Reconstructed by the author from data presented on p. 185 of Hahn, Smith and Block, "Moral Reasoning. . . . ."

the IP's sense of personal responsibility causes him to take roles in a double sense, not only understanding the position of others, but also questioning what he would have others do to him if the tables were turned. The highly developed sense of interpersonal obligation was reflected in the IP's description of the person he would like to be—sensitive, empathic, and altruistic or self-denying.[67]

The finding that activists tended to have a highly developed although unconventional manner of moral reasoning is supported by other research. Keniston's analysis is replete with instances of soul-searching among the radicals over moral issues, and leaves the reader with a sense of the high importance given moral principles as these inform or guide behavior toward others, particularly in the sense of fairness and justice. For example, when some of the secretaries on the Vietnam Summer project pointed out to the activists that they were not being treated justly, and in particular had been given no voice in project matters, the decision-making apparatus was immediately opened up to them and from then on they participated regularly. This experience, according to Keniston, was one of great import for the radicals and was assimilated quite consciously and deliberately into their process of self-examination.[68]

Such a sense of responsibility was brought out in McCloskey's study, in which liberals scored very high on a social responsibility scale: 47 percent were in the high range, as against 31 percent for moderate liberals, 22 percent for moderate conservatives, and 8 percent for extreme conservatives.[69] This suggests that the sense of

67. *Ibid*, pp. 199-200. An analysis of British and French students at the universities of Essex and St. Andrews in Great Britain and Montpelier in France provides very important and remarkable confirmation of these differences. In an able analysis, Robert O'Connor shows that most of those at all three institutions who were defined as "activists" exhibited post-conventional forms of moral reasoning. See his "Political Activism and Moral Reasoning: Political and Apolitical Students in Great Britain and France," *British J. of Pol. Sci.* 4: 53-78.
68. Keniston, *Young Radicals.*
69. McCloskey, p. 36.

responsibility among students on the Left has been partly the consequence of the substance of both radical and liberal ideology which, in contrast to conservative philosophy, places great emphasis on one's responsibility to eliminate or at least alleviate social injustice.

In this context one should understand the fact that radicals' moral systems reflect the values of the Left, and thus tend to be low in prejudice and to emphasize the theme of tolerance for others. McCloskey's research showed that liberals had hardly any contempt for weakness in others, and great tolerance for human frailty in general.[70] A study of student responses to the Cuban missile crisis disclosed that those favoring a hard line were more prejudiced than others.[71] The absence of ethnocentrism among radicals has been a rather obvious fact of their everyday lives—they have lived with and worked with blacks and other members of minority groups with a minimum of hang-ups (which is not to say, of course, that the relationships at the political level, say strategy vis-à-vis black militant students necessarily is congenial).

It must be said that the same cannot be said for sex role relations among radicals. Particularly in the early years, women in the movement found themselves typically relegated to the more menial, subordinate tasks, and found that the men often expected the conventional sex roles of the larger society to carry over into political activity. Many women, of course, revolted against this, and the resulting conflict was important in the genesis of the women's movement.[72]

The *general* pattern should not be allowed to obscure certain particulars. Along these lines, but more generally, the fact that the FSM arrestees in the Haan, Smith,

70. *Ibid.*, p. 38.
71. Mark Chesler and Richard Schmuck, "Student Reactions to the Cuban Missile Crisis and Public Dissent," *Pub. Op.* 2, no. 38 (Fall 1964).
72. For a discussion, see Marge Piercy, "The Grand Coolie Damn," in Robin Morgan, ed., *Sisterhood is Powerful* (New York: Vintage Books, 1970), pp. 421-37.

and Block study had the highest representation not only within the "principled" category, but in the "pre-moral" one as well, must also be noted. First, since their study was conducted at one institution, these figures—59 and 13 percent respectively—cannot be assumed to hold for activists generally. They may well have been higher or lower for this period. Second, neither can it be assumed that the later composition of the student movement was made up of any particular representation of these types. If anything, events suggest a decline in the numbers of principled and an increase in pre-moralist. There is, unfortunately, no evidence on this point, although it may be one of some importance for understanding the development and directions of the movement.

Self-awareness

The capacity to be aware of one's nature or of one's self is a highly variable one. Self-understanding, perhaps the most difficult of all forms of knowledge, has always been held up, by the great world religions and other systems of thought, as the very end of man's life. A quality characteristic of many student activists is that, although they may fall short in the matter of self-knowledge (who is to say, after all, when he has it?), they seem often to have esteemed its achievement as a value, and by various means have striven to increase their degree of understanding of themselves. Hampden-Turner makes the point that rap sessions, long group-discussion sessions, and the like, in which critical views are brought forward, are very similar to training groups ("T-groups") in their operative principles, and, in particular, in the manner in which they tend to force individuals to reconsider and reflect upon themselves in depth. The result of such experiences tends, at least in some instances, to be greater self-knowledge, in terms of grasping the real springs of one's actions, the real impressions one makes upon others, and the mechanisms by which one has covered up and papered over the basic conflicts in one's character.

The capacity for self-reflection has often been noted in the literature on activist students. Keniston found the Vietnam Summer radicals regularly holding themselves up for examination.[73] Barron's Rhode Island students scored low on a scale of extroversion (thus, inversely, were high on introspection),[74] Doress's Boston students exhibited a high rate of "self-discovery,"[75] and the relative openness of activists to criticism by others has been discussed by Flacks and Hampden-Turner.[76]

Again, these findings must be qualified. The trend of a certain segment of the movement in later years was doubtless away from such a reflective capacity, as some of the more publicized events at least seem to confirm. However, such characterizations must be made with great care. If restricted to Weathermen, "crazies," or other similar groups, an easy *prima facie* case can indeed to be made. If, however, it incorporates a broader delineation of activists, it must be questioned. In fact, the

73. Keniston, *The Young Radicals.*
74. Barron, *Creativity and Psychological Health.*
75. Doress, cited in Hampden-Turner, p. 353.
76. Flacks, "The Liberated Generation. . ."; and Hampden-Turner, *Radical Man* chap. 12. Is it necessary to note that the qualities of self-awareness and openness have little in common with the totalitarian technique of "self-criticism"? Many of those subjected to political trial in Russian courts, especially during the Stalinist period, have been made to be "self-critical" and not merely ones of "crime," but to renounce one's self by means of the self-critical confession. In so doing, the individual, in the name of the state, in effect renounces himself as a person, and makes himself into a nonentity that may then be casually scrapped. Other totalitarian systems have indulged in similar practices. This form of self-criticism is fundamentally unlike that which we are talking about. First, its object is to destroy the individual rather than to authenticate him. Second, it is practiced *on* individuals by others of much greater power, rather than by free individuals upon themselves. And, third, it exists to validate the ideological primacy and infallibility of the state, thus demonstrating to all, through terror, its capacity to overwhelm the individual. The self-awareness of the autonomous individual arises freely (although various forms of assistance may be employed—psychiatrists, T-groups, etc.—in the consciousness of the individual and ideally acts to free one for less conflictful relationships rather than to destroy.

failures of the movement up through 1968 probably brought into being, within some circles at least, a more reflective and more analytical concern over the relation of individuals and their groups and organizations to society.

Impulse Control

Related to self-awareness is the matter of self-control. Christian culture, especially its more fundamentalist Protestant variant, has to a large extent taken the form of impulse control in relation to the possibilities of sin. This complex of beliefs, rituals, and character traits was systematically analyzed by Max Weber, who referred to it as the "Protestant Ethic."[77] The appellation has stuck and the "Protestant Ethic," along with the id, the ego, and the superego, has long since passed into popular parlance. The highly developed expressiveness of the counter-culture opposes, often in highly deliberate fashion, the principle of self-control as a behavioral norm. But the "hippies" have no corner on expressiveness. Self-expression and impulse gratification as a fact and as a value have been central in the life-concerns of politically activist youth. This has been given particular emphasis by Flacks:

> Moralism and self-control were measured by studying implicit systems of morality, especially in the areas of sexual and other forms of personal expression. Students who scored highest in this category indicated an adherence to a control-dominated moralism and an inflexible personal approach to morality centered around absolute right and wrong. The low scoring end was for students who rejected conventional morality and who believed in free expression of impulses and emotions. Scores of non-activist students, obviously, were much higher than those of the

77. Max Weber, *The Protestant Ethic and the Spirit of Capitalism,* trans. Talcott Parsons (New York: Scribners, 1929).

activists. . . .This rating is powerfully related to activism in students and appears to be *at the core of value differences between the parents of activists and non-activists*.[78] (emphasis added)

The similarity in this respect between counter-cultural "drop-outs" and political activists has elicited this observation of Theodore Roszack:

> Beat-hip bohemianism may be too withdrawn from social action to suit New Left radicalism; but the withdrawal is in a direction the activists can readily understand. The "trip" is inward, toward deeper levels of self-examination. . . . One can discern, then, a continuum of thought and experience among the young which links together the New Left sociology of Mills, the Freudian Marxism of Herbert Marcuse, the gestalt-therapy of Paul Goodman, the apocalyptic body-mysticism of Norman Brown, the Zen-based psychotherapy of Alan Watts, and finally Timothy Leary's occult narcissism.[79]

In other words, student activists have tended to be expressive, and to set a high value on self-expression.

Impulse control in the West has historically been associated with the phenomenon of guilt. Only through self-control have Christians (especially the Calvinists, Lutherans, and similar types) avoided sin; by renunciation of the pleasures of the senses and, to some extent, of the mind as well. The psychological result of sin is guilt. Therefore guilt is linked to self-control in a most fundamental way: one controls the expression of one's impulses. This ridiculously brief characterization is intended only to point up the meaning of much principled expressiveness, directed as it is precisely against a culture that places a high value on self-control, and one in which achievement and advancement, in particular, are often linked to an ideal of the self-controlled man.

78. Flacks, "Student Activists. . . ." p. 21.
79. Theodore Roszak, *The Making of a Counter Culture* (New York: Doubleday Anchor Books, 1969), pp. 63-4.

It is therefore of some importance to note that young political activists have displayed very little in the way of guilt formation. The liberals in McCloskey's study scored lowest on a scale intended to identify the presence of guilt.[80] Doress reported that the Boston activists were the freest and most spontaneous in public situations and the least likely to suppress rebellious feelings.[81] Keniston characterized the Vietnam Summer leaders as highly spontaneous and expressive as they carried out their work[82] FSM arrestees in Trent and Craise's study scored highest on a scale of impulse expression.[83] Observations of this sort are to be found throughout the literature on student activists.

Dogmatism

It remains to consider the matter of dogmatism. It is a common notion, often maintained in the scholarly world, that radicals of the Left as well as the Right are dogmatic ideologues, and there is no doubt whatever that in many circumstances this has been true; e.g., Communists operating in hostile capitalist societies. However, the student Left is not the Old Left, and as everyone knows, or certainly ought to know, they have not had a great deal in common. Doress compared English student Communists with the groups in his Boston sample and found that they scored even higher on a subscale of the Rokeach Dogmatism Scale than did the Right-wing Americans.[84] The Boston University activists scored lowest of all. This fact alone points up the fallacy of attempting to cover all the Left with a single blanket (the same stricture, of course, holds for the Right; remember the differences between traditional conservatives who

80. McCloskey, p. 36.
81. Doress in Hampden-Turner, p. 351.
82. Keniston, *Young Radicals.*
83. Trent and Craise, "Commitment and Conformity...."
84. Doress, cited in Hampden-Turner, chapter 9.

were members of the Young Republicans and the "radical" conservatives of YAF mentioned earlier, a reflection of larger societal realities).

In fact, research on student activists shows them to be relatively undogmatic, and actually quite flexible across a variety of situations. The conservative students studied by Chesler and Schmuck in connection with the Cuban missile crisis were more dogmatic than those who took the Left-wing position.[85] And the work of others such as Keniston, Doress, and McCloskey revealed the same, that Left radicals (and liberals) have been consistently less dogmatic than *any* others, whether politically inactive or on the right. Watts and Whittaker made a distinction between rigidity and commitment, and argued that seeming rigidity often actually reflects not dogmatism, but the persistence with which radicals have fought for their ideals. Such stubbornness does not necessarily represent an intellectual or behavioral rigidity but, rather, a depth of commitment. They showed that radicals in fact exhibited a high level of ability in shifting frames of reference in their thought and for considering the viewpoints of others. Commitment to a cause, in short, is not necessarily accompanied by intellectual dogmatism.[86]

All this, of course, does not deny that there have been plenty of dogmatics in the movement, only that movement participants cannot generally be characterized as dogmatic. Neither does it deny the seeming trend toward increasing dogmatism among segments of the movement in the later period. Insofar as such segments have experienced increasingly attenuated ties to society and have lived an increasingly encapsulated existence, increased dogmatism has quite likely resulted.

Radicals have been charged with being dogmatic because both the style and substance of their protest became unbearably threatening to those they attacked. To

85. Chesler and Schmuck, "Student Reactions. . . ."
86. Watts and Whittaker.

insist on challenging the basic premises of the war was, in particular, for years regarded as unthinkable. To insist on a voice in university government is not necessarily dogmatic, but a simple assertion of rights. Radicals have seemed dogmatic primarily when viewed from on high, by those whose positions and interests have been challenged.

Authoritarianism and Autonomy

These qualities need not be understood merely as an array of isolated traits, but rather as a syndrome of interrelated personality functions defining a total world view and approach to life. Such an analysis exists in the study of authoritarianism.

Scientific analysis of authoritarianism in modern social science was begun by some of the members of the so-called Frankfurt School, which existed at Frankfurt University in Weimar Germany and was eliminated under Hitler, but has shown a great resurgence in the postwar-years.[87] Research into authoritarianism was the direct result of the Nazi experience, and was an attempt to find the roots in personality that proved so receptive to Nazi appeals. The fruits of this study were brought together in the volume *The Authoritarian Personality*, by Theodor Adorno, Else Frankel-Brunswick, and their colleagues.[88] In the main, the research demonstrated the existence of a closely related set of personality characteristics centering around the need either to submit to or assert one's power over others. That is, authoritarians were shown to be those who, depending on the situation, usually oriented themselves to authority—those who, as it were, reduced their fears and anxieties through im-

87. Two important contemporary representatives of this tradition are Jürgen Habermas in sociology and Herbert Marcuse in philosophy.
88. Theodore Adorno and Else Frankel-Brunswick, *The Authoritarian Personality* (New York: Harper, 1950).

mersion in an authoritarian system, as did so many Germans in the 1930s.[89]

To thus embrace authority involves a complex of personality characteristics. Authoritarians tend to be intellectually rigid, are unable to give serious, real consideration to positions other than their own. They generally lack the capacity for introspection, thus are more likely to be attracted to totalistic, authoritarian creeds as a king of externalization of the self. They tend to be compulsively orderly; disarray in anything is highly disconcerting to them. They exhibit a lack of personal capacity for independent action, needing the guides of unambiguous moral systems or the directives of others in order to act. Thus they make good, or perhaps one should say dutiful, bureaucrats. They tend to be cynical, pessimistic, and highly puritanical. They exhibit high levels of prejudice toward minority groups, and are intolerant of them, sometimes even of their very existence. They have little feeling for others, especially the poor or oppressed, tending to hold them in contempt because they are weak.

There have been frequent charges that radical students represent a kind of authoritarianism akin to Nazism, an authoritarianism that is at least implicit in their actions and demands. Louis Halle, for instance, has characterized the movement as a "drive to destruction."[90] Peter Berger finds that "one is confronted by an ideological constellation that strikingly resembles the common core of Italian and German fascism."[91] The issue is of great importance because of the fact that many revolutions made in the name of

89. For a rather different analysis that nevertheless emphasizes the authoritarian problem, see Erich Fromm, *Escape From Freedom* (New York: Rinehart & Co., 1941).

90. Louis Halle, "The Student Drive to Destruction," *New Republic* 159 (1969): 10-13.

91. Peter L. Berger, "Between System and Horde," in Peter L. Berger and Richard J. Neuhaus, *Movement and Revolution* (New York: Doubleday, Anchor Books, 1970).

freedom and justice have crystallized into authoritarian forms of social order controlled by authoritarian men. Have student radicals, then, been essentially destructive totalitarians who would transform our society into an authoritarian order? Or, alternatively, despite their "idealism," has there been an inherent jacobinism in their movement that prefigures such an order? These are questions that many would regard as having become largely academic in the 1970s with the demise of the movement. It is worth noting, however, that despite the shift after the 1968 election to violent rhetoric and action by some, it remains questionable whether this represented even then the center of gravity of the movement. The bulk of the more or less systematic evidence clearly suggests that the student movement has not been rooted in the authoritarian impulses as was true of Nazism. And New Left literature has, with some exceptions, been generally egalitarian and has displayed a sensitivity to the problems of institutionalized authority that beset socialism almost everywhere. In fact, these fears were generally so powerful in the movement that firm organizational structures were never created, but were effectively inhibited by the powerful anarchist ethos in which the movement was always grounded.

In connection with all such evidence having to do with the qualities of activists, a potentially powerful criticism has been raised. It has been argued that these "positive" characterizations reflect the bias of investigators—social scientists who are mostly liberal academicians holding precisely these values.[92] If so, it is a thoroughgoing indictment of contemporary social science, ironically emanating from the pole politically opposite the usual source of criticisms of liberal social science—the far Left. While there is little doubt that many social scientists have

92. See, for instance, Richard Blum, "Epilogue: Students and Drugs," in Richard Blum and Associates, *Students and Drugs,* Drugs II.

taken up such studies out of a sense of identification with activist youth, who seem to embody their own values, it does not thereby follow that their research is systematically biased. In fact, the mass of data, in its considerable consistency, suggests that it is not. Until some evidence supporting this line of criticism is advanced, we have only a choice between an interesting hypothesis and a substantial aggregate of data.

A Comparative Note

Whether these aspects of personality are limited to Left-wing radicals or are characteristic of activists generally is something about which we know little, mainly because so little research on the Right has been conducted. We have already noted that YAF members described their family relationships as even closer than those of SDS members. Kerpelman, in an analysis of Left, Middle, and Right activists and nonactivists found that

> all student activists, no matter what their ideology, are less needful of support and nurturance, value leadership more, are more socially ascendant and assertive, and are more sociable than students who are not politically active.[93]

However, Shiff's earlier work suggested otherwise. The YAF members in his sample were authoritarian, insecure, anxiety-prone, less open, and dogmatic.[94] The question remains unresolved.

Latent Radicalism

By no means all of those with radical views become activists. From both general sociological and political

93. Larry C. Kerpelman, *Student Activism and Ideology in Higher Educational Institutions* (Washington, D.C., Bureau of Research, Office of Research U.S. Department of Health, Education and Welfare, March, 1970), p. 85.
94. Shiff; also see David Westby and Richard Braungart, "Activists and the History of the Future," in Foster and Long, *Protest!*, pp. 158-83.

standpoints this is an important question, for it touches the matter of recruitment and more generally of active citizen participation. While there has been a good deal of analysis of the general conditions of political participation, and even of participation in radical movements, there is little understanding of those who hold radical ideas yet decline to participate. Recently, Sack's analysis has thrown some light on the question. Utilizing a three percent sample of the Pennsylvania State University student body in 1968, Sack analyzed a series of items discriminating, first, the degree of radicalism, and second, the extent of participation in movement activities, such as involvement in picketing, protest marches, and civil disobedience. This permitted him to discriminate between radical and moderate activists and nonactivists. Of the 552 usable schedules, Sack found that of 54 who satisfied the ideological criterion for radicalism, only 24, or 44 percent, reported any actual activity. This 24 consituted only 4.4 percent of the sample. However, the sample also yielded 39 who expressed only relatively moderate, essentially Left-wing liberal views, yet had been actively involved. One hundred and seventy-one, or 31 percent of the sample, held such liberal views but had never been involved actively. Thus, only 28 percent of all those with Left-wing liberal views reported any active involvement.

Sack then analyzed the sample in terms of the class origins of the students. The results appear in Table 4.[95]

95. Sack, *General Support...*, p. 125. It was not possible to analyze differences between activist and nonactivist conservative students because there were too few in the sample. This may be the appropriate place for a brief comment on the nature of most of the data used in this chapter. Much of the evidence I have presented has taken the form of frequency distributions for an array of variables. In the complexities of the social world our knowledge of relationships is always very imperfect; we must typically be satisfied, at least for the time, with statements of varying degrees of probability and considerable inexactness. We speak of "tendencies," "trends," "probabilities," and the like. Thus emphasis on, say, the incidence of particular personality traits among activists always means that such traits are more highly represented among them than in other populations. It does

The reader will note that the high-status backgrounds of activist students—both radical and moderate—are again revealed. However, the radical nonactivists, and even the moderate nonactivists, were comprised of students who as a whole were anchored considerably lower in the status order.

We could say that when students from upper-middle class homes developed Left-wing ideological views, they tended on the whole to carry them over into action of some sort. Those from lower class origins, on the other hand, even if they have developed ideological Left-wing views, more often have not converted them into action.

It may be that the lower-middle-class and working-class homes that have nurtured ideologically Left youth have less often developed the humanistic value pattern found among some upper-middle-class families. This is to locate the essential springs of activism in that pattern as I have described it, and to make the assumption that it is significantly less characteristic of middle and lower strata. There is reason to believe that this is true.

Closely related is the organizational situation of the upper-middle-class. Not only is it true that upper-middle-class people are far more often joiners of organizations in general, but also that the clustering of voluntary organizations that historically have espoused the panoply of humanitarian and "social" causes have been essentially upper middle class in character, even when they have been aristocratic in sponsorship. This is as true of conventional civic volunteerism as of the Left progressive movements: abolitionism, feminism, the

not mean that individuals exhibiting opposed or different traits cannot be found among them. Indeed, anyone who has had any contact with the student movement—or any movement—is familiar enough with the kinds of rigidity, dogmatism, and anti-intellectualism that are too often in evidence. The fallacy often indulged in is to generalize from such instances to the group as a whole. The analysis of the movement presented thus far can support no universal characterizations, only general ones relative to other groups or population.

Table 4

Class Backgrounds of Activist and Nonactivist Students,
Penn State University, 1968 (in percents)*

Type of Student

Class Origin

	Radical Activist (25)	Radical Non-activist (30)	Moderate Activist (40)	Moderate Non-activist (178)	Center and Other (299)
Upper-Middle Class	52	27	45	32	34
Lower-Middle Class	28	46	25	33	27
Working Class	20	27	30	35	40

*Adapted from Sack, p. 125.

peace movement, and so on. Within a sector of the upper middle class, there has been an ideology ranging from Left-liberal to socialist that has been anchored in a tradition of social and political activism.[96]

96. All this is consistent with a study by Coudry, which revealed that students who both opposed the war *and* were willing to sign an anti-war statement had fathers who, like themselves, were reported to be highly expressive and idealistic, while those who refused to sign even though they opposed

Political Activism and the Counterculture

The matter of recruitment into political activism versus the counterculture as alternative routes of protest deserves comment, if only because the latter, on one view at least, represents not only a withdrawal from society but a rejection of and alienation from politics as well. There is evidence that although "hippies," like Left political activists, have come from upper-middle-class homes, there is nevertheless a difference. This is well put by Keniston:

> Available evidence suggests that members of the political wing tend to be recruited disproportionately from among the children of professors, social workers, ministers, scientists, lawyers and artists. These young men and women are the ones most concerned with institutional, social and political change, and are also the most likely to express solidarity with the basic values of their parents. Recruits to the cultural, expressive, aesthetic, or hippie wing of the counterculture, in contrast, tend to be drawn to a much greater degree from the families of media executives, entertainers, advertising men, merchandisers, scientific administrators, and personnel managers. . . .the parents of the knowledge sector, whereas the parents of the "culturals" are the "newly arrived," whose membership in the knowledge sector is more tenuous and ambivalent.[97]

Keniston might have added that the former grouping is distinguished not only by the fact of their relative oldness, but by virtue of their relative independence from immediate involvement in the central institutions of industrial capitalism, the state and the corporations. This is not to say that such professions and occupations do not serve a social function, only that they have traditions that to some degree are independent of strictly capitalist economic and political development, and in some in-

war, reported their fathers to be quite otherwise. The determinants of belief are not the same as those of action. (Reported in Keniston, "Notes on Young Radicals," *Change* [November/December 1969], pp. 25-33).

97. Keniston, "A Second Look at the Uncommitted," *Social Policy* (July/August 1971), p. 18.

stances are in important ways even opposed to it, as in the case of artists. The newer professionals, on the other hand, serve occupational functions that arise more directly out of the economic or political imperatives of capitalism. To a considerable extent they can thus be characterized as occupations without histories or traditions. Their principal ideological meaning is service to corporation and state.

The implications of this may be considerable. Whereas more or less strictly political activists have been grounded in a tradition within which politics—radical, liberal, or whatever—makes sense, "hippies" would as likely have had no such roots within which they might locate themselves; thus, their apolitical and lost character. Whereas the earlier socialization of political activists probably has tended to sensitize them to the richness of humanist values in the Western tradition, strict counterculturalists may have been cut off from such influences because of the discontinuity from that tradition inherent in the occupational situations of their fathers. In this sense, the counterculture indeed represents more of a reaction against the spread of technology as such, and the dehumanization inherent in the elevation of the value of technicism to supremacy. This goes also with the tendency to embrace, at least outwardly, aspects of the culture of the East. Such an affinity is less likely for political activists, if only on practical grounds, even when their experience and analysis have pressed them to an ultimate condemnation of American society.

All this, of course, presents neither a moral justification nor a condemnation of the activists who have made the movement. Moral concern, and even a consciousness of one's own stance vis-à-vis moral questions, do not in themselves constitute objective moral justifications of political activity. This is inherently a matter each must judge for himself.

Conclusion: Societal Drift and the Origins of the Student Movement

The early movement participants can be understood both as consequence and to some extent as initiator of larger social change. The social origins of movement creators and participants have been rooted in massive changes in the evolution of capitalist industrial development. These changes have mainly to do with the shift from the situation of the enterprise in a time of scarcity to the emergence of the corporation as the creator and manipulator of affluence.

As Max Weber observed, the "spirit of capitalism" was not merely that of profit-taking, which is as old as man's economic enterprise, but rather meant a new kind of discipline for Western man: the functioning of an enterprise in which an ethic of achievement through self-disciplined work constituted a new secular religion. The requisites of industrial societies, whether capitalist or not, include some provision for acquisition of skills and some degree of advancement by merit. The willingness to work systematically in routinized ways as a manner of achieving personal success—and thus personal worth and dignity as well—is an imperative of earlier phases of industrial development; all societies in the early phases of industrialization have as a central problem the ideological motivation of the work force. In Weber's terms this meant the smashing of tradition and the substitution of acceptance of the rationality of the discipline of the enterprise. In the modern world ideologies of nationalism rather than a secularized Protestant Ethic are typically fostered to provide the motivational support for development. But in late phases of capitalist industrial development, so-called post-industrial society characterized particularly by affluence and increasing automation, the Protestant Ethic—or certain of its functional substitutes—has become less relevant. This is so especially since World War II. A spate of books beginning in the early 50s with Riesman, Denny, and Glazer's *The Lonely Crowd* through Whyte's *Organization Man* attested to aspects of this change. Clearly, for many, work has taken on a new meaning as advanced corporate capitalism has become increasingly productive. Affluence, in the sense of an increasing abundance of goods being distributed roughly among the top half of the population, has been decisive in determining the events of the 60s. For an increasing number, personal development through exploration of the nature of the good life rather than disciplined struggle for economic survival has increasingly become the value around which life is centered.

The withering of the Protestant Ethic as a basic life-orientation has meant the growth in the number of families that are oriented to "consumerism," which we may define as the economic condition in which sufficient discretionary income is available as to constitute a condition for regularly making market decisions not determined by basic economic imperatives. As we have seen, however, it is not this stratum of families relieved of everyday economic considerations as such, but rather that minority of humanist families within this stratum, all out of proportion to its numbers, which has produced our generation of activists.

Expansion of affluence has been important for at least two reasons. First, the sheer quantitative increase in families living beyond the margin has made possible that much larger a coterie of activists. But probably at least as important is the fact that when affluence comes to characterize a large segment of the population, and particularly when much of it is spent as organized waste in various forms of conspicuous consumption, moral indignation over the plight of those left out—minorities, poor, unemployed, blacks—becomes structurally "appropriate." Extension of a materially good life to all seems, at least, to have become economically feasible (although in the future the retrenchment due to dwindling resources will doubtless have a profound effect). When such a level of economic development has not been attained, ideologies such as social darwinism are more typical; the wretched condition of the masses is justified along with the moral superiority of their masters. The importance of this is nowhere more obvious than in the fact that the very consumerism of the middle classes is a principal object of protest and contempt, indeed, is a way of life rejected as a contradiction—as long as the class society with its poverty and exploitation is maintained.

In summary, we can say that, from the standpoint of the core values of American society the middle-class humanistic family is a "deviant" type. Modern humanism has its roots in the Renaissance, although its anti-capitalist variant, of course, is more recent. The contemporary humanist family is thus the bearer of both a traditional and an anti-capitalistic ethic. In recent times two converging trends have transformed this sector of society from a tiny elite into a numerically significant sector of society: (1) the sheer quantitative expansion of the upper middle class, an expansion rooted in a rapidly developing technology, and, (2) the undermining of the Protestant Ethic by growing affluence. The result has been rapid growth of a sector of the intelligentsia, a development that has meant an expansion of the disruptive potential of the periphery. As Joseph Schumpeter predicted years ago,[98] the contradictions of mature capitalism would more likely manifest themselves in regions remote from the experience and discipline of the industrial workplace, and particularly among the more intellectually liberated intelligentsia.

98. Schumpeter, *Capitalism, Socialism and Democracy*, 3d ed. (New York: Harper and Row, 1950).

3
THE ACADEMY

The question of the effects of higher education on college students was first treated systematically by Newcomb in his study of Bennington College (Vermont) in
the 1930s.[1] Newcomb concluded that at this liberal arts
college for women education generally had a considerable liberalizing effect. For instance, in the election of
1936 seniors voted overwhelmingly for Roosevelt and
the socialist candidates, while most freshmen voted for
Alf Landon.

However, a number of studies during the 1940s and
50s, some of which were quite comprehensive, seemed to
challenge Newcomb's findings.[2] In 1957 Philip Jacob
summed up the findings of his analysis of the values of
American college students as follows:

1. Theodore Newcomb, *Personality and Social Change: Attitude Formation in a
   Student Community* (New York: Dryden Press, 1943). It should be noted
   that Bennington was an experimental college for high-status girls. The
   success of such an effort at liberalization is hardly surprising, certainly
   much less so than if it had been instituted at a vocationally oriented public institution.
2. See, for example, Rose Goldsen, *Report on the Cornell Student Body* (Ithaca,
   N.Y.; Social Science Research Center, June 1951); A. J. Drucker and H.
   H. Remmers, "Citizenship Attitudes of Purdue Seniors, College
   Graduates and High School Pupils," *Journal of Educ. Psych.* 42, no. 4
   (1951): 231-35. and Robert Pace, "What Kind of Citizens Do College Students Become?" *Journal of Gen. Educ.* 3 (April 1949).

American college students today tend to think alike, feel alike and believe alike. To an extraordinary degree, their values are the same wherever they may be studying and whatever the stage of their college careers. The great majority seem turned out of a common mold as far as outlook on life and standards of conduct are concerned. This phenomenon, interpreted from one point of view, shows how limited has been the overall impact of higher education on the human character with which it has worked. Evidently college in general, or colleges in particular, do not break or alter the mold of values for most students.[3]

In fact, Jacob concluded that

There is more homogeneity and greater consistency of values among students at the end of their four years than when they begin. Fewer seniors espouse beliefs which deviate from the going standards than do freshmen....The impact of the college experience is...to *socialize* the individual, to refine, polish, or "shape up" his values so that he can fit comfortably into the ranks of American college alumni.[4]

And, what is very important,

For the most part, the values and outlook of students do not vary greatly whether they have pursued a conventional liberal arts program, an integrated education curriculum or one of the strictly professional-vocational options.[5]

Jacob did, however, note some exceptions to this molding process. A few colleges, "private ones with modest enrollments," or those with very special atmospheres or "climates," created a superior response to education. Likewise, he found students with an authoritarian cast to be virtually "impervious to education." And students were often deeply affected by participation in

3. Philip Jacob, *Changing Values in College* (New York: Harper, 1957), p. 12.
4. *Ibid.*, p. 4.
5. *Ibid.*, p. 6.

experiences which vividly confront them with value issues, and possibly demand decisions on their part whose consequences they can witness.[6]

Such is the flavor of pre-1960 research on the values and attitudes of college students. But how is it that such a state of affairs was transformed into the eruptions of the 1960s? Is there anything about the university that can help to account for the growth of political activism? Perhaps the beginnings of an answer lie in those *caveats* appended by Jacob himself: the type of college or university and the character of the student's experience there.

Various hypotheses invoking different aspects of the structure of the universities and colleges have been advanced as explanations of student activism. Of these, four themes predominate: (1) institutional size, (2) institutional quality, (3) structural coordination, and (4) bureaucratization.

The first parallels Marx's argument concerning the function of the factory in creating great and dense agglomerations of men, all of whom stand in the same relations to the means of production, thus facilitating the development of class consciousness among them. On this view, the university is the modern counterpart of the nineteenth-century factory, agglomerating students, not workers, in subordinate roles. The quality-of-institution hypothesis rests on the empirical observation that protest seems to occur more often and with greater intensity at superior institutions. By structural coordination I mean the extent to which the academic institutions have entered arrangements with government or business that tie them to policies and commitments that are at odds with idealized academic values. Contracts for military research are perhaps the prime example. The bureaucratization hypothesis asserts that bureaucratization leads to

6. *Ibid.,* p. 9.

depersonalization of relationships, thence to a loss of a sense of identity within increasingly machinelike, "production-oriented" institutions. After examining these structural features, we will turn to the second of Jacob's *caveats*, the character of the educational experience itself.

Institutional Characteristics

Size

The effects of the size of academic institutions on student rebellion has been incorporated in many of the demographic studies of the student movement. Utilizing a sample of 104 colleges and universities, Scott and El-Assal, in an analysis of the relative importance of institutional size, quality, bureaucratization, and size of the environing community, concluded that "school size accounted for almost all of the explained variance,"[7] although very significantly they noted that large size did not result in a higher rate of demonstrations per student. The Scott and El-Assal data suggested that institutional quality was only third in rank as a determinant of activism, falling below complexity as an indicator of bureaucratization as well as size. This was so in spite of the fact that complexity was very closely related to size—26 of the 29 large institutions were determined to be complex (that is, presumably more heavily bureaucratized in the sense of having more administrative units). An analysis by Blau and Slaughter utilizing a national sample of four-year institutions also demonstrated a relationship between size and the incidence of protest,[8] a

7. Joseph Scott and Mohammed El-Assal, "Multiversity, University Size, University Quality and Student Protest," *Amer. Soc. Rev.* 43, no. 5 (Oct. 1969): 707.
8. Peter Blau and Ellen Slaughter, "Institutional Conditions and Student Demonstrations" (Mimeo, Department of Sociology, Columbia University, Fall 1970).

conclusion reached also by Hodgkinson, who found that the larger institutions had exhibited a greater capability to maintain protest over time.[9] Analyses conducted under the auspices of the President's Commission on Campus Unrest,[10] and by Bayer and Astin,[11] arrived at essentially similar conclusions.

However, the preeminence of size was called into question by Peterson, who, as the reader will recall, surveyed the Deans of Men of all the four-year institutions in the country. Peterson concluded that

> size of student body proved to be unrelated linearly, to organized student protest to any meaningful degree.[12]

even though in a special analysis he did find that protest was more likely to occur in the *very large* institutions (those over 10,000).

Peterson was not the only one to produce such findings. In a survey of 946 students drawn from 97 institutions, Kahn and Bowers demonstrated that the incidence of student participation in protest demonstrations or civil disobedience was unrelated to the size of the institution, if its quality was controlled.[13] Basing their criterion of institutional quality on the degree of selectivity of the student body, the authors showed that *among quality institutions, the incidence of participation in demonstrations remained constant for those of all sizes,* except, interestingly,

9. Harold Hodgkinson, "Student Protest: In Institutional and National Profile," *Teacher's College Record* 71 (May 1970).
10. Garth Buchanan and Joan Brackett, *Summary Results of the Survey for the President's Commission on Campus Unrest* (Washington, D.C.: The Urban Institute, 1970), p. 18.
11. Alan E. Bayer and Alexander Astin, "Violence and Disruption in the U.S. Campus, 1968-69," *Educ. Record* 50 (Fall 1969).
12. Richard E. Peterson, "The Student Left in American Higher Education," *Daedalus* 97 (1968): 311.
13. Roger M. Kahn and William J. Bowers, "The Social Context of the Rank-and-File Student Activist: A Test of Four Hypotheses," *Soc. of Educ.* 43, no. 1 (Winter 1970). We should perhaps note that in speaking of "incidence" of demonstrations and civil disobedience, the authors mean the percentage of the student body as represented in their sample to report having ever participated in such activity.

for the very largest (defined as those over 5,000). There, the incidence was considerably *smaller*—15 percent as against around 40 percent for the other four-size categories.

The Kahn and Bowers's results suggest that the larger institutions, although they have produced more action than smaller ones, have nevertheless involved proportionally fewer numbers of their student bodies. This was confirmed in an analysis conducted by Keniston and Lerner, who found that in four-year institutions, the rate of student involvement was about four times as great for those with student bodies under 1,000 as it was for those with more than 5,000 students,[14] a result consistent with the findings of Scott and El-Assal.

The most important observation to be made seems to be that beyond a certain threshold there is a relationship between size and the incidence of and capacity to sustain protest, thus providing a kind of confirmation of the agglomeration thesis. However, it is important to keep in mind as well the fact that in terms of numbers involved, there is a proportional decrease as the size of institutions increases.

Quality

It has been remarked, with some real irony, that student activism is really elitist since it has occurred so frequently at all the best places. And the Berkeleys, Columbias, Harvards, and Wisconsins are indeed the elite.

Does the research confirm this impression? Yes, and rather emphatically. Blau and Slaughter, in the study referred to above, found the quality of the institution to be independently associated with the incidence of protest.[15] Hodgkinson discovered that institutions of higher quality

14. Kenneth Keniston and Michael Lerner, "Campus Characteristics and Campus Unrest," *The Annals of The American Academy of Political and Social Sciences* (May 1971), p. 395.
15. Blau and Slaughter, "Institutional Condition. . . ."

had very rapid rates of *increase* of protest over a 10-year period,[16] a finding confirmed by Bayer and Astin.[17] The Kahn and Bowers study mentioned above also provided evidence for the independent effect of institutional quality.[18] In fact, only the analysis of Scott and El-Assal fails to strongly confirm the finding.[19] Kahn and Bowers concluded that

> there is something apart from a student's social back-
> ground, his academic commitment, his field of study, or his
> intellectual orientation that promotes activists' involvement
> at the better quality colleges and universities.[20]

What can be said about this "something"?

High-quality colleges and universities include such in-stitutions as the eastern Ivy League and other private universities elsewhere, many of the state universities of the midwest, and a variety of smaller liberal arts colleges scattered throughout the country but somewhat overrep-resented in the East. These schools are known not only for their academic excellence but also for their relative freedom, lack of regimentation, and general liberalism. They tend, in contrast to most others, to be relatively faculty-dominated; that is to say, the faculties exercise a voice in various matters of university policy. Such institu-tions may be contrasted with those that may be termed "management-dominated," by which is meant merely that the faculties, relative to the administration, have lit-tle or no voice. Now, it would not do to overstate this distinction, for it is only one of degree, and it must be remembered that, even in the best of places—and this is particularly true of the public universities—faculty *influence* is exercised in the context of what, from a strictly legal standpoint at least, is a situation of almost

16. Hodgkinson, "Student Protest. . . ."
17. Bayer and Astin, "Violence and Disruption. . . ."
18. Kahn and Bowers, "The Social Context. . . ."
19. Scott and El-Assal, "Multiversity. . . ."
20. Kahn and Bowers, "The Social Context. . . ."

total subjection of faculties to administrative authority. And yet the distinction is important, for it is fundamental in any consideration of the quality of the institutions themselves. Faculty influence, it is important to emphasize, is closely related to faculty excellence. Institutions with reputations to maintain try to retain their better scholars, and this is done partly by assuring them relative freedom, not only in the sense of freedom to pursue their scholarly interests, but also in helping to shape the institutional conditions of their lives. The recognized intellectual leaders within the disciplines are therefore key figures—as an elite group—in establishing, maintaining, and renewing institutional freedom. The freedom or "looseness" of the elite institutions is an observed fact, in this double sense. Obviously, this does not mean that the management of such universities lies in the hands of the faculty. But it does mean, among other things, that the choice of administrators is influenced more heavily by faculty, and that the former are, therefore, more likely to think and act more like scholars and less likely to hold a strictly managerial image of themselves. In this sense, administrative perspectives to a greater extent tend to reflect the somewhat liberal views of the faculty, especially of the more prominent faculty, and this places greater emphasis on freedom in general.

In such a climate the possibility of student challenge to authority seems to be greater, partly because the liberal atmosphere encourages, may even require, individual expression of a somewhat nonconforming sort. This is the case not only because of fewer rules and the fact that those that do exist tend to be rather liberally interpreted, but also because such schools tend to select the potentially more rebellious in the first place. This latter is by no means to be regarded as unrelated to the nature of the institution. Many schools have traditionally deliberately sought out not only the bright, but also the involved and the relatively independent-minded. To some extent the "protest-prone" character of the student bodies of the superior institutions has been carefully and rationally selected precisely in terms of the more intellectual and liberal ethos of those institutions—surely an irony that should not go unnoted.[21]

Protest and the Quality of Instruction

It has sometimes been argued that protest has been generated by the *low* quality of instruction, but if this were so, the materials reviewed above would be inexplicable. In fact, relatively little protest has occurred specifically over the quality of education. Somers reported that only 17 percent of Berkeley students reported *any* degree of dissatisfaction with their education there, while 82 percent said they were satisfied or very satisfied. Furthermore, he found that

> the minority of students who *are* dissatisfied with the courses, the exams, or professors, are little more likely to be found among the militants than those who are satisfied.[22]

These sentiments have by no means been restricted to Berkeley. Trent and Craise reported that, despite some complaints over teaching, "most. . .found college basically satisfying."[23] And Peterson's nationwide data suggest that although the significance of protest over the quality of instructions may have been increasing (at the time), in the earlier years it was actually of little importance in comparison with a range of other issues (see items A-3 and A-4 in Table 5).

If good education is that process which inculcates a critical sense of mind, then the conditions in the better

---

21. The reader should see, in particular, Edmund Williamson and John Cohan's *The American Student's Freedom of Expression* (Minneapolis, Minn.: University of Minnesota Press, 1966).
22. Somers, pp. 549-50.
23. Trent and Craise, p. 38.

institutions can be readily seen to have fostered protest. The fact that protest has not been directed mainly against the high-quality instruction itself should come as no surprise.

The Nonteaching Professor

There is one special sense of educational deprivation that should be mentioned. This is the belief that student protest has been a consequence of the absence of senior professors from the classroom. It would seem that this explanation is supported by the fact of higher incidence of protest at better institutions, those that attract, support, and provide facilities for the research-oriented elite faculty members. It is a fact that such institutions are considered superior partly because they are able to attract and retain distinguished men, and that this often entails considerable relief from teaching duties. But there is little evidence to support the claim that their absence from the classroom is at all an adequate explanation of student protest. First, many such men actually do teach, although admittedly less than others, and frequently many aspects of teaching such as advising, constructing, and correcting exams are left to graduate assistants. Second, this corps of favored scholars constitutes a minority of the faculty even at the better schools, and to place such a heavy burden of explanation on their partial withdrawal would seem to be unreasonable in the extreme. Third, there is at best only some very shaky and desultory evidence concerning the relation between scholarly creativity and teaching ability. Indeed, all of us know of cases in which everyone agrees that, the creative brilliance of a man not withstanding, it seems the better part of realistic prudence to keep him well away from students, especially undergraduate students—and for their benefit. And finally, graduate assistants as a group cannot be considered to be either necessarily incompetent or greatly inferior to the professoriate. As anyone who has spent any time around a university knows, the range of competence among graduate students, just as among faculty, is enormous. But it is also true that at the better institutions graduate students are carefully selected and can be considered to represent more or less the cream of the crop. The typical or average graduate assistant at these institutions, therefore, cannot be regarded as incompetent, even though he may be relatively inexperienced. And this is by no means the same thing.

If the reader will again glance at Table 5, he will see that Peterson's data confirm empirically the thrust of these arguments. The item "Senior faculty not sufficiently involved in undergraduate instruction" seems to have been a negligible issue and in any case is probably on the decline. And Blau and Slaughter reached the identical conclusion: an institutional emphasis on research *as such* was unrelated to protest.[24]

It was one of Clark Kerr's major points, in his now-famous Godkin lectures, that the withdrawal of the faculty from the classroom seriously threatened the university. For Kerr the blame clearly lay with the faculties themselves and he therefore argued that there was an incipient revolt against that faculty. But Kerr was wrong in one important respect. He failed to perceive that the revolt would to a much greater extent be directed against *him,* that is, university management, than against his faculty.

Despite all this, there is an indirect relationship between the new class of research academics and student protest. The rise of this class is the direct consequence of business and government (including foundation) subsidization of research. The bulk of this research has been concentrated in a relatively few universities, those of high quality and large size. Here, and only here, reside

24. Blau and Slaughter, p. 14.

the requisite competence and facilities. A great deal if not most of this work has had to do, directly or indirectly, with military interests.

For the members of the disciplines, professional status has increasingly depended on publication, and publication depends mainly on research. University managers, often themselves former or even still part-time faculty members involved in research, encouraged the building of these relationships in the interests of maintaining or increasing the prestige of their institutions. Such men are typically highly committed to their institutions. Thus, a typically instrumental view of the university (unaccompanied by strong feelings of identification) on the part of elite mobile faculty members dovetailed with the strong institutional identifications and prestige interests often characteristic of administrators. It is thus not a matter of management *or* the elite of the faculty. Their interests have been to some extent identical, to some extent complementary. Together they have brought the big high-quality institutions into coordination with requirements emanating from political and economic core institutions, and in so doing have compromised much of the traditional albeit idealized autonomy of the academy.

In building these arrangements, the academic elite of university managers and research professors have not been unaware of what they were up to. They have surely had at least that degree of self-comprehension attributed to the lady celebrated in the limerick,

> There was a young lady from Kent,
> Who said that she knew what it meant,
> When men took her to dine
> Gave her cocktail and wine.
> She knew what it meant—but she went.

Structural Coordination and Value Emphasis

Student protest has occurred and recurred with the greatest intensity precisely in those institutions most highly coordinated. Many of the biggest and best publicized revolts have been assaults on the various forms of coordination. The revolt at Columbia was manifestly a protest against both the participation of the university in the Institute of Defense Analysis as well as in opposition to the Harlem "land grab" for the purpose of building a gymnasium (that would have been used part-time by Harlemites). At both Harvard and Wisconsin the biggest, bloodiest, and most publicized protests were attempts to stop Dow Chemical representatives from recruiting on the campuses. The Chicago sit-in protested collusion between the university and the draft boards, to which the former was releasing information regarding students' academic standing.

The incidence of protest among coordinated institutions, however, has not been uniform. Very high-quality institutions such as, say, the Massachusetts Institute of Technology or The California Institute of Technology, while they have not been "immune," experienced only minor levels of protest. As distinct from institutions such as Harvard, Columbia, Berkeley, and Wisconsin, which are in important degrees receptacles of *humanistic traditions,* such institutions are organized essentially around technical values. Conversely, many small, uncoordinated institutions are embodiments of humanist values. Absence of ties coordinating them with core institutions has meant that they have experienced less protest, and especially less directed specifically against more strictly local matters. Thus, two conditions: (1) humanistic vs. technical ethos, and (2) coordination with core institutions, serve to differentiate institutions with respect to generation of protest. Figure 2 renders these distinctions paradigmatically.

Institutions of the type designated in Cell D, the coordinated-humanistic type, have produced an enormously disproportionate amount of protest, as compared

Figure 2

Structural Relation to
Core

Dominant Values	Coordinated	Uncoordinated
Technicist	**A** Technically oriented institutions such as MIT, or Cal. Tech. and many state universities.	**B** Many state colleges, teacher training colleges, lesser technical colleges, religiously related and/or oriented institutions, etc.
Humanistic	**D** "Great" universities with fully developed faculties and facilities in all disciplines (Harvard, Columbia, Wisconsin, Michigan, Berkeley, etc.)	**C** Mainly high-quality liberal arts Colleges.

with those in the other three cells. Although the presence of either a humanistic ethos (Cell C) or a high degree of coordination (Cell A) accounts for more protest than situations where both are absent (Cell B), in combination they have constituted a truly volatile situation. From the standpoint of the *values* of the core, the humanistic institutions of Cells C and D stand near the periphery. However, the growing structural coordination of the "great" institutions, coupled with an intrusion of values centering around technicism and national priorities, has deepened and made more acute the sense of contradiction underlying student protest.

Bureaucracy

Bureaucratization is a master trend of all developed societies and has a great variety of effects that are by no means fully understood. We must therefore develop our concept of bureaucracy in a careful although necessarily brief exposition.[25]

At the outset it must be understood that this analysis is deliberately restricted to the specific effects of bureaucratization on the campus, and will not address the larger question of societal bureaucratization or rationalization. Student movements, of course, have often been characterized, by their leaders and by others, as anti-bureaucratic, and the literature of the New Left reflects this animus in uncompromising fashion. However, the ideological question of just what aspects of the old society must be eliminated in the building of the new one is distinct from that of the proximate effects of bureaucratic forms as conditions of movement mobilization, and much, if not most, of the arguments linking bureaucratization to the student movement have understood that link to lie in the conversion of academic institutions into impersonal, machinelike structures.

It is useful to distinguish, at the outset, between (1) strictly bureaucratic elements, (2) variable aspects of particular bureaucracies, and (3) bureaucratic effects. As an absolute minimum bureaucracy may be defined as a formal organization that is centrally controlled, hierarchically ordered so that communications move through set formalized channels both up and down, and conducted in terms of the application of rules that govern the activities of officials and that theoretically constitute bases of decision for all cases that are defined as lying within the organization's jurisdiction. Among variable aspects of bureaucracies are such factors as the degree of incorporation of scientific ("rational") principles, the de-

---

25. It is not possible to give here a reasonable listing of literature on the subject of bureaucracy. Some readers might wish to begin with Weber's classic formulation, "Bureaucracy," in Hans Gerth and C. Wright Mills, eds., *From Max Weber: Essays in Sociology* (New York: Oxford University Press, 1946), pp. 196-244.

gree of flexibility, and the degree of skill or training considered necessary for its functionaries. Bureaucratic effects have at one time or another been held to include apathy, mass behavior, depersonalization, the formation of primary groups, exaggerated concern over status, routine indulgence in violence (as in Hanna Arendt's treatment of Adolph Eichman—the "banalization" of violence), organizational oligarchy, elimination of democracy, technological development, and greater efficiency.

Since the issue for us here is just how bureaucratization is related to the intensity or incidence of student protest, the question may be formulated as follows: because of what specific aspect(s) of bureaucratic organization and through what specific effect(s) does student protest occur? The *routine* of bureaucratic functioning, it is often held, in regarding students as mere members of categories rather than tendering them consideration in the entirety of their individuality, violates their dignity or sense of self-esteem. One consequence of this organizational process, depersonalization, is presumed to be the proximate generator of protest.

On the organizational side matters may also be specified a bit further. Treatment of people as members of categories results directly from the existence of rules that define their statuses (with respect to the organization) and associated rights, duties, and so on. But rules may be interpreted with greater or less flexibility, which is to say that the ethos of an organization may encourage officials to give greater or lesser weight to particular rules and to interpret them more in the light of particular conditions. Such flexibility is a variable aspect of bureaucracy.

We can now approach the question of the effect of bureaucracy on student protest. We will look for evidence that links bureaucratic rigidity in the application of the rules, along with a sense of depersonalization among students, with activism. This is the sense of former Berkeley student-leader Mario Savio's cry, that the operation of the university "machine" becomes "so odious. . .you've got to make it stop." It is also, I think, the sense of the many academic or administrative constructions that parallel Savio's, such as that of Clark Kerr:

> The students find themselves under a blanket of impersonal rules for admissions, for scholarships, for examinations, for degrees. . . .The students also want to be treated as distinct individuals.[26]

What sort of evidence is there for the bureaucratization-protest hypothesis?

It is somewhat complex. Lipset and Altbach reported that 80 percent of the Wisconsin student body felt that that institution was depersonalized, and that 59 percent felt that they were no longer treated as individuals, but as "cogs in a machine."[27] Wisconsin, of course, has been a major locus of protest. And Blau and Slaughter found that the use of computers for administrative purposes was related to protest, although they then went on to argue that this was to a large extent a spurious correlation, being mainly a consequence of size.[28] An analysis by Astin and Bayer suggested that institutions exhibiting "little involvement in class" on the part of either students or faculty members had a greater incidence of protest.[29] Evidently the presence of concern for students tends to inhibit the development of protest, a point to which we will return in chapter 4. There is little doubt that the

26. "Selections from *The Uses of the University,*" by Clark Kerr, in Seymour M. Lipset and Sheldon S. Wollin, eds., *The Berkeley Student Revolt* (Garden City, N.Y.: Doubleday Anchor Books, 1965), p. 56.
27. Seymour M. Lipset and Philip Altbach, "Student Politics and Higher Education in the United States," in Lipset, ed., *Student Politics* (New York: Basic Books, 1967), p. 213.
28. Blau and Slaughter.
29. Alexander Astin and Alan E. Bayer, "Antecedents and Consequences of Disruptive Campus Protests," *Measurement and Evaluation in Guidance* 4 (April 1971).

universities have indeed become more impersonal and more mechanical, as have other public institutions of modern industrial societies, and that they have undergone relationalization at all levels. But this massive fact, and evidence such as that cited above, do not necessarily add up to a meaningful analysis.

First of all, despite the alienation of many students, this sort of evidence fails to demonstrate whether such sentiments are more typical of radical students, and whether students holding them have predominated in protest activity. Second, it fails to make the connection between the *experience* of depersonalization and the actual issues manifest in the protest.[30] And third, it is important to distinguish between bureaucratization of academic as against parietal aspects of university life. Astin and Bayer's data, for instance, emphasized the classroom situation and the nature of relationships within the student body. When we take these factors into account, especially the last, the connection between bureaucratization and protest becomes more tenuous. The distinction between the bureaucratization of the educational process itself and those other spheres of student life in which the universities typically interest themselves—living conditions in general, along with all manner of behavior it is thought necessary to bring under control in the interests of "morality"—is an important one. The latter may be termed the "parietal sphere" and the process by which the universities structure and control it as "parietal management."

Paulus's study of Michigan State University students constitutes one test of the bureaucratization hypothesis.

30. We should note that such feelings of alienation are quite widespread among the American population, even though the United States is exceeded, or at least was exceeded up until a few years ago, by some, perhaps many, other countries. But these feelings do not, for the most part, result in radical protest. For comparative data, see Gabriel Almond and James Coleman, *The Civic Culture: Political Attitudes and Democracy in Five Nations* (Princeton, N. J.: Princeton University Press, 1963).

The reader will recall that Paulus constructed matched samples of student government leaders, Left-wing activists, and a representative control group of MSU students. On scales of satisfaction with faculty, including student-faculty relations, and with satisfaction with major field work, the activists' scores were practically the same as those of the control group and quite close to those of the student-government leaders. However, their scores on a scale measuring their satisfaction with administrative rules and practices were much lower than those of the other two groups—in fact, two standard deviations below, which means that the possibility of this difference having occurred by chance was extremely remote.[31]

These data suggest that depersonalization is indeed experienced differentially by radicals but that it is felt much more onerously in the sphere of parietal management. From this alone, however, there is no way of knowing whether or not alienation is a consequence, a cause, or a condition of activism.

Some of Astin's data carry us a bit further. Astin defined a variable, "organization in the class," in terms of such things as having assigned seats, taking role regularly, and holding class only at specific times and places, all of which are features of education that are dealt with in some fashion by the rules but are subject to greatly varying interpretations and applications by individual instructors. If the bureaucratization thesis were correct, we could expect that institutions scoring high on these qualities would have more protest than others. The opposite is the case, those institutions with low scores had more protests and demonstrations than those scoring high.[32] Specifically, for a sample of 246 institutions, there was actually a *negative* correlation between bureaucratization of the academic side of life and the incidence of protest. In fact, protest seemed to have been related not to

31. Paulus, *A Multivariate Analysis. . .*, pp. 217-18.
32. Alexander Astin, "Determinants of Student Activism," in *Long and Foster*, pp. 98-101.

bureaucratization, but to the degree of "looseness," characterized as a lack of organizational tightness linking the student to his most important participatory milieu, the class. And this sounds very much like the kind of institutional climate discussed earlier in connection with the quality of the schools.

Other data support those of Paulus and Astin. Immediately after the Berkeley revolt, Somers found that only six percent of his sample of the student body mentioned such bureaucratic features as red tape, impersonality, or being treated like IBM cards.[33] In fact, despite Savio's rhetoric, the Berkeley revolt began not over the bureaucratization of institutional functions, but over a conflict concerning the rights of students. Prior to this, student political involvement had been directed into neighboring communities, especially Oakland, and the racist practices of businessmen there.[34] And in the study referred to earlier, Blau and Slaughter found only a relatively weak relationship between use of computers (probably a fair indicator of bureaucratization) for administrative purposes and the incidence of protest.[35]

Some nationwide data collected by Peterson are also useful here. The first and fifth items in Table 5 (A-1, A-5), which is taken unchanged from Peterson,[36] seem *prima facie* to approximate to some extent our criterion of bureaucracy-depersonalization. The reader will note that, in terms of their incidence in relation to protest, the first, dealing with the size and impersonality of classes, ranked 26th out of 27 different issues, and the fifth, curriculum inflexibility, ranked fourteenth. In short, they are not at all highly placed, and therefore fail to lend any support to the hypothesis.

All in all, evidence supporting a direct link between

33. Somers, p. 550.
34. In this connection see Hal Draper, *Berkeley: The New Student Revolt* (New York: Grove Press, 1965).
35. Blau and Slaughter, "Institutional Conditions. . . ."
36. Richard E. Peterson, "The Scope of Organized Student Protest," in Long and Foster, pp. 59-80. See Table 2, page 69.

bureaucratization and protest is tenuous at best, particularly if we understand this to mean the bureaucratization of specifically educational functions.

It should be recognized that administrative actions may often be specifically unbureaucratic in the sense of a management breaking, ignoring, or bending its own rules. A succession of actions by officials of a large state university regarding university disciplinary procedures is a good example of this.

After protest demonstrations during the spring of 1969, the university senate recommended that a nine-man board representing students, faculty, and administration be set up for the purpose of hearing student disciplinary cases. The university then did create such a board. This "court" was an example of a bureaucratic procedure in the sense of working in terms of a set of rules regarding its jurisdiction and its procedures and powers. The board had no power to actually suspend or expel, only to report its findings to the president and recommend action. The president remained free to act on them or to disregard them at his pleasure.

One year later, following a sit-in and demonstrations protesting the killings at Kent State University and the invasion of Cambodia, a number of students were remanded for discipline. But the Board of Trustees of the university, along with the president, decided to circumvent the board and appoint a new three-man panel of lawyer-politicians to sit in judgment. Since all three members of the board were lawyers, the administration could argue that legal knowledge was being brought to bear, (even though the procedure was not a trial and the "defendants" were not accused of breaking any civil laws). The reluctance of the president to utilize the existing and recognized board was widely attributed to the fact that, during the proceedings of the previous spring, the members of the board had been confronted with a mountain of actual evidence clearly proving that those

Table 5
Percentages of All Institutions and of 50 Large Public Universities
Reporting Some Degree of Organized Student Protest in Relation to
27 Issues, for 1967-68 and 1964-65

	All Institutions 849 in 1965, 859 in 1968		50 Large Public Universities	
	1967-68	1964-65	1967-68	1964-65
Undergraduate classes typically too large, instruction too impersonal	03	04	10	10
Senior faculty not sufficiently involved in undergraduate instruction	02	03	08	16
Poor quality of instruction—in general or specific instances	13	12	18	10
Generally prevailing system(s) of testing and/or grading	12	09	20	12
Curriculum inflexibility	15	08	18	14
Academic freedom for faculty—in principle	04	04	08	16
Faculty tenure policies, e.g., "publish or perish"	04	04	06	08
Controversy surrounding a particular faculty member	20	16	26	26
"Censorship" of certain publications, e.g., student newspaper	10	14	20	18
Campus rules regarding speeches, appearances by "controversial" persons	08	09	06	24
Actual appearance by a particular person of leftist persuasion	05	05	08	22
Actual appearance by a particular person of rightist persuasion	04	05	06	18
Dormitory and other living-group regulations, e.g., women's hours	34	28	30	22
Food service	25	29	18	28
Dress regulations	20	20	06	20
Policies, regulations regarding student drinking	11	11	08	10

	All Institutions 849 in 1965, 859 in 1968		50 Large Public Universi	
	1967-68	1964-65	1967-68	1964-
Policies, regulations regarding student use of drugs	05	xx	08	xx
Disciplinary action against particular student(s)	16	18	16	18
Alleged racial discrimination: in admissions, nonaction on frat. discrim., etc.	18	24	48	24
Student-administration communication: students unable to voice grievances	19	24	28	24
Insufficient student participation in establishing campus policies	27	26	36	26
Civil rights: local area (off campus)— protest and/or work	29	38	46	56
The draft	25	xx	46	xx
On-campus recruiting by one or another of the armed services	25	xx	56	xx
On-campus recruiting by any other firm or agency, e.g., Dow, CIA, etc.	20	xx	68	xx
U.S. policies regarding Vietnam	38	21	64	68
Classified defense and related research on campus	04	xx	16	xx

brought for discipline had done practically none of the things alleged by the university, evidence brought out by the faculty members representing them. Faced with the lack of evidence, the president had been able to apply only token sanctions. So it was widely believed that the board, the president, and others in the administration wanted to risk no rerun of this scenario.

Institutions that circumvent their own rules and procedures are not (technically, at least) acting bureaucratically, and the ability to exercise power in capricious, extra-legal ways may be a greater threat to substantive justice than the most mechanical and impersonal of administrative procedures. The fact that Astin's data show greater alienation in the sphere of parietal management suggests that not bureaucratization so much as the contradictory expectations associated with the student role are implicated in student uprisings. The contradictions defining this role became extraordinarily acute particularly under conditions involving the administration of justice or protests concerning civil liberties. This has been well summed up by Keniston:

> In contrast to their relative satisfaction with the quality of their education, however, activists *are* distinctively dissatisfied with what might be termed the "civil-libertarian" defects of their college administrations. While no doubt a great many American undergraduates distrust "University Hall," this distrust is especially pronounced amongst student protestors. . . .Furthermore, activists tend to be more responsive than other students to deprivations of civil rights on campus as well as off campus, particularly when political pressures seem to motivate on-campus policies they consider unjust. The same responsiveness increasingly extends to issues of "student power"; i.e., student participation and decisions affecting campus life. Thus, bans on controversial speakers, censorship of student publications, and limitations on off-campus political or social action are likely to incense the activist, as is arbitrary "administration" without the consent of the administered.[37]

This interpretation can be readily placed within the paradigm presented earlier in Figure 1. Such a sense of rights and of injustice is probably "apt" to take root within the humanistic ethos of those institutions falling in Cells C and D.

This discussion suggests that any relation between bureaucratization of the university and student protest is, at best, highly problematic. However, it must also be reiterated that this analysis has been deliberately restricted to the effects of bureaucratization specifically within the university, and has not attempted to confront the issue of bureaucratization as a societal process.

---

37. Keniston, "The Sources. . .,", p. 118.

Furthermore, we are not done with consideration of organizational structure. In chapter 4 we will return to some organization questions in connection with the analysis of confrontation.

Political Activism and the Educational Experience

The reader will recall that back in the 30s Newcomb found that a Bennington education had a liberalizing effect, but that the findings of others challenged this. More recent evidence suggests that this problem can be resolved in good part by analysis of the courses of study in which students are enrolled, and the kinds of careers they envision. Student political activists have been heavily concentrated in the social sciences and humanities and, in a sense, this is a continuation of a long-standing situation.

Prior to the 1960s some scattered research was already suggesting that Newcomb's Bennington findings could be interpreted in such a curricular sense. Both the Pace study of 1949 and that of Nogee and Levin a decade later found that those who had gone through a general education course scored higher on liberal or "good citizenship" items than those who had been enrolled in more strictly vocational tracks.[38] And Holtzman found that students in education, the social sciences, and humanities were less supportive of racial segregation than those in business, engineering, and natural science.[39]

Earlier research at Berkeley showed that those scoring high on "libertarianism" (fifteen statements embodying principles of the Bill of Rights stated in such a way as to conflict with other values) were heavily overrepresented in the social sciences and humanities, with those

38. See Pace, and Philip Nogee and Murray B. Levin, "Some Determinants of Political Attitudes Among College Votes," *Pub. Op. Q.* 22 (1958): 449-63.
39. W. H. Holtzman, "Attitudes of College Men Toward Non-Segregation in Texas Schools," *Pub. Op. Q.* 20 (1956): 559-69.

in business, engineering, and business administration scoring lowest.[40] In a review of these materials Edelstein concluded that they demonstrated "a continuing shift by most college students, particularly in the general education areas, toward more tolerant and flexible attitudes toward politics and the political process," but that even in 1962 (as the Port Huron Statement[41] was being written), "there was very little in the studies to show a trend toward ideology of the extreme right or left."[42]

Edelstein misread the meaning of his own conclusion. Research of the later 60s clearly demonstrates the connection between the liberalism associated with study of the social sciences and humanities, and the emergence of Left radicalism. The connection between the intellectual liberalism rooted in these modern world views and political activism is now a firmly established fact. Somers reported that at Berkeley "social science and humanities students. . .are most likely to be found in the more militant camp. . . ,"[43] and they were heavily overrepresented in FSM itself.[44] The anti-bomb peace march revealed that two-thirds of the students participating were social science and humanities majors.[45] Braungart's study of student political organizations in ten institutions clearly showed the same pattern (Table 6).

The particular value of Braungart's data, as indicated earlier, lies in the fact that they cover a range of institutions and provide comparative information over a range of political groups. Thus, while it is clear that SDS members were overwhelmingly social science and humanities majors, and this holds as well for the liberal

40. Hannan Selvin, and Warren O. Hagstrom, "Determinants of Support for Civil Liberties," in S. M. Lipset and S. S. Wolin, eds., *The Berkeley Student Revolt* (Garden City, N.Y.: Doubleday and Company, Inc., 1965), p. 512.
41. The Port Huron statement was the original manifesto of the Students for a Democratic Society, drafted at Port Huron, Michigan, in 1962.
42. Alex S. Edelstein, "Since Bennington: Evidence of Change in Student Political Behavior," *Pub. Op. Q.* 26 (1962): 575.
43. Somers, p. 51.
44. Watts and Whittaker, p. 51.
45. Solomon and Fishman, p. 57.

Young Democrats, as we would expect, it also applies with considerable force to the Young Republicans and even to the members of the Young Americans for Freedom. It thus appears that even the far Right activists have been drawn quite heavily from the social sciences. Table 7, in which creative and fine arts, humanities, and social science majors have been grouped together as "liberal," and business, education, and engineering majors as "vocational," indicates this clearly.

Table 6

Percentage Distribution of Student Group
by College Major*

College Major	SDS	YD	YR	YAF
Bio. & Earth Science	3.2	3.0	6.3	6.9
Business	0.0	9.0	9.9	13.7
Crative or Fine Arts	6.3	1.0	.9	2.9
Education	2.3	5.0	4.5	5.9
Engineering	.4	3.0	3.6	7.9
Humanities	29.0	20.0	17.0	12.7
Mathematics	.4	2.0	2.4	2.5
Physical Science	1.8	0.0	3.6	3.9
Social Science	56.6	57.0	51.8	43.6
Total	100.0	100.0	100.0	100.0
N	(221)	(100)	(112)	(204)

*SOURCE: Richard G. Braungart, "Family Status, Socialization and Student Politics" Doctoral Dissertation, Penn State University, 1969), p. 333.

The linear relationship shown in Table 8 indicates that vocationalism is to some extent related to the form of political expression but, perhaps more important, that it may be even more strongly related to no political expression at all. The fact that YAF drew more heavily from business and engineering than education, which is also vocationally oriented, suggests that to some extent

Table 7

Liberal and Vocational Curricula for Four Student
Political Groups (percents)

Group

Type of Curriculum	SDS	YD	YR	YAF
Liberal	85.6	77.0	68.8	56.3
Vocational	2.7	17.0	18.0	27.5

vocationalism as such, but beyond this, vocationalism of a specific ideological type, has provided the more fertile recruiting ground for the students on the Right. Education as a profession and as taught in the colleges is today highly suffused with progressive and liberal ideas that stand in some contrast with those generally prevalent in schools of business and engineering, with their corporate connections and subsidies. This remains so despite some reformist inclinations, particularly in the former.[46] Equally as important, these distributions also suggest that inherent political implications of the social sciences in particular seem by no means to be as monolithically Leftward-leaning as some have supposed. In this connection we would do well to remember, although they cannot be developed here, the conservative social and intellectual origins not only of most of economics and political science, but of mainstream sociology as well.

It seems, then, that the relationship between the sort of intellectual materials one is confronted with and Left-wing activism is a more complicated matter than it

46. The seemingly low rates of participation of students in education present an especially interesting case, although I can do no more than speculate about it here. Perhaps the liberalism of modern educational ideology has tended to drive students in the direction of Left political activism, but the vocationalism has inhibited the kind of free-wheeling approach to the social and cultural affairs that the social sciences and humanities inherently encourage.

has sometimes been thought to be. The Braungart data suggest that those materials dealing with the questions of society and culture are very highly conducive to political activity *in general,* not just on the Left, and that in this instance, when political activity does result, it is generally in a conservative direction. In any case, Left and Right students would seem to have at least something in common.

None of the material thus far discussed clearly establishes that factors in education are determinants of political activity, for the relationship could, in fact, be the other way around. As we have seen, strong predispositions toward Left-wing politics exist prior to college, and these predispositions are themselves related to interests in the social sciences and humanities. Thus, it has been maintained that both college major and political activism are consequences of prior experiences and interests. Lipset, for instance, has argued that these differences in curriculum or major subject "appear to be a product of selective entrance into difficult disciplines than of the effects of the content of the fields on those pursuing them as students or practitioners."[47]

Such evidence as exists bears this out only partially. Edelstein pointed out that a series of studies showed consistently that changes in political viewpoints do result from exposure to different sorts of educational materials and situations. One study compared engineering students to science majors, both of whom had been exposed to a broad liberal arts course. The engineers retained their essential conservatism, while the science majors became more liberal. Another showed "extensive" changes from quarter to quarter during a two-year course in economics. Edelstein concluded that the results of these and other researches indicated that "the direction has

47. S. M. Lipset, "American Student Activism," in Philip S. Altbach, *Student Politics and Higher Education in the United States: A Select Bibliography* (St. Louis, Mo.: United Ministries of Higher Education, 1968), p. 11.

been toward increasing liberalism."[48] However, as noted above, the effects of some curricula are definitely not in a liberal or radical direction. Webster's study of engineering students showed that they become *more* conservative while at school,[49] despite the fact, clearly shown elsewhere, that at the time of entry they might have been the most conservative of all students.[50]

Although this evidence is by no means conclusive, it does suggest that involvement in the social sciences and humanities (including the creative arts) can have substantial independent effect. We might better view the relationship, then, as one of intensifying and expanding whatever knowledge and understanding are already brought to the college experience, which further builds and fortifies the actual or latent radicalism (or, in the case of at least some conservative students, latent *conservatism*) of such students.

It may well be the case that whether the characteristics of students (or students-to-be) or of the institutions are decisive depends on the type of issue. Astin's analysis, in which an attempt was made to weigh their relative importance, suggests that this may be so. He found that protests against the war or racism were predictable on the basis of the personal characteristics of those who participated in them. Protests against aspects of university management, on the other hand, were found to be much more closely related to "environmental characteristics," that is, structural, demographic, and other aspects of the institutions themselves.[51] This is important, be-

48. Edelstein, p. 521.
49. H. Webster, M. Freeman, and P. Heist, "Personality Changes in College Students," in *The American College*, ed. N. Sanford (New York: John Wiley & Sons, Inc., 1962).
50. We should perhaps note in passing that there is some evidence suggesting that it is those students who do better in their academic life who tend to become more liberal, and perhaps, radical. See Selvin and Hagstrom, p. 332.
51. Alexander Astin, "Personal and Environmental Determinants of Student Activism," *Measurement and Evaluation in Guidance* 1 (Fall 1968).

cause it suggests that many university reforms, tried and untried, would have little if any effect on protests directed against outside events or constellations of power.

Of course, the relationship between radicalism and courses of study must be comprehended in terms broader than the career; it tends to involve the whole of life. The "vocational" ambitions of radicals, as generally distinct from almost all others, have tended to be directed toward teaching, the social sciences, and "creative" careers generally.[52] We should keep in mind the fact that many radical students, and quite a few others as well, have not attended college for primarily vocational reasons in the first place, a phenomenon that is only partly a survival of the very unvocational dilettantism of older upper-class education. It is the commonest of observations that the values of many Left-wing students have been nonvocational, which is to say that they have not thought about or organized their activities mainly in terms of their future careers. Education has commonly been viewed essentially as a thing that is good or rewarding in and of itself. In varying degrees such students have rejected on moral grounds the possibility of working within at least those structures of society viewed as responsible for the war, for continuing racism, and for pollution—essentially the economy and the government. The fact that virtually no other organized institutional base for radicalism exists in American society has meant that they have continued to fall back primarily on the university itself, thus contributing to making it a battleground for all the struggles of the times.

I will return later to the question of the larger meaning of the counterculture. It will suffice here merely to emphasize its connection with the idea of a career and, through this, to the disciplinary structure of the academy. For radicals, rejection of the middle-class idea

52. See, for example, Braungart, p. 335.

of a career, with its trappings of status, power, and personal corruption within American institutions, is a rejection of something larger than just vocationalism. To reject careerism is to reject the achievement ethos itself, and this goes to the core of the meaning of America. Flacks has gone so far as to argue that this is a form of blocked mobility,[53] in which the barrier is not "objective" in the sense of rejection because all the slots are filled, but of a moral revulsion so deep that to participate would be a personal calamity psychologically reducing oneself, in one's own eyes, to a moral cipher. It can be posited that all societies exhibit norms and values relating to the social necessity of work. When a society provides substantial numbers of its citizens only with situations in which they feel they are forced to relinquish their sense of moral worth—to become nothing—it is indeed in crisis.

These patterns are consistent with the core-periphery model. Students in vocational-technical curricula are in training for quite specific kinds of slots in the occupational world, primarily in corporate and government worlds, and their values and politics reflect this fact. Those in social-humanistic, nonvocational settings are organizationally and culturally remote from such milieux, and the experiences commonly associated with them. The curricular structure reproduces, in microcosm, structural forms—and consequences of these forms—analogous to those defining the academic world as a whole.

All this is by no means to denigrate the significance of occupational life. Quite to the contrary, it implies that the creation of socially constructive jobs and occupations—work designed to build a humane society—and that thereby provides a meaningful framework for individual self-actualization, is a most

53. Richard Flacks, "Some Social and Cultural Meanings of Student Revolt: Some Informal Comparative Observations," *Social Problems* (Winter 1970).

urgent priority. But it is clear that the political framework that would make this possible has yet to come into being.

Conclusion: The Societal Context

Like that of the humanist family, the role of educational institutions in creating protest and struggle can be understood in the larger terms of master trends in advanced capitalist industrial development. In educational terms this has meant a shift from elite to mass education, and it subsumes three interrelated processes: (1) agglomeration, (2) institutional coordination, and (3) differentiation. All are related to the rise of student protest and struggle.

At least up until the Second World War, and probably beyond, educational institutions served mainly the needs of the elite, although the Morrill Act had created important inroads with the establishment of Land Grant Colleges. But for the most part, education was financed by private money in the interests of the upper class. This meant two things. First, the size of the educational establishment remained very small. At the time of World War I probably less than two percent of all college-age persons were enrolled in college. This figure is now around 40 percent. Second, this system was not one upon which industry and business were fundamentally dependent, although it was beginning to produce significant numbers of engineers and other technicians. Rather, it served status and leisure needs of the elite. Higher education during this period included the very important component of "character building," by which was meant training in the various facets of upper-class lifestyles. Closely related was the fact that, for men in particular, college provided a few years of youthful irresponsibility before assumption of the sobriety required for adult responsibilities—an aspect of what Veblen called "conspicuous waste."

Agglomeration of vast numbers of students, in some cases 20,000 and more in a relatively concentrated space, is one *condition* facilitating development of protest. Some have spoken of a "critical mass," an unspecified number beneath which organized protest is not possible, because not enough individuals sensitive to radical political appeals would be present. Although the magnitude of such a critical mass is obviously highly variable, depending on characteristics of the population as well as other aspects of the institution itself, we can accept the notion in principle. We have seen that larger institutions produce more protest than smaller ones, although the *proportion* of students involved in the larger institutions has been lower than in smaller liberal arts schools.[54]

Although it cannot be demonstrated directly, this fact may stem from the bureaucratization that typically accompanies institutional growth. We have already noted the rather ambiguous relationship between bureaucratization and protest. Bureaucratization is a way of integrating individuals and their functions through extension of control over their activities. This is to say that the conditions of struggle are in fact made more, not less, difficult. It seems reasonable to interpret the evidence in such fashion: while agglomeration has provided an increasingly significant *technical* condition of organized protest, bureaucratization in its *direct* effect, has tended, if anything, to inhibit or restrain its incidence and intensity.

It has been argued, and in some degree demonstrated, that bureaucratization can inhibit development of class or group consciousness in various ways: for example, by functional departmentalization or fragmentation, by encouraging a sense of difference and/or competitiveness

54. The findings of Scott and El-Assal, and Kahn and Bowers.

between units, and by creation of a graded hierarchy through which advancement is at least theoretically possible, thus encouraging a personal mobility orientation that is inherently competitive and that therefore tends to separate men. If bureaucracies in these and other ways serve to disguise or conceal interests, they can hardly as such, be causes of revolt. This is not to say that bureaucratization is not a source of alienation and dehumanization or that one should not struggle against bureaucratic domination; only that it is not a sufficient cause of the student movement.

Dramatic increase in institutional coordination dates essentially from the end of World War II. The Cold War years of the 1950s saw immense growth in the relationships between the government and business on the one hand, and the colleges and universities on the other. While some of them, mainly the elite schools in the East, continued to perform their class-related functions of socialization, the rapid expansion of the bulk of the system meant that large sectors were moved toward increasingly technical, occupational, and ideological coordination with the economic and political orders. The most important aspects of this development have been: (1) business and industrial determination and support of all sorts of programs, curriculums, schools, and colleges in the interest of turning out technical personnel appropriate for the work requirements of the system; (2) creation of a university-based system of research units for varied purposes, but increasingly serving war-related interests, of government agencies directly or of government-subsidized corporations such as Lockheed and General Dynamics; and (3) proliferation of an extensive system of government-and-business-consulting on the part of a growing class drawn from among the professoriate in all fields, ranging from the technical or hard sciences to the disciplines relevant for social policy-making and implementation. These processes

THE ACADEMY • 125

meant that many institutions, especially the larger and better ones, became increasingly dependent on and thus subject to the influences of government and business interests.

Along with its immense growth, the differentiation of the system has proceeded rapidly—a process that somewhat imperfectly aligns the structure of the educational system with the societal class system. With the entrance of so many students from the middle ranges of society, and recently increasingly even from lower strata, the changes in the system have been designed so as to serve what are perceived to be the highly differentiated needs of the different classes. The California system is the most highly developed, a vertically differentiated structure designed to prepare students from different class levels for entrance into the occupational world of achievement and reward at the appropriate level. Thus, many trained people of differing talents and resources are made available at the different levels. In California, the amount of public money spent on a student at the Berkeley campus is at least three times as great as it is for a student at one of the state-supported junior colleges. So, while the system supposedly guarantees a free public education to anyone, it does so on the terms of the perpetuation of existing societal inequalities. The junior colleges are mostly for working-class youth; the majority who complete the two years will be unable to go on to higher education. Their primary function is thus to maintain the class system as it is. This is true as well of the meritocratic elements that the system includes. The tracking that begins much earlier is thus carried forward within the system or elsewhere toward a baccalaurate degree. The system is meritocratic to the extent that it allows a number of superior achievers from the lower reaches of the society to enter schools that are mainly for those from the middle and upper-middle classes.

This practice serves several important functions. First, it allows for the perpetuation of the myth of equality of opportunity, a very important legitimation of the system as a whole. Successful minority members serve as models for those at the bottom generally, demonstrating by their success that the possibility exists for any and all. For those in the white middle classes, it remains possible to believe that anyone can pull himself up by the bootstraps if he puts out enough effort. Second, some degree of meritocratic selection drains off considerable potential for political leadership, thus contributing to the general disorganized and divided state of those at the bottom. In this fashion the increasing differentiation of the educational system responds to the needs of the societal system, for the most part contributing to its perpetuation.

While the growth in size and scope of the system has been an important technical condition facilitating protest, bureaucratization has tended to keep masses of students wedded to their routines, even when they may have been touched by the ideological currents of the times. Atmospheres in which bureaucratic control has been relatively lax have facilitated protest, and these are strongly related to the educational quality of the institutions themselves. At the same time, coordination of universities with political and economic orders, and their continued functioning as perhaps the most significant vehicle of class inequality, have increasingly expanded the consciousness of students. Thus, the concatenation of these circumstances, (1) high-quality educational institutions that (2) have been coordinated with business and government needs, but with (3) relatively loose or lax bureaucratic control, have been the most fertile breeding grounds of protest. Originally, those students which constituted the vanguard were already sensitized and prepared in their homes for perception and understanding of societal contradictions. Later, this base expanded beyond the original minority, and, in spite of the decline of the movement, one may say that not only large numbers of college students, but many others as well, have become ideologically sensitized to these questions.

4
DYNAMICS OF CAMPUS CONFRONTATION

The growth and decline of the movement have been comprised mostly of events occurring in local milieux and displaying a kaleidoscope of political activity. It is important to analyze these confrontations because their inner dynamic illuminates much about the ebb and flow of the movement. Specifically, the key issue lies in the relation of protest and violence, and the creation and destruction of meanings in this context. I will treat this question in terms of two related aspects: (1) factors affecting protest and violence, and (2) the relation of protest and violence to different institutional environments and responses.

Common conceptions of and rhetoric about the relation between protest and violence have emerged either out of the immediacy of being in the center of the storm, or from press accounts. But the immediate experiences of those involved in a particular clash not only very often give rise to quite inconsistent accounts of the events themselves, but are less than objective bases for generalizations about campus confrontations in general. Let us look now at the available data.

A comprehensive analysis of this relationship was undertaken by Long and Foster, who mailed questionnaires to the presidents of all the universities and colleges belonging to the American Council of Education, obtaining a return of 47 percent.[1] Their data indicate that up through the spring of 1968 protests had occurred at 43 percent of the responding institutions,[2] although this may be a somewhat inflated figure since larger institutions had both a higher return rate and a higher rate of violence. In 1968 the actual figure was probably no more than 40 percent—let us put it conservatively between 35 and 40 percent. This means that around 1,000 institutions had experienced some kind of protest up through the spring of 1968. The events in the aftermath of the Kent State and Jackson State killings and the invasion of Cambodia in the spring of 1970 increased this figure considerably. A study by the Carnegie Commission showed that the latter events caused student-faculty strikes on 21 percent of campuses with more than 5,000 students. And this does not include institutions where protest demonstrations but no strikes occurred. The Harris poll conducted at the same time revealed that over half of all students participated in the uprising in some way.[3]

What of more recent years? It has been commonly assumed that the academic year 1970-71 was one in which

1. Durward Long and Julian Foster, "Levels of Protest," in Long and Foster, eds., *Protest: Student Activism in America* (New York: William Morrow & Co., Inc., 1970), pp. 81-88.
2. The sample may be biased in at least three ways: (1) larger institutions had a greater return rate, possibly because many presidents undoubtedly had their assistants complete the questionnaires and return them, and presidents of larger institutions have more staff assistance available: (2) presidents and their assistants, as Long and Foster recognize, may have had a biased view of events (although Morgan's analysis of questionnaires returned by administrators, faculty members, and students yielded high agreement (see Morgan, n16, this chapter); and (3) the reports of violence refer to the occurrence of any violence whatever, regardless of the number of protest demonstrations or activities on any particular campus. The authors evidently did not attempt to elicit information about the incidence of protest or violence at particular institutions.
3. Harris *Poll of Students,* May 20-128, 1970.

there was a great decline in protest. Compared to 1969-70, this is true, due mainly to the response to the Kent State killings and the invasion of Cambodia. However, compared to 1968-69 there was, somewhat surprisingly, scarcely any decline, as Bayer and Astin have shown.[4] Evidently, the decline was in press coverage. By 1971, we may assume, over one-half of all American institutions had experienced some degree of protest, and the figure may be considerably higher. Student protest has clearly been a mass phenomenon. One change noted by Bayer and Astin was a shift in the locus of protest to institutions of "Low Selectivity," by which they mean those of lower quality.[5]

So much for the incidence of protest in general. What about violence? The presidents reported violence at only 17 of the 535 institutions at which protest occurred, a rate of less than three percent. And even obstructive action (generally meaning civilly disobedient activity of some kind, particularly sit-ins) occurred in only 48 instances, or nine percent of the total.[6] Clearly, while the incidence of protest has been high, violent or obstructive actions have constituted only a small part of it. Furthermore, if we preferred to revise these figures as proportions of the total range of about 2,580 institutions belonging to the A.C.E., we would conclude that protest of some sort occurred in over fifty percent, civil disobedience in perhaps five percent, and violence in about one percent. These figures reveal the overwhelmingly nonviolent character of student activism up to 1968.[7]

4. Allen E. Bayer and Alexander Astin, "Campus Unrest 1970-71: Was it Really All That Quiet?" *The Educational Record* (Fall 1971), pp. 301-13. See Table 1.
5. *Ibid.*, Table 2.
6. Long and Foster, "Levels. . .,", p. 84.
7. In considering the issue from the sheerly quantitative standpoint, I should make some mention of possible administrator's bias in completion of questionnaires. It is possible, on the one hand, that some presidents or their assistants reported as violent events that could only on the most meretricious criterion be so designated, because of the tendency of some

In this connection the reader should understand that in this discussion, and throughout the remainder of this chapter, I speak exclusively of the violence arising out of situations of campus confrontation, and not that associated with guerilla-type activities. Both politically and organizationally the two types differ significantly. Guerilla actions have been the work of revolutionaries organized in small, highly fragmented "cells," having little or no connection with larger movement organizations. Violence occurring within campus confrontation, on the other hand, has to be understood in terms of the process of confrontation itself and the nature of the issues at stake.

The Long and Foster materials also address the question of the relation between issues and violence. Data in

to stigmatize peacefully *disruptive* actions as violent. Thus, it may be that some essentially nonviolent activities are here reported as violent, thus inflating the reported rate of violence to some extent. On the other hand, it is possible that reports of both violence and protest have been underreported to some degree because of administrators' presumed unwillingness to admit that there are issues worthy of protest, or their unwillingness to have such matters bandied about in reports, scientific or otherwise, prepared by various investigators (to say nothing of the press). Large publicity given to protest has sometimes been considered undesirable and financially unhealthy by administrators, and, indeed, state legislatures have in many places arranged financial (and legal) punishments for state institutions. To some extent this is also true of private ones. Furthermore, there is some evidence that widely publicized protest brings in its aftermath a decrease in applications for admission and, particularly in the case of such institutions as Columbia, has an unwanted negative effect on prestige. Again, reports of protest have often tended to reflect in an unfavorable way on administrators, unless they can manage to cast themselves in the role of heroic defender, as in the case of President Hayakawa at San Francisco State. Inept handling of protest, from the standpoint of outsiders, can thus have ramifications for the professional and career possibilities of administrators. All this would seem to suggest a bias in the direction of underreporting. This remains a matter of speculation, however, particularly in view of the fact that in Long and Foster's study only very small proportions of university presidents reported that the protest had worsened relations with the community, or that the State legislature had become less supportive. But this, of course, was 1968. See Long and Foster, "Dynamics of Institutional Responses," in *Protest: Student Activism in America*, p. 443. An analysis by Morgan also suggests that university presidents are not necessarily biased. Their accounts of activity centering around on-campus recruitment did not depart significantly from those of students or faculty members. See William R. Morgan, "Faculty Mediation in Campus Conflict," in *Protest!* . . . , pp. 365-82.

Table 8, which I have taken from their analysis, suggest that there has been little violence over strictly local issues such as educational and *in loco parentis* matters. However, neither does it seem to be the case that national issues have *as such* been occasions of greater violence. The draft and the war have been national issues but seem to have occasioned little violence (practically none at all, if Long and Foster's data are to be accepted as exact, which of course, they should not be). Obviously, the war and the draft have differed somewhat from issues like on-campus recruiting and race in terms of the likelihood of engendering violence.

Table 8

Types of Issues and Levels of Protest*
(in percents)

Level of Protest	N	Recruit-ment	Race	Vietnam and Draft	Education Policies	In Loco Parentis
Violent	17	8	10	0	1	1
Obstructive	48	27	12	13	6	3
Physical	174	49	38	55	28	25
Diplomatic	296	16	40	32	65	71
	535	100	100	100	100	100

*My title. I have changed Long and Foster's original title because it suggests that the data have substantive implications that I regard as imprecisely delineated. The original title was "National Issues Stirred More Violent Protest than On-Campus Ones." See Long and Foster, "Levels of Protest," p. 85.

There is at least one major difference between issues such as the draft and the war, and those such as race and on-campus recruiting. The latter are matters over which the university itself could exercise some real influence: recruiters could be kicked off the campus, or even, as more often occurred, relegated to a more inconspicuous location; discriminatory policies against blacks can be changed through new programs and imaginative and enlightened recruiting. This is not so of the propagation of the war or of draft policy; over such matters the university has only the most remote influence. Violence, insofar as it actually has been perpetrated by students, is in this sense "rational"; it has occurred mostly in connection with protest over issues within the effective power of the university. Indeed, violence against an institution over issues remote from its competence or jurisdiction, except in the minds of the most ideological of men, would seem tactically misplaced.

To the extent that they have perpetuated racially discriminatory policies, recruitment on campus, and war-related research and connections with the government and private industry—which is to say, permitted themselves to become coordinated—the universities have made themselves the immediate and direct targets of rage engendered not by university conditions as such, but by the great issues of national life and policy. Bad teaching, paternalism, and impersonal bureaucracy are common enough, but except where matters of fundamental moral significance intrude, they have rarely resulted in violence.

Related to this is the fact that university authorities have been more likely to call in police (or National Guard) to put down protests over issues having to do with the outside links of the university than they have over purely internal matters. Police on the campus, more than any other single event, symbolize for students in immediate concrete form what they take to be sheer repression. Police "electrify" the student body, create an immediate shift of masses of previously uncommitted students to active protest, and thereby have created a *condition* for violence not theretofore present.

Why have authorities called in police on "external" issues more often than "internal" ones? The answer may lie in the fact that, while students have always been totally shut out of the management of the former, they have participated to some extent in both educational and parietal practice. This has been so in both formal and informal ways. Students have been involved, even if in very limited ways, for instance, in both policy-making and administration of dormitory regulations, thus providing possibilities for both some degree of formal influence over and informal evasion of the rules (the latter often taking on the character of sport). The potential influence of students on teaching is obvious and makes itself felt in many, if small, ways, too numerous to go into here. The important point is that in the case of both teaching and parietal management, students have experienced degrees of institutionalized relationships to those in power, and to some (admittedly small) extent have even managed to affect these policies.

The same cannot be said about many other matters, particularly those involving high-level relations with government and private industry. Here, students have never participated and have never had any influence. The difference, from the standpoint of sociological theory, is instructive. I would argue that the actual institutionalization of relations in educational and parietal spheres has acted as a strong reinforcing factor in making this a common and intense but nonviolent sphere of student protest.

Dahrendorf's analysis of organizational conflict is useful in understanding these differences.[8] He has argued that violence tends to occur in situations where relationships between superordinate and subordinate groups within an organization are *not* institutionalized. The intensity of the conflict, however, is related not to institutionalization but to the presence of overlapping or

8. See Ralf Dahrendorf, *Class and Class Conflict in Industrial Society* (Stanford, Calif.: Stanford University Press, 1959).

reinforcing statuses. Thus, the theory would characterize students as a subordinate group with respect to their role specifically as students *and* as a politically subordinate group with respect to their role as citizens, which is to say, as members of the state. This condition has intensified their sense of oppression in general. It is youth who have been drafted and sent to be killed in the war (the median age of American soldiers killed in Vietnam is around twenty), and who have been politically powerless to do anything about it, just as they have been powerless to do anything about the larger relations of the university. In neither instance are there real channels of communication or influence, or even potential influence.

In these terms, the *intensity* of protest over societal but campus-manifest arrangements is great because the statuses of student, and of youthful citizen, who may be required to fight and kill, have reinforced one another. The higher rate of *violence*, on the other hand, has resulted from the absence of institutionalized relations in these spheres. In the case of national issues over which universities have little or no control, this is so simply because of their organizational irrelevance. In the case of strictly local matters, it has resulted, in part at least, from the fact that to some extent institutional relations have in fact been present.[9]

9. Since there seems to be a reasonably clear relationship between protest and violence on the one hand and issues on the other, since protest demonstrations over strictly local issues seem to be larger than those over national issues (see Astin), and since there is an obvious relationship between the size of institutions and the size of demonstrations, it seems a bit strange that the Long and Foster data show a relationship between the size of institutions and the incidence of violence. This is, however, the case. Fourteen percent of the protests at large institutions (those over 10,000) involved violence, but this was true of only two percent at medium-sized ones (2,500-10,000) and less than one percent at those below 2,500. The same pattern prevailed for obstructive action or civil disobedience, which occurred at twenty-two percent of the large, eight percent of the medium-sized and only one percent of the smaller institutions. Violent and disruptive protest, then, seems to have been a function of institutional size. But since we have seen that there is a relationship between institutional size and the incidence of protest, this is surprising. Among other things, it suggests that violence and the size of protest demonstrations have been unrelated, and

Conditions of violence may thus be seen to be different from those of protest. While protest in general has occurred disproportionately in contexts of large numbers, emphasis on personal freedom, and high depersonalization (see chap. 3), violence has been fostered more specifically by situations where institutional relations relative to national but campus-manifest issues have been attenuated or nonexistent. And the salience of these issues has obviously been much greater in the coordinated-humanistic institutions (Figure 1). This has obvious implications for student participation in the governance of the university.

Protest and Violence:
Administrative Responses and Effects

In the simplest possible formulation, administrations could respond to protest in at least four ways: (1) by attempting to repress it, (2) by making concessions, (3) by bargaining, or (4) by attempting to ignore it. However, simply to ignore protest, although it might seem to achieve a tactical advantage for the movement, cannot in itself effect a resolution of issues, unless the protest itself is greatly constricted in scope and intensity. I will therefore not consider it as a viable tactic of conflict resolution. It is not possible to know the relative incidence of these different responses. Long and Foster on the one hand tell us that bargaining has been frequent, but also that

> few administrations have been particularly imaginative in their efforts at persuasion. The method typically involves

that the relationship between institutional size and violent or disruptive protest may have resulted from characteristics of the universities themselves. It is, of course, primarily the big state universities along with some of the bigger private ones that have the big contracts and that constitute the most fruitful recruiting grounds, especially for technical and scientifically trained people.

the issuing of formal statements to the press, couched in official and restrained language, and appealing to norms which are patently unrelated to the protesters.[10]

However, Bayer and Astin, comparing their 1968-69 and 1970-71 data, concluded that "there was less negotiation of issues with students" (from 78 percent of the institutions experiencing severe incidents in 1968-69 to 52 percent in 1970-71).[11] In any case, administrative responses have varied with circumstances, such as the intrusion of outside political force—the best example of this perhaps being in California, where Governor Reagan and the Board of Trustees took a personal hand in both the Berkeley and San Francisco State uprisings, firing presidents and generally dictating policy. It is possible, however, to say something about the general process of confrontation, within which repression, concession, and bargaining have occurred.

Morgan analyzed the dynamics of confrontation at 106 institutions where there had been confrontations over on-campus recruitment by representatives of the Department of Defense or war-related industries.[12] The results of his analysis bear immediately on our problem.

First, the demonstrations did not occur without many prior attempts at communication with the administrations. Administrations were practically uniformly indifferent, despite the fact that objections to recruiting had been pressed in an average of four of seven different ways: campus newspaper editorials, meetings reported in the student paper, student government resolutions, petitions, leaflets, conversations with administrators, and conversations with faculty members.

Second, the incidence of civil disobedience in the ensuing demonstrations was related to the extent of attemp-

10. Long and Foster, "The Dynamics...," p. 423.
11. Bayer and Astin, pp. 309-10.
12. Morgan, "Faculty Mediation...."

ted communication in the predemonstration period. Where communication was low, that is to say, where fewer than three channels of communication were utilized, civil disobedience occurred in only 12 percent of the protest demonstrations. Where it was at a medium level (3-4 channels), civil disobedience occurred in 36 percent of the protests, and where it was above this, in 43 percent. In other words, civil disobedience occurred in the wake of situations where numerous unsuccessful attempts to communicate with administrations had been made. Insofar as administrations did respond, it was to "confine themselves to affirming existing recruiting policy and warning against interference during the impending recruiting visits."[13]

The consequences of one manner of mixing concessions and repression strategies can be seen in events at Columbia. There, protest had begun two years before the events of the spring of 1968. Students had already been protesting university policies vis-à-vis the community and various government agencies including the military.

> The administrators responded first with concessions, and later with repression, but they failed to re-examine their basic policies—or to make any reforms in the way the university's policies were determined. The public policies of the university (as opposed to its internal academic issues) were being determined by only a few administrators, after little or no consultation with the faculty, let alone the students.[14]

During the years preceding spring 1968, the university

---

13. *Ibid.*, p. 369.
14. Ellen Kay Trimberger, "Columbia: The Dynamics of Student Revolution" *Trans-action* (September 1969); reprinted in *Campus Power Struggle*, ed. Howard S. Becker (Chicago: Aldine, 1970), pp. 27-55. The quotation is taken from pp. 27-28. All subsequent reports of events, unless otherwise indicated, are drawn from the Trimberger account. However, none of these events has, to my knowledge, been contradicted *factually* in important ways in other published accounts of the Columbia insurrection.

had been declining in prestige, and the proposed expansion into Morningside Heights, adjacent to Harlem, was part of a major program attempting to reverse this trend. As at practically all institutions of higher learning, student influence in the university was practically nonexistent. The students had voted to abolish the student government some years preceding, and in fact, even before the demonstrations, both the president and vice-president of the student council had resigned their positions, saying that the body was ineffective. The series of resolutions passed by the council had been totally ignored by the administration, which failed to consult either formally or informally with the council. Furthermore, faculty influence has evidently been quite weak at Columbia. The faculty council included at that time a majority of administrators, was chaired and run by administrators, and dealt hardly at all with other than routine matters. Faculty committees had little influence on the administration, their reports and recommendations having been generally disregarded.

In this situation a coalition of student organizations in 1966-67 confronted the administration over a series of issues, conducting mass demonstrations and threatening to strike. The university administration made the following concessions: (1) instituted a policy of withholding class ranks from local draft boards; (2) established a commission comprised of administrators, faculty members, and students to try students who had participated in demonstrations against the C.I.A.; and (3) canceled army recruiting on the campus and the annual Naval Reserve Officers Training Corps ceremony. Although the student newspaper generally hailed these concessions as a major breakthrough, Trimberger notes that not the slightest change in fostering structural reforms in university governance was initiated. The university administration resisted such change until the very end.

It is not possible here to recount in detail all the sig-

nificant events of the Columbia uprising. As everyone
knows, there were two police actions, the first occasion-
ing considerable violence by the police and the second
involving a return in kind by students. In the first action
many bystanders were clubbed by police, who also
smashed furniture and other articles in the rooms that
had been occupied by the students. The administration,
which during the academic year had failed to enforce its
own regulations against demonstrations, during the confrontation determined that calling in the police was the
only way to preserve its authority. Indeed, the administration defined the situation as one in which it was essential, at all 'costs, to retain its authority. During the period
before and after the police actions, the administration
refused to bargain on the issue of amnesty (raised as always, immediately upon the arrest of students) and generally took a "hard line" on all issues. During this period
it was evidently almost totally isolated from all other
elements in the university, although its members con-
ferred regularly with outside figures such as Mayor Lind-
sey. The administration never admitted any need to consider restructuring the university, and Vice-President
Truman stated that the most important lesson he had
learned was to call the police immediately in the future.

The administration's belief that a policy of repression
would restore its authority was erroneous. In the first
place, the very fact of such massive action, involving at
least 800 students (a very conservative figure) along with
several thousand sympathizers backed by *all* the moderate student leaders, indicated that that authority had already suffered extensive erosion. And after the police
bust, a survey showed that support for the sit-ins increased by 17 percent among faculty and by 19 percent
among students. Calling in the police, far from providing an antidote to eroded authority, was the occasion for
its almost total obliteration.

The developments at Columbia can perhaps be thought

of as occurring in three phases. First, there was a period during which attempts to utilize existing means of communication were made. During this phase there was considerable ambiguity in the position of the administration with respect to the actual enforcement of regulations, and some concessions on particular issues. The second phase was that of direct confrontation initiated by the students, a time of dramatically increasing polarization. During this period the definitions of the situation by both students and administration were confirmed in the manner of a "self-fulfilling prophecy." Since the confrontation tactics of the students were unable either to wring concessions from or to bring the administration to the bargaining table, the initial student definition of the administration as irrevocably rigid by reason of its being locked into the larger power structure of America, was reinforced. Likewise, from the standpoint of the administration, the radical and intransigent character of student protesters was confirmed by their escalation of confrontation tactics. This resulted in the emergence of various myths, particularly those of the protesters being a small band of students organized by a few "outside agitators" (in spite of the great numbers involved), and that they "were out to destroy the university."

The third phase was initiated by the administration's attempt at repression, which exacerbated greatly the already polarized situation. This phase is notable in that attempts at intervention by members of the faculty proved totally ineffectual and resulted only in increasing the alienation of the students from the faculty as well as the administration, thus confirming the belief of many of the students that the faculty were not to be trusted and, at worst, were no better than administration stooges.

Trimberger concludes that it had been the polarization itself that had prevented a rapprochement at Columbia. In this process the moderate positions were destroyed: student moderates became radicalized, administration moderates became rigid and conservative, faculty moderates failed in attempts to mediate and became alienated from both sides. The weakness of the moderates was a result of the institutional weaknesses of Columbia—authority, the lack of effective faculty and student governments, and the attenuation of faculty-student relations. These institutional weaknesses led to a general lack of administrative and faculty responsiveness to student grievances and to the students' attempt to compel response by dramatic action.[15]

It is interesting that, although he approached the situation from a more conservative stance and in some particulars disagreed in his interpretations, Daniel Bell arrived at essentially the same conclusion.

The true difficulty is that the Columbia administration, both in its experience and in its conceptions of politics, was ill equipped for either the Machiavellianism of Brzezinski or the politics of persuasion that I think would have served the university far better.[16]

in a community one cannot regain authority simply by asserting it, or by using force to suppress dissidents. Authority in this case is like respect. One can only *earn* the authority—the loyalty of one's students—by going in and arguing with them, by engaging in full debate.[17]

Even after suspension of many strike leaders, Bell tells us, the university

still did not completely recognize the need to engage students in debate; in part, simply for lack of an adequate apparatus—the administration's public relations were singularly inept. The university never presented its own case for the gymnasium.[18]

15. Trimberger, p. 54.
16. Daniel Bell, "Columbia and the New Left," in *Confrontation: The Student Rebellion and the Universities* (New York: Basic Books, 1968), p. 101.
17. *Ibid.*, p. 101.
18. *Ibid.*, p. 104.

Although Bell here seems to reduce the problem of communication with students to one of public relations, in connection with the question of the manner in which the university throttled or frustrated the voices of all except those of the administration, he nevertheless argues that

the major lapse of the administration was its failure to respond to the evident desire for structural change which became so manifest [that] one of the buildings [was] seized.[19]

Vice-President Truman had attempted to address himself to this question by arranging a greater voice for the liberal arts portions of the university as against the professional schools, but not, apparently, by in any way attempting to democratize student-administration relations. According to Bell,

Truman worked cautiously, cards close to the chest, and consulting only a few senior persons, instead of involving the faculty and even the student body in broad discussions.[20]

My point here is not to show that Bell is in any fundamental ideological agreement with Trimberger, which he most decidedly seems not to be (since his analysis is, in part, an attempt to stigmatize the protestors as using "desperado tactics [that] are never the mark of a coherent social movement, but the guttering last gasps of a romanticism soured by rancor and impotence, ... impelled not to innovation but to destruction"[21]). Rather, I merely attempt to show that, in spite of his general view of things, along with other liberal or even conservative critics of student radicals, he emphasizes the university's lack of institutional ways for students (and faculty) to press their views with some

19. *Ibid.*, p. 105.
20. *Ibid.*, p. 106.
21. *Ibid.*

hope of exerting actual influence. From the narrow situational standpoint of confrontation, this is what university protest has been all about. In the absence of such institutional modes of participation, many students and some faculty members have been driven progressively to insurrections like Columbia's, although most such affairs, of course, have not occurred on such a scale or involved such violence. In the absence of institutional means of participation (excluding, of course, the symbolic ones such as student government), definitions of the situation harden and are confirmed by actions of those on the other side—actions that were initially responses to the rigidity and stereotyping present in the original situation. In situations where there is no "third force" (such as the faculty, which has practically everywhere been disorganized and essentially powerless), this process was free to go on unchecked. Even when "peace" has been restored, the situation has typically remained one of untrusting standoff. And even in those modal situations in which confrontation has not reached such intensity, the process has been essentially the same.

I cannot in this work present a series of additional cases in the descriptive detail necessary to convincingly demonstrate inductively the pattern of confrontation in student protest. Available space permits the description of only one additional case.[22] At the University of Indiana a group of students protested the presence of the Dow Chemical Company recruiter on the campus in October 1967.[23] After a protest march, in which 75 to 100 participated, about 45 or 50 students arrived at the Business Building, where the interviewing was scheduled to

22. But see, for example, practically any of the accounts dealing with Berkeley, Wisconsin, San Francisco State, or Howard.
23. The Faculty Forum to Investigate the Dow Incident of Indiana University, "Indiana: The Anatomy of Violence" in Long and Foster, *Protest!. . .*, pp. 229-45. I use the Indiana case partly because it is the product of a *faculty committee,* and therefore can perhaps reasonably be assumed to be a balanced, objective presentation and analysis.

take place. The students made repeated requests to speak with the Dow Interviewer, all of which were refused—after all, they had no appointment. The Dean of the Business School is reported to have said that he believed the interviewer's life would have been endangered if he had come out to meet the group. The students, who had been sitting in the hallway in nondisruptive fashion (that is, in such a manner that access was not blocked), voted to enter the anteroom of an inner room in which the interviewing was taking place. After the vote was taken, the officer in charge requested assistance in the form of further police reinforcements, and told the students they would be arrested if they entered the room. Although two officers tried to hold the door (which had for a time been locked, but then apparently unlocked from the inside), the students pressed in, brushing the officers aside. Once inside they did not attempt to force their way into the interview room, which was only a few feet away.

Meanwhile, the campus police chief had called for outside help, and advised that riot equipment be brought to the scene. Shortly, a number of Bloomington police, some in full riot gear—including gas grenades —arrived. When the student nearest the door was told to leave or be carried out (and probably "get hurt" in the process), he elected to walk. Thereupon, most of the students got up and prepared to leave. These were escorted to a waiting bus and placed under custody. Some 15 students who remained in the room were then attacked and beaten by the police, in some instances with obvious relish but without provocation. Cameras that had been set up earlier recorded this and the antecedent proceedings on film. Although several students were seriously injured from being beaten about the head and neck, they were for several hours deprived of medical attention. In the aftermath followed the plethora of civil legal action and campus quasi-legal activity that has everywhere typically followed such events. In their analysis the faculty committee wrote:

> If there was one cause that contributed more than any other to the violence, it was the previously laid plan to cope with a riot. Conceived on a tough line, inflexibly structured, and left to low-level administrators to administer, this plan determined most of the events of October 30. The off-campus police were called when the possibilities for violence were difficult to assess. But once the students had entered the room and it became obvious that there would be no riot, there was no reason to bring off-campus police inside the Business Building. What authority Dean Smith and Professor Snider possessed was relinquished early, and the orders that Captain Spannuth gave had been previously determined when the plan was made.[24]

As at Columbia, the insistence on retaining "authority," and the definition of the situation as one involving students who would "riot," determined the hard line of administrative procedure. The self-fulfilling prophecy, dominating administrative conceptions of the situation in which no channels of communication or influence existed, resulted in violent police action. Although the account of the Faculty Committee concludes at this point, it is well known that this event was a major one contributing to the polarization of the university. Students and faculty generally supported the students and in varying degree condemned the administration, whose actions, like those of the Columbia administration, were self-defeating.

The effects of repressive administrative policy over a large number of cases is shown with remarkable clarity in the study by Morgan referred to earlier. For 102 instances of administrative response to protest over on-campus recruiting, the more severe the action taken, the greater was the likelihood of an expansion of the protest. When police were called in and demonstrators ar-

24. *Ibid.*, pp. 244-45.

rested, the protest expanded in more than 50 percent of the cases. If measures of medium severity were employed (taking names for later disciplinary action, or giving warnings to the demonstrators), expansion of the protest occurred in only about one-quarter of the cases. Where administrations made promises to deal with the issues, only seven percent of the protests were expanded.[25] One wonders what Vice-President Truman had in mind.

All this supports the common observation that much of the protest of students has been sustained by the sheer clumsiness and bullheadedness of administrative repression. It is even possible that in a quantitative sense it has been at least as important as movement ideology. In fact, the predictability of college administrations has been an essential factor in the escalation of local protests, particularly where movement leaders have employed the tactic of eliciting a police bust. Police on the campus have represented for students a complete vindication of their darkest conceptions of the administration, and a confirmation of its utter disregard for the validity of the issues about which they have attempted to express themselves. As such, police have been a virtual guarantee that the definition of the situation on both sides will be escalated in self-fulfilling fashion. Police or National Guard on campus have constituted the ultimate step in an ascending scale of noncommunication.

Most of the dynamic of confrontation has occurred not in terms of police or national guard intervention, but in terms of increasingly intense verbalization on both sides. The increasing loss of legitimacy of a university administration can be seen in the raising of the verbal ante through such statements as that of Mark Rudd: "Up against the wall, motherfuckers—this is a stick-up!", or simply in denouncing administrative statements as so

25. Morgan, p. 373.

much "bullshit."[26] Likewise, administrators and others
have commonly stigmatized demonstrators as children,
cautioning them that their youthful energies would be
better spent in panty raids or, as Vice-President Truman
characterized Mark Rudd, "an adolescent having a
temper tantrum."

As the semantics increasingly polarize the two sides'
views of one another, the positions taken become more
rigid and more ideologically impregnated, thus making
communication of any type much more difficult. Sometimes concessions have been made and the protest run
its course, but the general pattern that pervaded the
situation in the early 1970s was one of continued frustration on the part of students, and a wary untrusting
toughness among the administration. The faculties have
scarcely moved at all from their general noninvolvement.

From the standpoint of the administration, a repressive policy is in some ways a dubious one, since it tends
to align major elements of the university against itself.
In many cases it can be doubted whether even the support of trustees and politicians is sufficient to counter
such a breach. Repression has necessarily created situations of rancorous conflict and made it impossible to
deal with the issues.

It is doubtful whether a policy of concession is much
better, but this depends on the nature of the concessions. Ritual participation, a form of cooptation predict-
ably instituted in many places, many parietal reforms,
certain changes in educational procedures such as pass-
fail grading, seem to have been of some significance to
at least certain sectors of the student bodies, but do not
involve a change in students' role in policy-making. At
very few places have the administrations or the faculties

26. For Rudd's statement discussing the meaning of this and similar locutions,
see his "Symbols of the Revolution," in Jerry L. Avorn, *Up Against the
Wall: A History of the Columbia Crisis* (New York: Atheneum Publishers,
1968).

been prepared to stand for extensive participation in policy-making. Furthermore, the simple granting of concessions has been likely to bring trustees and politicians on head-hunting expeditions, as presidents Smith and Summerskill of San Francisco State, among others, discovered.

Most important, a policy of concession to particular demands has the great weakness of failing to establish an institutionalized relationship—regardless of the nature of the concessions—with the others in the academic "community." If the concessions are not very meaningful, it is unlikely that the aggrieved will be silenced. Indeed, even if they seem more substantial, this may, in the manner of raising expectations anywhere, foster more militancy. And regardless of whether they have or have not been significant, it is generally the case that administrations have recognized the power, but not the legitimacy, of both protests and protesters. Such a condition is one that tends to foster continuing rancorous conflict.

It would seem that, as Daniel Bell and others have argued, the most rational policy of the administration is to bargain. Bargaining, so long as both parties believe they can gain from it (which may by no means be the case), is the strategy most likely to establish a relationship through which students can make their influence felt in the future. But this depends, of course, on the concrete results of the bargaining. The end result of bargaining is not only that one's power has been applied with some effect, but that one's gains are more likely to be recognized as legitimate as well. Furthermore, since bargaining proceeds by rules and recognized procedures, it is perhaps less likely to elicit repressive storms from trustees and politicians. We have, however, no good analysis of campus bargaining, in part because there has been so little of it, and so all this must be regarded as speculation. Impressionistically, administrations, faculty senates, and academic departments in the late 60s and early 70s seemed everywhere to be in motion over questions of student rights, student participation, student power. But if Bayer and Astin are right, all this has proceeded increasingly independently of bargaining.[27] Such "reform from the top," without fundamental student participation, is undoubtedly a major factor in maintaining the deep alienated mood that continues to characterize the campus.

In what relation, then, to post-protest events has protest itself stood? There is evidence that, at least in terms of a number of specific concrete changes, disruptive protest has been more likely to force administrative and faculty action than lower levels of confrontation. Morgan showed that disruptive protests over on-campus recruiting were more than twice as likely to elicit faculty and student-body responses in the form of resolutions evaluating administrative action; and in these resolutions, "the administrative position...gained little sympathy."[28]

Further, faculty involvement (resulting mostly from raising of the ante by militants) tended to have a very strong effect on the position of the administration with respect to imposing restrictions on recruiters.[29] Wherever faculties took a position on restricting or limiting recruiting, the administrations were very likely to go along. Where only student resolutions were brought forward, the effect on administration policy was much less marked. Clearly, the potential role of the faculty, as everyone has recognized, is great. But the tendency of all faculties is to become aroused only during crises, and then to lapse back into customary routine. Student protest did not succeed in awakening the beast into a state of permanent involvement, a condition only now being approached in the movement toward collective bargaining.

27. Bayer and Astin.
28. Morgan, p. 371, and Table 1, p. 372.
29. *Ibid.*

Nor was there much reason to expect that this would come about. Faculties realize at least certain of their interests at the expense of students. These interests—lowered teaching loads (a somewhat ironic frequent consequence of student protest), low accountability with respect to job performance, maintenance of their power within the strictly academic sector of the university, a general tranquillity within which activities in general are carried out—all are at odds with student political interests. For the most part, only on the most highly charged issues revolving about the war have significant elements of the faculty found themselves in concert with students, and then only at moments of crisis. Faculty have been activated by actions that have touched their moral sensitivities, usually sensitivities of a rather conventional sort and frequently evoking their middle-class and intellectually rooted horror of violence. The reason that this moral indignation has displayed such an ephemeral quality is mainly that it is not rooted in the *interests* of the faculty; it arises out of the rather purely ideological sphere dominated by the liberal and banausic self-regard so characteristic of the university-based salaried professoriate.

The process of polarization may be defined as one in which definitions of the enemy become progressively more rigid, and in which the parties' own response then acts to confirm the other's initial view, thus increasing the rigidity, a process orchestrated by progressively escalating language. This scenario often reached at least a temporary conclusion in many different ways: by a police bust, by mediation, in a few cases by faculty action, by administrative promises or concessions, or by simply closing the university—this often regarded as a defeat for the administration. But even when immediate protests died down or were forcibly stamped out, the situation typically remained essentially unchanged, with little or only token reform.

Two final points. Those whose voices have been raised

in defense of the traditional academic prerogatives —administrators, faculty, and others—commonly argue that to force issues in the fashion of student militants is to destroy the fragile value of reason, in effect, to eliminate rational discourse as the guiding norm of academic procedure. But it can first of all be seriously questioned whether, given the nature of the exercise of power in academia, there has been any substantial degree of such discourse. Certainly students have never been invited to participate. And the relation between attempted coercive protest and reason is by no means so clear. Morgan concluded his analysis as follows:

> The conception of reason and coercion as separate entities incompatible with one another in the academic world is symptomatic of the polarizing tendencies of the current era of student protests. Clearly the findings presented in this chapter confirm that student coercion has bred faculty and administration reasoning.[30]

The future may see faculties reasoning not only with one another, but with students as well. But if and until this occurs, and particularly until students participate significantly in their own governance, the university will continue to be an institution based heavily on coercion.

Second, there is the matter of "politicization of the university." The argument holds that this is the doing of the students, who have intruded on a nonpolitical consensus in which reason and scholarship move forward independently of political alignments or arguments. But this argument has so often been shown to be untenable that the rebuttal should scarcely require mention once again.[31] War-related contracts with government and private industry, cooperation with the military, and the sundry other involvements of the universities can hardly

30. Morgan, pp. 377-78.
31. See, for instance, Immanuel Wallerstein, *University in Turmoil: The Politics of Change* (New York: Atheneum Publishers, 1969).

be held to be nonpolitical. If the actions of the government and its industrial handmaidens are political, then the assistance of the universities in the policies they make and implement is necessarily also political. The universities have not been politicized by students, but by the patterns of power and the imperatives of its exercise, and by the historical structural commitment to these policies pursued by those in charge of the universities. And this has been so because it has been to the advantage of many, in terms of careers, prestige, and money. It is not a question of being political or nonpolitical —only of what the politics will be.[32]

Conclusion: The Societal Context of Protest and Violence

The findings of this chapter, like those of chapter 3, can be interpreted within our paradigm of structural coordination and value emphasis. The heaviest protest[33] has occurred more often in those institutions I have called coordinated-humanistic (cell D of our paradigm) and in the uncoordinated-humanistic institutions (cell C of our paradigm). *Violence* has occurred mainly over those matters that *are* the very forms of coordination —recruiting on campus, ROTC, war-related research, etcetera, on the one hand, and the race question on the other. And it has occurred most explosively in the coordinated-humanistic institutions (those in cell D), where the contradiction between structural fact and value ethos is greatest. Violence developed out of absolutely attenuated relationships as administrations sought not to communicate, but rather to defend their preroga-

---

32. For a treatment of this issue see Robert Wolff, *The Ideal of the University* (Boston: Beacon Press, 1969).
33. The reader should recall the qualification regarding the *per student* degree of protest.

tives relating to issues involving the institutional coordination with state and corporations.

All class societies, perhaps all complex societies, rest ultimately on coercion and the threat of coercion. The integration of functions essential to all complex societies and industrial ones in particular, is actually highly precarious. The capacity of industrialization to significantly expand the reward system has made it possible to rely more heavily on the carrot than the stick than has been the case in earlier times, but it is also true that industry has created conditions under which withdrawal from or revolt against routinized functioning is somewhat easier. Thus, the system of force and coercion must always be readily at hand wherever the value consensus breaks down. Since the contradictions inherent in the myths as against the realities of inequality sometimes become blatantly obvious, overt repressive violence remains common in many industrial societies, a last resort to enforce continued functioning and maintenance of inequality.

It is within the perspective of larger institutionalized violence of America that the protest and sometimes violence of the students should be understood. Violence initiated by those identified with the student movement reached its peak between the fall of 1968 and the spring of 1970, the latter in response to the Kent State killings and the invasion of Cambodia. But even during this period the extent of violence was not very great, and was only rarely directed against people; rather, as in the case of the ghetto rebellions, it was mostly against property.

All this is to say nothing about either violent *impulses* or violent *rhetoric* among New Left or student activists. Movement literature during the period 1969-70, in particular, reveals the depth and intensity of both. Given such rage, the surprising thing, perhaps, is not the actual amount of violence, but the extent to which it was suppressed. Those who were anywhere near the movement during these years know well that the question of violence, in tactical, political, and moral terms, dominated much debate. Even in the midst of this most intense period, it was widely and clearly understood that violence as an official tactic could only be self-defeating and exacerbate the already great fragmentation of the movement.

5
THE SOCIETAL COURSE
OF THE MOVEMENT

Introduction

In the previous chapters I have analyzed the student movement in terms of its genesis and activation within specific social *loci,* the structural conditions in class, family, and campus settings, and its political form. These characterizations, however, do not provide us with an analysis of the growth and vicissitudes of the movement from a macrocosmic standpoint, that is, as a developmental societal phenomenon. The factors discussed in the preceding chapters were present in their essentials during the 50s and earlier, yet failed to produce a movement among students until the 60s. The southeast Asian war is not in itself adequate to account for the rise of the movement, for the simple reason that it was antedated by the movement. The focus in this chapter will be on the changes in the course of the movement's development and the relation of these to society.

The first phase of the student movement can be traced to the decline of the reformist impulse of the early civil rights movements, from the early 60s roughly up to 1965. The Port Huron Statement was written in 1962, but there were already significant signs pointing to the coming politicization of American students, and the movement became a nationally relevant phenomenon at least as early as 1963, by which time students, black and white, had long been engaged in the racial struggle in the South. The course of this struggle in the early 60s is a decisive factor in understanding the growth of the movement, for the seeming failure of racial reform politics that marked its end was also the condition of its transformation. The second phase began with the shift to the campus in the fall of 1964. With Berkeley, a radicalism limited to salon discourse was at an end. This transition is a relatively clear-cut one, but the drift toward "cultural politics," the third phase, is less so. Beginning in the middle 60s, the countercultural revolt began to intrude into the public conscience. Widespread public awareness of the cultural movement can be dated at least from the summer of 1967 with the pilgrimage to San Francisco of thousands of "hippies." At least from this time on, the politically activist branch of the movement lived both in tension and accommodation with the cultural rebels, for there have been powerful affinities as well as conflict-filled between them.

We can characterize these three phases of development in terms of the ideological assumptions at their root, assumptions that I will refer to as contradictions of inequality, of power, and of culture.

I use the term *contradiction* here in the sense of a situation in which social reality is perceived to be at variance (and particularly where it is perceived to be radically at variance) with its manner of representation. Somewhat more concretely, it refers to situations in which the values and norms that define the "official" character of social structures are perceived to depart radically from the way in which they actually function or are perceived to function by others.[1]

Contradictions of Inequality, Power, and Culture

There is general agreement that the student movement has its roots in the South of the late 50s and early 60s. During this early period the movement differed in at least two important respects from its later manifestations. First, it did not separate youth or students either from their elders or from the larger community.[2] Protest activities such as sit-ins and voter registration were practical ways of action (whether successful or not), and necessarily involved protracted work with people. Sit-ins, wrote Robert Taber,

> operated in a community context involving people of all ages, eventually involving the resources, organizations and manpower of the community in its success.[3]

There is irony in the fact that among all the big issues, southern race relations by the mid-1970s may have undergone the greatest change of all; for it was precisely the growing perception and belief in the absolute intransigence of the southern racial system on the part of black and white civil rights activists that was crucial in preparing the ground for the subsequent growth of the movement.

Second, the assumptions of the movement in the

1. It should be noted that I am not here using the term in its more general Marxian sense, in which it refers (mainly) to imperatives inherent in capitalist economic institutions that produce class polarization, growing conflict, and opposition movements.
2. See Robert A. Taber, "From Protest to Radicalism: An Appraisal of the Student Movement," in *The New Left: An Anthology* (Boston: Beacon Press, 1966), pp. 34-42. For a detailed study that demonstrates this, see also Merrill Proudfoot, *Dairy of a Sit-In* (Chapel Hill, N.C.: University of North Carolina Press, 1962).
3. Taber, p. 30.

South were essentially liberal and reformist. Sit-ins, voter registration, even the various tactics of civil disobedience, were attempts to change racial exploitation from within the system. For many, perhaps most, the hopes associated with these assumptions were maintained even after the murders of Evers, of Schwerner, Goodman, and Chaney, and of four black children in a Birmingham church.

The understanding of American race relations in this early period was essentially that of a defect in the system, a defect that, however iniquitous, was reformable essentially within the ideological assumptions and political structure of American society. With only slight distortion we might say that Myrdal's much earlier characterization of racial subjection and exploitation as an "American dilemma" constituted the basic parameter of the movement's definition of the situation. This "dilemma" presumed that the value of equality of opportunity was substantially more than an evanescent rhetoric, and could be advanced in basically liberal, pluralist ways. It assumed a degree of openness in the system that after a few years came to appear to many of those who had early thrown themselves into the struggle as having been an incredibly naive conception.

The significance of the southern experience for the then-nascent movement, however, was to deepen the original consciousness of contradictions of inequality, contradictions that had for years been well documented in works of Myrdal and others.[4] It was in the South that students, and very importantly many northern students, learned that behind inequality, behind the inequity and exploitation of the southern racial system, stood local and national structures of power. When white students from the North were thrown into jail and beaten up by southern sheriffs, when Federal marshals stood by and,

4. Gunnar Myrdal, *An American Dilemma* (New York: Harper, 1944).

acting on Federal orders, watched passively as southern blacks were manhandled and rejected while attempting to register to vote, a changing appreciation of power and its workings began to grow in their minds. Much of the radicalization of the movement leadership had its roots in the South. It is important, however, to remember that this radicalization occurred only after years of community work that seemed to be accomplishing nothing. One recalls that Stokeley Carmichael, while a member of SNCC, worked for years in the communities of the South, and that Mario Savio was a prominent northern student active in the movement before his moment at Berkeley.

This is not to say that only those who actually worked in the South were affected—far from it. Although detailed proof is not available, southern resistance to the movement probably had just as great an effect on others throughout the North. Many later participants date their shift to the Left from the rage they felt on reading of the violence visited on civil rights workers or others in the South. So while many early student leaders-to-be received their political baptism in the South, many others were undoubtedly psychologically prepared by the growing prominence given the movement by the media. For them as well as the direct participants, the seeming inability of the civil rights movement to dent the power structure of the South had the consequence of destroying the liberal assumptions about legitimate procedure and accessibility of leaders to influence, assumptions that had underpinned the movement in the South up until the middle of the decade.

The movement in the South up to about 1965 divides readily into two phases. The early period involved mostly efforts to improve the *social status* of southern blacks, especially through sit-ins. Beginning very early in the 60s, the sit-in movement gave way to conceptions of political action, which meant mainly voter registration activity. But this political action was still carried out within the "rules of the game." White students from the north were, of course, involved mainly in the later political phase, and this was the condition of their disillusionment. Both SNCC and SDS were in the early years reformist, committed to political action within the system, organizing, tutoring, building in a myriad of ways.

As one might expect, the civil rights activists of the early 60s were much like later campus radicals. A study carried out in 1963 showed them to be young, well-educated, upper middle class, and acting mainly out of a sense of rage at violence being done to values they cherished. And surprisingly, particularly in view of the strong religious component of the movement in the South in those days, many were agnostics or only nominally religious.[5]

The failures of the early New Left led students (and others as well, of course) to despair of reformist tactics and their liberal assumptions as a way of achieving significant change in inequality. This shift, occurring during 1964-66, was concurrent with the escalation of the war and led students to radical reevaluations of the basic structure of power in American society. During this period C. Wright Mills was rediscovered, and for a while *The Power Elite* was perhaps the main political tract informing the ideological development of the New Left.

What earlier murders had not achieved, the "Orangeburg Massacre" probably succeeded in accomplishing. On February 8, 1968, South Carolina State police killed three black students and wounded 30 others, after students at South Carolina State College at Orangeburg had demonstrated against segregated public facilities in the community. More than any other, this event probably created new campus militancy on the

5. Alphonso Pinckney, *The Committed: White Activists in the Civil Rights Movement* (Storrs, Conn.: University of Connecticut Press, 1968), chap. 1.

part of blacks, for it seemed at that point that working within the system was only to invite greater violence from white society.[6]

Parallel to and perhaps just as important as the seeming failure to achieve significant changes, was the fact that the civil rights movement failed to establish an organizational base that could provide meaningful careers for potential activists in the immediate future. SNCC itself never became a mass organization and even the SCLC faltered after the murder of Martin Luther King.

This phase can be characterized as one of increasing realization of the contradiction of power, a contradiction between the liberal rhetoric of a politically pluralist society and the massive fact, or at least seeming fact, of the vast network of centralized state corporate power, a structure fully incorporating and thus set to defend the economic and political interests of the southern white ruling class. For increasing numbers of students and others, it meant the growing conviction that inequality could never be successfully attacked within the existing political and quasi-political arrangements, for these were increasingly perceived to be so undemocratic as to preclude any possibility of their use in instituting major social change. The rules themselves, along with the informal manner of their implementation, were such that they prevented effective expression of democratic activity on the part of the exploited, especially blacks the country round.[7] And if this were so, how could the politics of reform ever hope to really affect the distribution of power?

The relation between radicalization and movement participation is clearly seen in some of Pinckney's findings. Those who had been involved for longer periods of

6. See David Steinberg, "Black Power on Black Campuses," *Commonwealth* 88 (April 19, 1968).
7. For example, no charges were pressed against the killers of the Orangeburg students, even though it was soon established that the police had not been fired upon, as they had initially claimed.

time perceived their goal—at that time, integration—as being further away than did short-term participants.[8] This is tantamount to saying that belief in the real possibility of achieving one's goals is a function of the length of the period during which one has been frustrated. The longer the frustration, the greater is the likelihood of belief that success is not achievable through the means being utilized.

Campus confrontations, as we have seen in the last chapter, have been directed primarily at the power structure of American society in its varied aspects —connections to the campus, imperialist adventuring, the draft. Ideologically, the main difference between the early phase of the movement and the second was the emergence of a conception of total and complete involvement of all institutions of American life in perpetuation of racism and, by then, the war. Increasingly, universities and colleges came to be seen no longer as scholarly sanctuaries but rather as closely tied to and implicated in, perhaps even essential to, the maintenance of the interests of American capitalism at home and around the world. Therefore, attacks on the universities were increasingly perceived to be attempts to breach the outer ramparts of the state. This was true from Berkeley on. There the legal and political ties of the university to the state quickly became a major issue in the confrontation, even though the struggle began as an internal one over free speech. Three-and-a-half years later at Columbia, relations with the Federal government and the local community were the central concerns from the outset.

Concurrent with its ultra-Leftist ideological shift, the movement became increasingly divorced from the community, and from its potential constituencies as well. Indeed, the failure to reach a broader constituency was the reason for the ideological shift. This development then

8. Pinckney, chap. 6.

became to some extent a circular process. Further alienation from the community resulted from ideological and
rhetorical storms that failed to truly represent the actual
feelings and aspirations of the many. Rather than reaching the white working class as a constituency, the movement succeeded only in alienating it[9]—the condition for
the rapid emergence of "hard-hat" politics.

Thus, throughout the later 60s, the movement seemed
increasingly ineffective. The high point, in the early
spring of 1968 when Lyndon Johnson announced that
he would not run again, seemed at the time to be a victory of a sort, but a victory quickly snatched away with
the assassination of Robert Kennedy and the failure of
Eugene McCarthy (not that those on the far Left would
have considered McCarthy's election a victory). The
Democratic convention of 1968, with its bloody struggles
in the streets and its political machinations, seemed only
to underscore with greater finality and futility of reformist politics. The thousands of students who had "gone
clean for Gene," had, at that moment, it seemed, nowhere to go except the revolutionary wing of the movement or deeper into the counterculture.[10] In late 1968
the possibilities of system reform seemed more remote
than ever before, and Richard Nixon's victory, even for
those who could in the circumstances accept Hubert
Humphrey, seemed to represent a complete victory for
militarism and domestic conservatism. The movement
seemed to have failed in all of its major aims. It could be
demonstrated that black gains nationally were practically
nonexistent (for example, black income in proportion to
white had failed to rise); Nixon's formula for the war

9. A parallel process was occurring in the black community. The violent
   rhetoric of the Black Panthers and their early rapid spread around the
   country brought not only police repression, but alienation from the black
   community as well, an alienation that engendered fears still not eradi-
   cated. This is so despite later rhetorical pullbacks and efforts such as the
   children's breakfast programs instituted in many cities.
10. A parallel to the situation of civil rights workers of only a few years back.

was clearly one of reducing the American casualty rate while maintaining the struggle through the South Vietnam puppet regime, in order to undercut growing resistance to the draft; the military budget would continue to rise; poverty was to be ignored and the cities abandoned; the repression of dissident groups would be stepped up.

The failure of the movement to reach any significant segment of the population was clearly indicated in the results of survey research. For example, an overwhelming majority of the American people, most of whom had watched the proceedings on TV, thought that the Chicago demonstrators either deserved everything they had gotten or had not been put down hard enough, and sided strongly with the police and Mayor Daley. This was so despite the fact that the networks' presentations were slanted in favor of the demonstrators. The TV graphics, like those of atrocities in Vietnam, were unable, in the moral isolation of the living room, to generate a significant political meaning. Up until 1970 a majority supported the war, and even then only growing demoralization—through military defeat, vast corruption, drug use among GI's, and finally publication of the government's own study of its systematic deception of the people—finally brought a majority to oppose the war. And most of this opposition rested on the limited grounds of resentment against American boys' dying in the Asian jungles. The automation of the war that began in 1969 successfully undercut this opposition and placed a solid majority behind the policy of "Vietnamization." In 1970 a Gallup poll revealed that in the minds of the people, campus unrest had become the most important problem facing the country.

The third phase of the movement, the emergence of so-called cultural politics, resulted to a large extent, in my view, from the political *malaise* just described, although important influences from the bohemian communities of the 50s were present. I am referring here not to just any manifestations of the "counterculture," only to those having a political meaning. Although such distinctions are rather difficult to make in specific empirical contexts, I wish to differentiate from the larger phenomenon only those actions that in some manner oppose the dominant culture of American society —displays intended as messages of defiance and rejection, and as harbingers of a radically different way of living. Long hair, way-out clothes (or none at all), drugs, rock music, and so on, can all be and often have been countercultural politics, but they need not be. Much of what passes as counterculture is simply escape, or often even the sheerest conformity to an advancing style. This everyone recognizes. But all this shades off into the more politically meaningful segment, and a great many of those who are found here were (and often still are) activists.

The sense of contradiction in culture may be defined as the belief that the culture of one's society is totally bankrupt and that the lives people actually lead are based on premises totally remote from ideal public norms and values. One of the "discoveries" of the movement in the 60s was that received value systems are immensely powerful in determining thought and action at the political level. Political persuasion and confrontation having failed, many shifted toward some version of cultural politics, toward a total rejection of the cultural patterns of American society. Many activists embraced the counterculture and invested it with a political myth, that the growth and spread of the counterculture would undermine the politics and institutions of repression, an idea celebrated by Charles Reich in his *The Greening of America*. Although the beats of the 50s rejected American culture in a total way, they never imagined that this rejection would have any significant political consequence toward changing it. They simply withdrew.

While the confrontation politics of the 60s was radical in the sense of demanding totalistic changes in the structure of power, it was not necessarily opposed to American society *in toto*. The essential premise of cultural politics is that changes in power relations and subsequent elimination of inequality cannot come about until the basic underlying cultural patterns are swept away. Implicitly at least, the culture of capitalism is thought to be fundamental to the maintenance of the capitalist economic system and its inherent inequality.

Many analyses emphasize those aspects which separate the political from the cultural wings of the movement, and this is true for many at quite different points along the political spectrum. But it is also argued that a countercultural life-style may be a distinctive and important form of politics; in fact, that a radical politics is not possible without a culturally radical life-style within which it can thrive. A culturally radical style may in this sense be a form of witness. This is an argument that in contemporary circumstances seems compelling—the agencies of capitalist culture do indeed seem to do much of the work of political repression rather well—but that nevertheless contains certain theoretical and practical dilemmas. In its experiential root, the counterculture movement is the more radical in the sense of its total rejection not only of the structure of power, but of a complete way of life. As such it is both political and nonpolitical, since it rejects participation in both the conventional system and as old fashioned political revolutionaries. It hopes to undermine through the very power of its message and example the culture of capitalism, and thereby, through changing men radically, to change society. This may be a naive vision. For the present there are trends into which one can read quite varying futures. Some have indeed responded to the force of example. On the other hand, the deliberate confrontation of radically different cultural styles has probably more often than not been counterproductive. This latter bears some discussion.

One of the more significant aspects of cultural protest is that in its situational aspect elders, authorities, or others generally, have often responded with greater hostility to the style or form of protest than to the positions taken on the issues themselves, a kind of confrontation for which German students invented a most delightful word, *Bürgerschreck*, or the outraging of "solid citizens." Police, for example, are often far more outraged by the language used publicly by protesters (which they themselves regularly use in private) than by their purposes, with which they have found themselves in agreement more often than is commonly supposed.

It is important to note that politically suffused cultural confrontations are inherently public in nature—the political intent requires this. Frequently this involves a transformation of what is conventionally considered to be "private" into a public display. The reason that dirty language and sexual experimentation, for example, seem so offensive to many is not because they are *intrinsically* bad or wrong. All languages include a whole lexicon of "dirty" words and phrases. These styles offend because they have been shifted to the sphere of public life, thereby outraging very fundamental values having to do with the way our culture *compartmentalizes* segments of experience. What ideally constitutes public versus private dimensions of experience is a basic parameter of any culture, around which virtually all cultural meanings are organized.

This suggests that the norms of etiquette and presentation may at times, at least, have an important repressive function,—in this instance, that of making highly intense or emotional displays indicating powerful commitment difficult if not impossible. It is this inability of the common language, when rendered in terms of a standard etiquette, to convey the depth of feelings of outrage, anger, pain, or joy, that Marcuse has referred to as "one-dimensional." Such an etiquette serves the purpose of deflecting one's concern with the substance of protest in the direction of the niceties of social engagement itself. No one really wants to realistically contemplate the horrors of the systematic slaughter of hundreds of thousands, or even the facts of oppression and hunger here at home. The situational etiquette makes it possible to reject the protesters themselves without ever coming to grips with the issues.

Those who engage in public protest, of course, have been faced with an interactional dilemma. Presentations carried out in terms of the prevailing etiquette fail to convey the existential qualities of the forms and depth of one's feelings; on the other hand, the language of outrage deflects concern onto the style. A word such as *genocide*, for instance, as a description of American military policy in Vietnam, was almost always rejected, not only as representing a moral impossibility for Americans, but also as being a frightening extremism of language going beyond the boundaries of the norms of etiquette. There is a sense in which sheer linguistic expressions concentrate, as it were, a panoply of traits that would otherwise be in and of themselves tolerable. The language of outrage sums up and condenses all diffuse qualities of dissent or revolt in an incredibly volatile message.

All this suggests that displays of culturally deviant lifestyles have been as much of an obstacle as a base in the movement's struggle to transcend itself, that is, to reach broader constituencies for mobilization on relevant political issues. Yet, to play at the game within existing stylistic modalities has commonly seemed not only fruitless, but even a sellout, at least insofar as this has meant accepting even the outward forms of conventional behavior. This has been a dilemma of the most profound sort.

The countercultural side of the movement—and to a lesser extent the political side as well—has meant, as Flacks[11] and others have argued, a profound rejection of the Protestant Ethic, a rejection in favor of a far more open, expressive, free, hedonistic, and, hopefully, humane set of values.[12] As such, it has been fertilized by and exhibits important continuity with the beat philosophy of the 50s—a bohemianism powerfully impregnated with political imagery and intent.

Ultra-Leftism and "deviant" styles of life, of course, have been inherently in opposition to what is most fundamental among the working classes generally, their work ethic, and are surely the principal reasons for the failure of the movement to transcend itself by gaining footholds in sectors of society other than the campuses. Life-styles and political ideologies (often totally foreign to Americans, such as Maoism and Fanonism) have developed on the basis of essentially cultural or ideological experiences, and have not, on the whole, reflected the objective interests of students. Coming overwhelmingly from economically privileged strata and finding themselves in educational institutions holding out bright occupational futures, radical students have often failed to understand, and in so doing to reject much that is central in the lives of working people generally. The latter live and struggle under conditions of scarcity, and the work ethic remains central in their management of scarcity. Students from upper-middle-class homes who often never had to struggle for anything failed to understand

11. Richard Flacks, *Youth and Social Change* (Chicago: Markham Publishing Company, 1971).
12. For an extreme interpretation, see Theodore Roszack, *Sources: An Anthology of Contemporary Materials Useful for Preserving Sanity While Braving the Great Technological Wilderness* (New York: Harper & Row, Publishers 1972).

this imperative. Their radicalism resulted from their *socialization* under conditions of affluence and the freedoms created by affluence.

The Later Period

The Democratic convention of 1968 was a watershed in the course of the movement. Clearly, the murder of Robert Kennedy and the defeat of Eugene McCarthy were traumatizing events, events that shattered the hopes of multitudes of activist students. After Chicago a segment of the movement shifted to violent rhetoric and violence in fact, thereby sowing the seeds of the movement's dissolution. This time, however, had not yet arrived; in fact, the single most massive campus-based effort—the work of a coalition of Left and peace groups—lay almost two years in the future.

According to the Carnegie Commission study, the May 1970 uprising had a "significant impact" on 57 percent of the nation's campuses, resulted in student-faculty strikes on 21 percent of campuses with 5,000 or more students, and occasioned peaceful demonstration on 70 percent of them. The Harris poll of May 1970 revealed that 58 percent of those at colleges where protests occurred said they had participated, and 75 percent that they supported the goals of the protests. What occurred, of course, was a momentary but massive activation of students beyond the core and first ring (see Figure 1). But after the academic year 1969-70 everything in the movement was downhill.

Paradoxically, and somewhat ironically, the organizational dissolution of the movement was accompanied by a corresponding radicalization of student attitudes generally. This trend is reflected in the Yankelovich surveys of 1968-70. Compared with the 1970 survey results, for example, those from 1971 showed that students were:

1. more concerned about what was happening in Vietnam.
2. more sceptical of the integrity of government leaders.
3. more discouraged about the chances for bringing about deserved changes in the society.
4. more fearful of repression.
5. more angry and determined to do something.
6. more radical in their political thinking.
7. not confident about the underlying health of the country.
8. less conservative in their thinking.

Yet, at the same time, fewer students reported that they were:

1. alienated from society.
2. accepting of violence as a legitimate tactic to achieve social change.[13]

Apparently as social and political awareness spread among students, willingness to utilize violence declined. If this was so it may well have indicated the onset of a recapitulation of the fate of earlier movements in U.S. history (and elsewhere as well, of course). As the constituency grows, militancy of tactics subsides. In the case of the student movement, ideological diffusion accompanied by organizational demise[14] meant that militant

13. Daniel Yankelovich, *The Changing Values on Campus: Political and Personal Attitudes of Today's College Students* (New York: Washington Square Press, 1972), p. 23.
14. Organizational fragmentation has often occasioned pronouncements declaring the end of the movement. However, while all movements require organizational vehicles of *some* sort, it would be sociologically naive to *identify* any movement with a particular organization or organizations. The breakup of an organization is not necessarily the end of a movement; to suggest this is to implicitly accept an essentially Leninist view of politics, where all things are achieved only by a tightly organized party. Particularly in an age of instant mass communication, movements may be kept alive and even grow quite independently of the survival of particular

impulses were, on the one hand, becoming transformed into a variety of liberal reformist activities (PIRGs, ecology groups, etc.), and, on the other, becoming sublimated in various stylized forms of withdrawal, the most important of which is the drug subculture. The decline was also clearly a mark of a kind of success, of the actual achievement or partial achievement of major movement goals, particularly the Vietnam pullout, the suspension of the draft, and some campus reforms.

It has been suggested that the movement in its later years underwent a shift in its social and academic base, a shift related to the diffusion of some of its conceptions. The evidence for this, however, is mixed. In an analysis of SDS and YAF members at the University of Oregon in 1969, Dunlap concluded that there existed

> only moderate and rather inconsistent support for the political socialization hypothesis regarding SDS activists, but strong and consistent support for its applicability regarding YAF members.[15]

In particular, he found that the social-class backgrounds of SDS and YAF members, and those of a cross-section of University of Oregon students, were quite similar.[16] Furthermore, there seemed to be less in the way of political continuity between SDSers and their fathers than was true of either YAF members or the student cross-section (although, of course, the *political* identification of

organizations. The powerful anarchist trend within the student movement has reflected this. In fact, the organizational anarchy of the student movement has always been one of its central realities and has constituted the basic condition of its ideology of "consciousness-raising." At least in terms of the spread of radical sentiments, this has been by no means entirely unsuccessful. For an argument that there was in fact no student movement, based on the organizational fallacy, see Burgess and Hofstetter, "The Student Movement: Ideology and Reality," *Midwest Journal of Political Science* (Nov. 1971).

15. Riley Dunlap, "Radical and Conservative Student Activists: A Comparison of Family Backgrounds," *Pacific Sociological Review* 13 (Summer, 1970): 171-81.

16. *Ibid.*, p. 178.

both SDS and YAF members was shown to be predominantly Left and Right respectively[17]). At the University of Wisconsin Mankoff and Flacks found that in later years both the middle-class and left-wing political origins of activists had undergone considerable shift.[18]

Similar results were obtained by Clarke and Egan in an analysis of Florida State University students. There, little difference was found in the social background of activists and others. Furthermore, they reported no difference in academic achievement, although no data on either of these relationships were presented.[19] The evidence from Yankelovich's analysis of a national sample of 1,244 students interviewed at fifty colleges in 1971 seemed to bear this out. Those identifying themselves as "New Left" (11%) were distributed over the class structure in essentially the same frequencies as those characterized as having "post-affluent values," or being "career-minded."[20]

Other evidence, however, suggests that it would be a mistake to completely discount the continuing significance of social-base factors. An analysis of a large national sample of students by the Gergens at the time of the Kent State-Cambodia uprising showed that those participating in the demonstrations tended rather strongly to come from upper-middle-class backgrounds and to be Jewish or nonreligious.[21]

17. *Ibid.*, p. 176.
18. Milton Mankoff and Richard Flacks, "The Changing Social Base of the American Student Movement: Its Meaning and Implications," *The Annals of the American Academy of Political and Social Sciences* (May 1972): 500-523.
19. James W. Clarke and Joseph Egan, "Social and Political Dimensions of Campus Protest Activity," *Journal of Politics* 34, 2 (May 1972): 500-523.
20. Yankelovich, pp. 117-18. These designations, unfortunately, probably incorporate a strong spurious element. The "post-affluence values" and "career-minded" categories are derived from responses to a single item, a procedure likely to produce substantial empirical unreliability. The self-identification with "New Left" is also suspect: 51 percent of these so identifying also responded to a political identification item by labeling themselves "liberal," surely a historic and heretofore unrevealed mass transformation of New Left identity.
21. Mary and Kenneth Gergen, "How the War Affects the Campuses," *Change* 3 (Jan-Feb., 1971).

Although some change in the social origins of activists very likely did occur after 1968, the nature of academic influences seems to have changed little if at all. The Clarke and Egan Florida State data showed that a considerable preponderance of activists were still drawn from social science and humanities curricula. Thirty-two percent of a sample of "Arts and Sciences" students had been involved in demonstrations, compared with 19 percent in social welfare, 17 percent in education, and hardly any from the more vocationally oriented fields such as "engineering, business, library science, law and music."[22] In fact, national survey research has consistently demonstrated the continuing effect of institutional factors. The Yankelovich data showed that curriculum differences remained powerful discriminators. Fifty-six percent of "New Left" self-identifiers were found to be in the social sciences or humanities, as compared to 48 and 32 percent for "post-affluent-values" holders and "career-minded," respectively.[23] The data also showed the continuing importance of a basically secular home experience in the lives of student activists.[24] The pattern of these findings is supported by other research.[25]

Growth and Decline of the Movement:
Analytical Considerations

The decline of the movement in the early 70s has been interpreted in a variety of ways. From a theoretical standpoint, I would contend that three factors in particular have been of importance: (1) the relation between the movement's goals and its participants; (2) the relation between movement ideology and mobilization; and (3) government repression.

22. Clarke and Egan, p. 512.
23. Yankelovich, p. 118.
24. Yankelovich, p. 118, and the Harris Poll of Students, May 20-28, 1970.
25. See Clarke and Egan, "Social and Political. . . ."

Movement Goals and Participants

Analysis of the relation between movement goals and participation will be facilitated by two sets of distinctions; the first, between what I will term interest-based as distinct from culture-rooted participation; and second, between single-issue and multiple-issue participation.

Interest-based participation in social movements rests on economic, status, or other conditions that link individuals within a community of fate, and that create situations such that they may come to perceive their condition in terms of collective self-interest. Interest-based movements pursue goals the achievement of which would clearly benefit participants individually and collectively. Culture-rooted participation arises from situations in which common interests are absent or minor. Its unity is achieved through general moral-humanitarian principles rather than a recognition of a community of fate rooted in common interests distinct from those of others. Culture-rooted movements pursue goals in the name of the community or of larger abstractions, and achievement of these goals does not advance the condition of the participants relative to nonparticipants.[26]

Single-issue participation is practically self-explanatory.

26. This distinction is not the same as that between instrumental and expressive activity, a common basis for distinguishing among types of movements (see, for example, Frank Parkin, *Middle Class Radicalism*). Whether political activity is instrumental or expressive would seem to be unrelated to whether movements are more interest-based than culture-rooted, or vice versa. Expressive movements are defined as those in which individuals participate for the satisfaction of the participation itself, mainly that gained from taking a stand or displaying one's commitment. But it is probably the case that many kinds of satisfaction can be gleaned from participation, including the sense of being a moral witness. This does not mean that the participation is thereby noninstrumental (although one might argue against the specific tactics of a movement on the grounds of their likely ineffectiveness: moral witness itself can be and often has been a specifically political tactic, as in most nonviolent movements). Furthermore, since all movements have some goal or goals, making judgments on whether a movement is instrumental or not seems at least to imply the possibility of evaluating the goals themselves as realistic or attainable, as well as whether the participation serves some need that is itself unrelated to the goal or goals. And these are among the thorniest of questions.

Many movements have multiple goals, but some members may be interested in only one, while others pursue several. The distribution of these types may be an important consideration in analyzing the tactics and politics of a movement. This has been the case with the student movement.

The vanguard of the movement was a mix of single-issue and multiple-issue culture-rooted participants, who pursued goals that had little to do with their self-interest. Civil rights for blacks and opposing the war were both matters of sheer moral-humanitarian principle. The later growth of the movement, however, was to a considerable extent based on an influx of interest-based single-issue participants of several types, two of which are of special significance: (1) draft-avoiders, and (2) campus reformers. Organized resistance to the draft became probably the largest and best-organized single activity carried out within the radical Left. And as was shown earlier (in chapter 3), organizers were generally able to mobilize larger numbers around specifically campus issues—dorm rules, dress regulations, food service, student power, etcetera—than for national ones.

Insofar as the movement was comprised of either interest-based or culture-rooted single-issue participants, it was vulnerable to success. Elimination of the draft and perhaps to some degree the 18-year-old vote, clearly addressed the interest of draft-avoiders. Reforms of various sorts on the campuses, particularly in the sphere of parietal management, even though they often incorporated large elements of administrative cooptation, have clearly been responsive to the interest of campus reformers. Later, disengagement from Vietnam resulted in withdrawal of the many who had all along wanted only an end to the war.

Ideology and Mobilization

Related to the foregoing is a problem that can be for-

178 • THE CLOUDED VISION

mulated as the relation between ideology and mobilization. This is one of the master problems of social movements, raising as it does the issue of ideas as they relate
to the bases and reasons for participation. It is a question that is particularly salient for student movements,
within which the role of ideas is so significant.

We may begin by permitting ourselves the assumption
that any ideology must somehow be appropriate to or
"fit" the situation of its creators or those to whom its appeal is directed. This assumption, of course, must be
understood to be a very general one. In all social movements are found "deviants" who are attracted for a wide
variety of reasons but for whose personal objective situation the ideology is inappropriate. The creators and
early participants in the student movement, imbued with
the democratic humanism discussed earlier (in chapter
2), projected this ideal as a societal goal, a goal substantially embodied in the Port Huron Statement, written in
1962. It is important to recognize that the argument and
appeal of that document stand squarely in the indigenous American democratic tradition. Although these values were never fully developed theoretically, they were
nonetheless, in the early days, at the root of a variety of
activities central to the movement, particularly civil
rights actions and community organizing.

In its later years, of course, movement ideology
shifted away from this early stance toward radical neo-
marxist conceptions that grew out of Third World experiences of Western colonialism and imperialism. On
the face of it, at least, Fanonism, Maoism, Castroism,
and other forms of neo-marxist theory, however powerful they may be theoretically, are at least *prima facie*
inappropriate as rallying ideas or mobilizing conceptions
for the mass of students, and certainly for the great bulk
of the American working class. As has often been remarked, the New Left never developed ideas indigenous
to American experience that could in a meaningful way

represent the movement to its relevant potential constituencies and supporters. One may say that movement ideology never reached beyond a relatively narrow circle of the already culturally liberated. During its later years its thrust was always toward points remote from the actual consciousness of those it attempted to reach.

The ideology-mobilization question is better understood if placed in context in terms of the constraints inherent in social organization. Not only the pull of ideas but the presence of objective conditions facilitating or enabling people to respond underlies active participation in a social movement. This is a point that has recently been formulated parsimoniously by Oberschall. In his terms participation in movements is more likely under conditions of high segmentation, by which he means an absence of effective means of social control by authorities.[27] Assuming, as Oberschall does (rightly, in my view), that political action is for the most part a rational enterprise, it is sensible to formulate the question of movement participation as an outcome that involves the weighing of risks and rewards. Participation will occur only when men perceive an advantage to be attained that is greater than the risk that must be run. New Left ideology never developed a program of radical reform that held out reasonable concrete advantages, even for students, whose objective situation, compared with most work milieux, is in general one of a relatively great flexibility and freedom. In this sense the movement suffered a double failure. Not only did it fail to reach beyond those whose experiences had prepared them to respond, into the cultural mainstream, but particularly in terms of program, it failed to address itself meaningfully to those who were basically in sympathy, but who were constrained by their subjection within societal structures of domination.

27. Anthony Oberschall, *Social Conflict and Social Movements* (Englewood Cliffs, N.J.: Prentice-Hall, Inc., 1973). See chap. 3.

Repression

There is little doubt that the government at all levels, but the federal government in particular, was for some time provoked into a state of near-paranoia by the growing protests during the late 1960s. And there is no doubt that government social control activities, particularly its clandestine operations, reached massive proportions.[28] It is nonetheless very difficult to assess the significance of official repressive actions in the demise of the student movement.

On the one hand, a variety of policies ranging from official 'violence to general economic cutbacks in some types of funding for higher education have doubtless had substantial impact on the movement. University authorities have generally been permitted by the courts to exercise an almost totally arbitrary authority over students, including the right to expel them, without any semblance of due process, practices that have undoubtedly had some deterrent effect. To a lesser extent the same may be said for the application of political tests for recipients of federal grants and loans. Furthermore, many local exercises in social control are obscured from the often-embarrassing exposure to the public view, and when carried out against small and weak segments of the movement have frequently been effective. (In this connection, recall the analysis of administration tactics presented in chapter 4).

Repressive policies against faculty members who have been activists have also undoubtedly been of considerable importance. That faculty members have played an important role in student protest from the beginning is a documented fact. The Long and Foster data, for instance, showed that faculty members were involved as supporters in over 60 percent of protests against the

28. See, for instance, Frank Donner, "The Theory and Practice of American Political Intelligence," *New York Rev.* 21 (April 22, 1971):9.

Vietnam war and against the educational and censorship policies of their institutions, and that they were often leaders of these protests.[29] Aside from direct participation, they have often played *sub rosa* roles as advisors, counselors, and organizers of post-demonstration efforts to collect bail money and organize legal aid, and even as deliberate *agents provocateurs*.

Involved faculty members have typically been younger and untenured, and thus exceptionally vulnerable. The thousands of political firings during the late 60s and early 70s without doubt played an important part in the demoralization of the movement.

To look now at the other side of the picture, it must be observed that many attempts at repression were incompetently carried out or otherwise ineffective, a fact demonstrable from a variety of sources, including the FBI's own files stolen from its Media, Pennsylvania, offices. Often these efforts were truly ludicrous in their effects.[30]

Even the net effect of the principal repressive legislation to be directed against radicals and dissenters generally, the "Rap Brown law," which prohibited the crossing of state lines for presumed conspiratorial purposes, is by no means clear-cut. The resulting political trials, of which threat of the Chicago 7 was the most celebrated, certainly succeeded in deflecting and using up movement resources for defensive purposes. But from another standpoint they were anything but successful. Not only did they usually fail in the narrow legal sense, but they came to serve as focal points of identification for many, and became demonstrations of the limits of official repression conducted openly through legal institutions against financially well-supported defendants.

Probably as important as the objective dimensions of

29. Long and Foster, "Levels of Protest," p. 86.
30. See, for example Paul Cowan and Nick Egleson, et al., *State Secrets: Police Surveillance in America* (New York: Holt, Rinehart, and Winston, 1974).

the repression has been the paranoid tendency of much of the Left itself. In the later years especially, with many radicals living underground, the tendency to greatly exaggerate the extent of government surveillance and infiltration became incredibly destructive. This psychology was as much the product of the organizational weakness and ideological fragmentation of the Left as it was a consequence of government repression.

In all, the net effect of official repression remains difficult to assess. I am not able to prove it, but in my opinion it has been a less significant cause of movement demoralization than either of the factors discussed earlier.

Conclusion

The natural history of the student movement can be thought of in terms of four relatively distinct but overlapping periods: from its early roots in the southern civil rights movement, through its confrontation with power on the campuses, its dalliance with "cultural politics," and finally its period of organizational dissolution.

Three points seem worth extracting from this history. First, although some change in social bases of recruitment is demonstrable for the latter years, the continuing significance of academic departmentalization—an important bureaucratic element—is evident. Radicals, whether active or not, continue to be found in nonvocational social science and humanities bailiwicks. This fact, in its historical persistence, points up the importance of intellectual and knowledge factors in the genesis of at least certain types of movements.

Second, the movement's demise has occurred to a considerable extent in consequence of its limited success, particularly in the suspension of the draft, troop withdrawal from Vietnam, and the 18-year-old vote, and because of the remoteness of its emergent ideology from the consciousness of the great majority of students (and others), as well as the actualities of government repression.[31] Among other things, this decline demonstrates once again that the most intense feelings and most powerful commitments were always in connection with the war and related issues, and did not involve the universities as such.

Finally, and ironically, the critical perspective on American society developed in radical student circles (among other milieux) has become widely disseminated among students generally, just as the movement was experiencing organizational breakup. Whether this critical perspective can be mobilized into a new force remains problematic. From the standpoint of the remnants of the movement, the Watergate disclosures and oil conspiracy represented political windfalls that offered enormous political potential, but a potential unfulfilled because of organizational and ideological demoralization.

31. *Ibid.*

6
THEORIES OF THE STUDENT MOVEMENT

From among the many interpretations of the movement, we can, I think, distinguish between three general types of theories: (1) psychobiological theories; (2) functionalist and mass-pluralist theories; and (3) Left-institutional theories. Particular representatives of each are not necessarily exclusive of one another, but in a formal sense they do embody different principles of explanation. The psychobiological theories assume that certain constants of "human nature" of one sort or another, often conceptualized within a psychoanalytic framework, are at the roots of student activism. Functionalist and mass-pluralist theories on the one hand, and Left-institutional theories on the other, share the assumption that various aspects of the institutional orders of societies are the generators of movements (as well as other kinds of change), but differ in their conceptions as to just what is most fundamental about those orders. Functionalist and mass-pluralist theories presume that societies are basically orderly or "integrated"; conflict is usually treated as a form of deviance, or strain, or is considered to be "dysfunctional."[1] Left-institutional theories, on the

1. Some functionalist theorists have attempted to incorporate conflict formu-

other hand, assume that conflict is *inherent* and *ubiquitous* in human society, and that analyzing its forms, intensity, sources, and consequences is central to social analysis. The reader should understand that the rather cumbersome designation "Left-institutional" is employed first of all to avoid discussion of what are and what are not "Marxist" theories—a sterile debate—and second, because to speak of "conflict" versus "order" theories is somewhat misleading, since no general theory elaborates one such set of ideas to the total exclusion of the other.

I will consider representatives of each of the three types in turn, and evaluate them on the bases of logical consistency and capacity for interpreting and integrating the empirical evidence.

Psychobiological Theories

The most important psychobiological theory of student revolt, the celebrated analysis of Lewis Feuer, relies heavily on Freudian psychoanalytic ideas, particularly the oedipal principle and even the myth of the primeval killing of the father by the sons, as expounded in *Totem and Taboo.* To some degree it may reflect the recent resurgence of biological thinking in social analysis. The protest of youth, Feuer argues, is essentially a sublimation of their hatred for their fathers and their way of destroying them symbolically:

> The conflict of generations is a universal theme in history; it is founded on the most primordial facts of human nature, and it is a driving force of history, perhaps even more ultimate [*sic*] than that of class struggle. Yet its intensity

lations into functional theory. The most important of these is probably Lewis Coser, in his *The Functions of Social Conflict* (Glencoe, Ill.: The Free Press, 1956). It is questionable, however, if such works, although they succeed in interpreting *certain* forms of conflict within general functional assumptions, really cope with other forms, particularly those involving radical or absolute opposition.

fluctuates. Under fortunate circumstances, it may be resolved within a generational equilibrium. Under less happy circumstances, it becomes bitter, unyielding, angry, violent;
this is what takes place when the elder generation, through
some presumable historical failure, has become de-
authoritized in the eyes of the young. Every student movement is the outcome of a de-authoritization of the elder
generation.[2]

He writes a bit later:

Student movements have been the chief expression of generational conflict in modern history....They have attained
the greatest heights of idealistic emotion even as they have
been enthralled by compulsions to destructions."[3]

The unconscious ingredient of generational revolt in the
student's idealism has tended to shape decisively their political expression.[4]

Feuer goes on to explain that student movements are
an example of what he calls "projective politics," by
which he means that they are dominated by unconscious
drives. This differentiates them in a fundamental way
from movements rooted in the class structure. The latter
exhibit well-defined patterns of interests and, in contrast
to student movements, they are conscious of the bases of
these interests and the goals that express them. In Feuer's
view, such a politics of the unconscious carries with it
great dangers for civilization.[5]

Essential to Feuer's conception is the element of
idealism within the movement. All student movements
are "idealistic," and invariably take some kind of "back
to the people" form. Thus, the Russian movement in the
nineteenth century romanticized the peasant, and the

2. Feuer, *The Conflict of Generations* (New York: Basic Books, 1969), pp.
   527-28.
3. *Ibid.*, p. 528.
4. *Ibid.*
5. *Ibid.*

American white student movement attempted to use the civil-rights movement as a "carrier." All student movements require a "carrier" movement, partly because there is no hope of making revolution on their own and partly because there can be no genuine issues arising from students' social position. As Feuer is fond of saying, student movements are unlike the labor movements of the West in that "consciousness determines existence," rather than the other way around. In any case the "idealism" of the students is important for Feuer's thesis because, not being anchored in objective interest situations in the social structure, it easily becomes corrupted into fanaticism and eventuates in terror and "suicidalism." Terror as a tactic and suicidal tendencies among movement members are inevitable, according to Feuer, because the "back to the people" ideology is everywhere doomed to failure, particularly in industrial societies where the working class is well integrated. The entire process is rooted in the original abstract idealism of youth.

Because student movements result from universal drives and only find expression in "abnormal" societies, the issues they raise cannot be credited as genuine.[6] Idealism is rooted in the unconscious, not in any real comprehension of the oppressiveness or inequalities of the social order; therefore it ultimately drives the movement to destruction. The ways of interest-based politics—compromise, sharing in power, and gradualism—are intolerable. It is because the movements refuse to play the pluralist political game that they become, in Feuer's characterization, threats to civilization itself. itself.

These themes can be perceived in Feuer's conception

6. It must be said that on this point Feuer is contradictory and ambiguous. For example, he recognizes that Czarist Russia was authoritarian and oppressive, obviously the general condition for all sorts of issues, yet adheres to his formula that, like all the others, the Russian movement was caused by unconscious drives.

of the natural history of all student movements. According to him, they always originate in small circles of intellectuals, emerge in an "issue-searching" phase, develop into organizational forms capable of autonomous political action that engage in the "back to the people phase," and finally, after failure, degenerate into terrorism and suicide. Actual issues seem to be of little or no importance.

There are a great many more details, and a great deal of what Feuer regards as analysis, but the essentials are stated above. Most of the book is devoted to analyses of the German, Bosnian, Russian, and United States movements. What can be said about all this?

First of all, Feuer's approach is almost entirely unsystematic. There is no reason given for the selection of the movements included in the analysis, or for the exclusion of others. More serious, Feuer has no discernible *method* of analysis. He simply quotes endlessly from all sorts of documents, letters, and other materials that suit his purpose. Most of this material illustrates the activities and thought of a *very few* student leaders of the movements in question. There is no attempt made either to find materials that might challenge the theory, or to face the issue of sampling. This is a quasi-historical procedure that cannot be credited with much scholarly objectivity.

Feuer even neglects to apply his own theory systematically. The circle concept is probably potentially the most fruitful idea in the book, but like much of the other conceptual baggage introduced at the beginning, it is never put to use. The phases of the development and demise of student movements should, according to the theory, occur in all cases, but Feuer is clearly not interested in such a test. Thus, the several elements that are alleged to be universally characteristic of student movements, such as issue-searching, terror, and suicide, are never established. Feuer simply picks a few student leaders—suicidal ones—and ignores completely the question of representativeness or sampling.

This matter of the suicidal tendency of students exemplifies a more general defect. Nowhere does Feuer ever give us any criteria for actually determining whether a particular movement is in fact generational, whether particular students are suicidal, whether "deauthoritization" has actually taken place. He merely asserts this by fiat, or assumes it by implication. But such absence of any sort of scientific criteria for the empirical establishment of basic concepts call the entire work into question. Another example of this is his practice of constantly asserting that statements of various sorts are "generational" in nature, although in many cases this is far from obvious, judging from their simple manifest content.

Feuer's single-mindedness about his generational explanation has the consequence of never permitting him to even consider the possibility of alternative explanations. This means that no structural analysis of social conditions is to be found anywhere in the book. Of course, in this studied kind of blindness, Feuer is only following his own dictum that movements are independent of social institutions, including the class structure. One suspects, however, that to have engaged in such analyses would have placed, at least implicitly, Feuer's basic objective in writing the book—total condemnation of the student movement—in jeopardy. Analysis of conditions of student revolt implies that there may be real reasons for it in the social and political world—reasons that in themselves might be at least partial explanations.

The principle that student movements are somehow independent of societal institutions has one particular significant consequence. Feuer cannot, in fact, completely ignore social conditions; he apparently does recognize that since movements are a variable phenomenon, they cannot be adequately explained by a constant, and therefore he introduces a few factors that allegedly provide the conditions for their emergence. These are, most importantly, gerontocracy (literally, the rule of the old), political apathy among the masses, and "de-authoritization" of those in authority (by which he means the older generation). The latter is especially important. But, as I have said, Feuer provides no *analysis* of these factors, and no demonstration whatever that they really are the crucial ones in allowing political manifestation of oedipal hatred. There is nowhere any indication of *why* "de-authoritization" occurs, nor is there any attempt to establish its presence independently of student movements. Thus we remain unconvinced. One suspects that to have developed such an analysis would have led Feuer far from his generational theme, and might even have suggested that there might be conditions in the social order that would justify the goals of the movements.

Among the problems presented by Feuer's analysis are some curious distortions of fact. For instance, he has the peace movement in the United States at its height in the fall of 1961. This could be construed as a matter of judgment. But there are more serious matters. He uses the New York City survey of Columbia that was done following the spring revolt, but ignores the technically superior one performed by the Survey Research Center. The former produced results favorable to Feuer's position, while the latter did not. None of the excellent work of the leading American scholars of the movements —Flacks, Keniston, and many others—is ever cited or used. Indeed, there is no indication that Feuer is even aware of it.

The analysis proceeds in terms of a highly emotive vocabulary. Evidently Feuer believes that if something is repeated often enough it must be true. This magical labeling formula is seen in his endlessly repetitive assertions that particular movements are generational, suicidal, and terrorist. Denigrating phrases are constantly in evidence: the movements are "irrational," "elitist," and "the last outposts of the children's world." They are, furthermore, the causes of various major political events (all bad), such as bringing to an end the movement toward constitutionalism in Germany.

How does Feuer's thesis square with the evidence presented in earlier chapters? On the face of it, it might seem as though at least some aspects of the theory would apply. Clearly, Feuer is at least partially correct on several points. First, student movements do sometimes attempt to ride the crest of other "carrier" movements. Both the early civil rights phase and later attempts of white students to ally themselves with and adopt the tactics of black campus militants exemplify this principle. Second, there is indeed a sense in which consciousness does determine existence, although it is not precisely Feuer's sense. I have discussed earlier how life-styles and ideologies of students were consequences of their socialization, not their basic interest situation, and the fatefulness of this fact for the movement.

The terrorism-suicidal tendency occurring after 1969 seems also to fit within Feuer's formulation, and there is, indeed, a sense in which a policy of terror resulted from failure to introduce the principles of the early idealism. But it is also true that terrorism became the *métier* of only a small segment of the movement. Furthermore, there is not much evidence for Feuer's suicidal thesis, although a few people, often religiously connected but generally not centrally located within the movement, have immolated themselves.

Despite these objections, one must grant some degree of truth to Feuer's suicidalism thesis. Participants in radical social movements, especially those totally encapsulated within them, are without doubt extraordinarily vulnerable to self-destructive impulses when the movement collapses. This is a truth that applies in any sphere of social life, as Durkheim demonstrated over 70 years ago.[7] People commit suicide when their lives become

7. Emile Durkheim, *Suicide: A Study in Sociology*, trans. George Simpson (Glencoe, Ill.: The Free Press, 1951).

meaningless, and the collapse of a movement can be an extreme form of the destruction of meaningfulness.

Beyond these points, serious difficulties arise. Although the evidence clearly shows the intellectualism of student rebels in general, the circle notion itself may not be very applicable to the United States. The early phase of the movement—involvement in the civil rights struggle in the South—resulted not from anything very much like a *circle* of intellectuals, but rather was a movement of young from all across the country united more by contagion. And the early movement can only be understood as having formed *around* the civil rights issue. There was no "issue-searching" phase.

I have shown earlier that in terms of their politics and other aspects of belief and behavior, student activists, particularly the earlier ones, have been in rather close political proximity to their fathers. This is hardly a condition we would expect if Feuer is correct about sublimated hostilities in the oedipal situation of the family. Of course, Feuer might reply that these are unconsciousness drives and therefore naturally do not show up in research analyses of manifest attitudes, feelings, and aspects of interaction. However, if this is the case, there would seem to be no way in which the family situations could be empirically revealed (except, perhaps, through psychoanalysis). And it is perhaps of some significance that even the more or less psychoanalytic approaches have failed to find among the activists any appreciable degree of father-hatred. So, on this score, the evidence does not seem consistent with the theory.

Is Feuer's characterization of student movements as irrational accurate for the American movement? Insofar as this question can be treated in terms of the nature and incidence of violence in or in connection with the movement, it would not seem so. In chapter 4 we saw that the incidence of violence in the movement was not particularly great, and that, furthermore, the proportion attributable to the movement was essentially unascertainable. Its terrorist phase was short-lived and the work of a small minority. Even beyond this, there is in any case no reason to regard violence as necessarily irrational, since it has often been employed successfully in the achievement of political ends. Finally, we saw in chapter 4 that campus violence occurred mainly in connection with national or societal issues as these were manifest on the campus, and thus amenable to local administrative action. On purely local or purely national matters the incidence of violence was slight. There is thus at least a sense in which campus violence incorporated a rational element, that is, in its relation to attainable ends. In the light of all this, Feuer's stigmatization seems misplaced.

One final criticism can be leveled against Feuer's theory. While there may be some sense in which youth are exceptionally idealistic, or even liberal, this is not borne out by at least certain kinds of evidence. Recent opinion polls, for example, show that *attitudinal* opposition to the war has actually been greater among older age groups, although for the most part these older people have never been willing to convert their views into active resistance.[8] Middleton and Putney, in reviewing the evidence for this idea in connection with their study, concluded that

> At least two studies cast doubt on the assumption that conservatism increases with age. Lazarsfeld and associates found that older people were not necessarily more conservative than younger people, but were merely more closely aligned with the political attitudes prevalent in their ethnic or religious group, and Centers failed to find a tendency for older people to be more conservative than younger people among laboring groups.[9]

8. See Hazel Erskine, "The Polls: Is the War a Mistake?" *Public Opinion Quarterly* 34 (Spring 1970).
9. Russell Middleton and Snell Putney, "Student Rebellion Against Parental Political Beliefs," *Social Forces* 41 (May 1963).

The idea of youth as inherently idealistic is as much a part of the higher as it is of the popular culture. A voluminous literature—Turgenev and others in Russian, Conrad and Melville in English, the suddenly popular Hermann Hesse in German are only a few—supports this notion in academic and intellectual circles generally. Whatever the degree of truth—and there surely is some—it is pretty clear that youth as a whole do not seem to be particularly liberal or idealistic. In any case, the question of whether youth, or even political activists, are idealistic or not is a matter that is probably best approached developmentally, that is, in terms of the development of the individual in relation to the movement within which he finds himself. In this regard Keniston's comment that "the same person, depending on circumstances, is invariably both an idealist and a nihilist," seems most cogent.

There is another version of the psychobiological theory of student protest, a version anchored in our conventional conceptions of adolescence as a period of turbulence. The idea that youth is a "period of restlessness, or searching, of unbounded energy,"[10] is one that is firmly implanted in the conventional wisdom of our culture. It is an ideal that is much older than Freudian psychology and has its origins not in academic thought so much as in ordinary life. And its power as conventional wisdom has led to its adoption, even by scholars, as an explanation of student unrest. Thus E. Wight Bakke writes:

> Student activism is a function of the universal search of adolescent youth for an adult role in society, for self-identity and social integration, and of their predisposition to energetic self-assertion at this stage of the maturation process.[11]

10. Edward E. Sampson, "Student Activism and the Decade of Protest," *Journal of Social Issues* 23 (July 1967): 1.
11. E. Wight Bakke, "Roots and Soil of Student Activism," in S. M. Lipset, ed., *Student Politics* (New York: Basic Books, 1967), p. 58.

Joseph Katz and Nevitt Sanford, respected students of education, put forward essentially the same idea:

> The time between 17 and 21 is often one of nagging self-doubt, of intense conflict in relations with other people, painful and sometimes rebellious struggles for independence from one's parents, of an uneasy search for one's eventual occupational and sexual roles. Such emotional struggles and discomfort upset the individual's equilibrium and thus free considerable energy for either creative or destructive acts. . . .Adolescence is the time of life when a new generation defines itself. Not only does it have to find its own values and come naturally into some conflict with the older generation, but there are implicit expectations on the part of the older that the one coming along will do something different—and we hope, better.[12]

There are several difficulties with this view. First, the idea of "emotional struggles and discomforts" that "upset the individual's equilibrium and thus free considerable energy for either creative or destructive acts," is a crude, mechanistic mode of understanding the complexities of personality development, that has, in the judgment of many, never proved itself very useful in social psychology. The root idea itself—that of adolescence—is as Aries and Musgrove,[13] among others, have shown, a product of the industrializing forces of the nineteenth century, forces that created the idea in response to the increasing demand for greater skill and education in the industrial and occupational orders. "Adolescence" was the name given to this stretched-out period in a revised social definition of youth. But adolescence is anything but universal; prior to industrialization no notice was given to the peculiar discomforts and emotional struggles of those between, say, 15

12. Joseph Katz and Nevitt Sanford, "Causes of the Student Revolution," *Saturday Review* 48 (December 18, 1965): 64.
13. F. Musgrove, *Youth and the Social Order* (Bloomington, Ind.: University of Indiana Press, 1965); and Phillippe Aries, *Centuries of Childhood* trans. Robert Baldick (New York: Random House, Vintage Books, 1965).

and 20. The concept and phenomenon of adolescence are culturally specific.

Even if adolescence were a universal phenomenon, these theorists would be hard put to answer an even more basic criticism: If adolescence is a universal, and therefore a constant in the biopsychological composition of youth, why is it that youth protest is so variable? This is, of course, from a formal standpoint the same basic criticism that goes unanswered by Feuer, and the adolescence-as-turbulence theorists do no better with it than he does.

Even if we interpret the theory in the more limited sense as an essentially social phenomenon peculiar to modern industrial or perhaps even modern capitalist societies, there are serious difficulties. If protest stems from the upsets of the adolescent years, why is it so often manifest so much later in life? The median age of SDS members in Braungart's study was 20, and they reported that they came to their political awareness rather late, in fact, fully two years later than YAF members. The theory cannot explain the large number of radicals that are well beyond adolescence, or the fact that many, if not most of them, became radical after adolescence (except perhaps, by the sheer semantics of such phrases as "delayed adolescence").

A final critical point has to do with the relevance of some of the material presented earlier in chapter 1. If this explanation of student protest is correct, I suppose we could legitimately expect that the protesters would be those who had experienced particularly difficult times during adolescence, and especially in their later teens. But if the evidence of various kinds of psychological tests is accepted as a reasonable indicator of this, it seems not to be the case. (See chapter 2 above for the details.) Suffice it to say here that in terms of a variety of personality traits—dogmatism, autonomy, self-awareness, expressiveness—activists as a group appear to be reasonably capable of handling their personal lives. They do not appear to be projecting archetypal problems of adolescence into the political arena.

In some of his writings Keniston has suggested that we think of youth as a new developmental stage in the life cycle itself, a stage anchored in the vast numbers involved in the educational stretch-out. As such, "youth" have the vastly extended freedom, in comparison with those who must work for a living (in the conventional sense, for study can also be defined or interpreted as work), provided by the conditions of study. Youth is in this sense a new stage beyond adolescence prior to attaining sociological adulthood, during which beliefs about the possibilities of the good society and their place within it have not been compromised by the realities of marketplace, the work organization, and the darker side of politics.

Student political activism makes more sense within this conception than through attempts to comprehend it in terms of psychobiological constants. We may well be undergoing nothing less than a major social redefinition of the life cycle itself. The idea of an emergent life-cycle state makes it unnecessary to search for the root of student political protest in some presumed factors of human nature. Indeed, much of student protest has centered on struggles over aspects of both student and youth status roles. The principal problem would seem to be the fact that youth protest is at least 150 years old and has manifested itself in many societies under rather different conditions.[14] The way around this objection is to argue that while earlier protests were merely incipient, perhaps only anticipatory steps toward creation of a stage of youth, modern mass education has created the widespread base necessary for its institutionalization.

Considerations involving the functions of the life cycle

14. See Anthony Esler, *Bombs, Beards and Barricades* (New York: Stein and Day Publishers, 1971).

within changing social structures have also been emphasized by some members of the functionalist school, to which we turn next.

Functionalist and Mass-Pluralist Theories

Functionalist and mass-pluralist theories have dominated general sociology and political sociology respectively since the end of World War II. While functionalism is a general theory of society, mass-pluralist theory can be thought of as the political theory of functionalism, especially as applied to industrial societies.

The Functional Analysis of Age-Grading

The basic tenets of functionalism are: (1) that all aspects of a society are somehow interrelated with and in some fashion important in the functioning of at least some other elements; (2) the value systems of societies are the primary basis for their cohesion or integration, and other organizational aspects of society can be best understood in terms of the ways they are brought into relatedness through these value systems; (3) societies tend toward a condition of equilibrium, stability, or homeostasis, mainly through the mechanism of consensus on values; and (4) activities within society that are not somehow integrated are regarded as "deviant" or "dysfunctional."[15]

15. Any epitomization of an intellectual structure so complex and extensive as sociological functionalism is necessarily an oversimplification. The summing up I have given here borders on the ridiculous, mainly because space does not permit the kinds of detailed elaborations of these points that would otherwise be desirable. The reader can consult such standard works as Talcott Parsons, *The Social System* (Glencoe, Ill.: The Free Press, 1951); Marion Levy, *The Structure of Society* (Princeton, N.Y.: Princeton University Press, 1953); and Robert Merton, *Social Theory and Social Structure* (Glencoe, Ill.: The Free Press, 1957). A recent powerful critical work is Alvin Gouldner, *The Coming Crisis of Western Sociology* (New York: Basic Books, 1970).

The principal functionalist analysis of youth groups is found in the work of S. N. Eisenstadt.[16] Eisenstadt sees youth groups as a peculiar response to problems of socialization in modern industrial societies. On the one hand, children acquire knowledge and skills first of all within the family. And the family is a unit in which relationships are diffuse, particularistic, collectivity-oriented, and ascriptive, in the jargon of functionalism. This means that relations are not restricted to specific or specialized functions, that individuals are not subjected to evaluations based on standardized or "functionally specific" criteria or norms, that the worth of activities from the standpoint of the group rather than the individual is emphasized (and this is paralleled by a high sense of identification with the family group), and that statuses are defined in terms of achievement norms and goals. We might say that in the family individuals are treated more in terms of their generally esteemed worth as individuals than for their abilities as performers of roles or functions. Within this context children acquire the various skills, knowledge, and behavior patterns that are essential for their later integration into the nonkinship spheres of society. Although the general significance of kinship in its ramifications throughout other spheres of social structure varies tremendously in different types of societies, the family is everywhere constituted in terms of these principles.

In modern industrialized societies, with their large-scale organizations and instrumental orientation, the problem of making the transition from family life and experience to effective participation in the economic, occupational, political, and other spheres of life is particu-

16. S. M. Eisenstadt, *From Generation to Generation* (Glencoe, Ill.: The Free Press, 1956). The account presented here is drawn entirely from this work. A later piece, "Generational Conflict and Intellectual Antinominism," in Philip G. Altbach and Robert S. Laufer, eds., *The New Pilgrims* (New York: David McKay Co. Inc., 1972), adds little to the earlier statement.

larly difficult. This is because of the relatively great discontinuity between the organizing principles applied within and outside the kinship sphere. In the occupational world particularly, men are judged categorically, or according to "universalistic" criteria (in theory, at least), and they are valued according to their capacities to perform functions rather than by virtue of their nature as whole men. The primary function of the school is to mediate this transition from the family to the occupational and other instrumentally oriented spheres. But schools, since they are oriented only toward inculcation of correct values and formal acquisition of skills and knowledge, are no substitute for the diffuseness, particularism, and solidarity of the family. Although students are not held "responsible" in the way they will be upon attaining adulthood (for school, after all, is only training or practice), the basic principles governing the operation of the school must nevertheless be universalistic, functionally specific, individualistic, and achievement-oriented. Experience at school is therefore inherently one of drastic discontinuity, of disjunction from the principles that supposedly govern life in kinship spheres.

It is at this point that age groups have their peculiar relevance. They provide a focus for *group* identity beyond the family, a vehicle for the experience of solidarity that makes the (very long) transition to life in the larger community easier. Age groups grease the skids, so to speak, of what would otherwise be an intolerable period of growing up and getting ready. They thus have the *function* of mediating the discrepancies in values and norms that are particularly acute in modern industrial societies.

Although youth groups (and age-grading in general) appear in all but the most simple societies, it is only in modern industrial ones that they have no more than a temporary age-specific life and significance. In virtually all preindustrial societies, age groups remain relevant for life and determine the life fate of individuals in a variety of ways. Although Eisenstadt does not say so, the withering away and adult irrelevance of age-grading systems as bases for experiences of solidarity and group identification are probably the source of romantic and sentimental recollections of "the good old days." It is precisely the solidarity of the age-group-based experience that makes it irrelevant, even positively dysfunctional for participation in the instrumental spheres of society. Therefore, unlike preindustrial societies, even complex ones, there is inevitably a great discontinuity between the requirements of this period and those of adult life. The conflict between the solidarity of youth groups and the necessity to strive for achievement in later life is a crucial one.

Because age-grading, and age groups based on age-grading, are antithetical to or dysfunctional for the basic principles of occupational, economic, and political systems in industrial societies, they can never become fully institutionalized, a fundamental difference from pre-industrial societies. But the strong group identifications characteristic of the tender school years, along with the learning of abstract values apart from the reality of their application in specific social roles, results in a common sense of cynicism, rebellion, and deviance of various types. And the situation is more acute in societies with a low communal orientation, by which Eisenstadt presumably means the United States, as distinct from, say Russia, China, or many smaller societies.

All this applies only to youth groups that are essentially adult-sponsored and located within the fundamental consensus of society. But the question in which we are really interested is: How does functional theory account for radical protest by students? It is clear that student protesters are deviant,[17] but there seems to be more to it than this.

Eisenstadt's analysis of revolutionary youth groups is

17. Cf. p. 307.

unfortunately limited to the German movement of the twentieth century up until Hitler, after which, of course, there were no more independent movements of any kind in Germany. He holds that the principal condition lay in tensions within the family itself:

> On the one hand, the family was still based internally on relatively strong authoritarian and ascriptive values, and strongly oriented towards the old traditional collectivity images. On the other hand, its ascriptive status orientation could not be fully upheld in the occupational (more achievement-oriented) sphere. Thus the father's authority became undermined in a way, and he could not serve as a full model for status aspirations; yet his authority was still strongly upheld by the formalized educational system. Internal tensions within the family became very strong, both between the "authoritarian" father and the submissive mother, on the one hand, and between them and the children, on the other. The children could not fully identify themselves with the father, whose authority was thrust upon them, nor with the mother, whose image was highly ambiguous because of the mixture of "love" (towards the children) and submissiveness (towards the father). This internal tension was one of the main reasons for the lack of development of a fully integrated sexual image or the capacity for heterosexual relations, which manifested itself, as has been shown, in the development of the German youth movement.[18]

Along with these tensions within the family were parallel ones toward participation in German society and toward achievement norms accompanying industrialization. According to Eisenstadt, these parallel conflicts caused great tension among youth, a tension that "could not always find release within a sphere of secondary institutionalization or within an adult rebellious movement." The root of the German movement is found, then, in the peculiar tensions generated by Germany's very rapid industrialization essentially within the valua-

18. *Ibid.*, pp. 318-19.

tional and normative framework of feudalism and the monarchy.

There are several weaknesses in all this. Perhaps in part because it was performed in such a cursory and off-hand manner, Eisenstadt's analysis of revolutionary youth groups seems unconvincing. But more than this is involved. Autonomous political movements of youth are conceptualized (from a formal standpoint) in essentially the same manner as are the instutionalized ones—in terms of the problem of discontinuities between kinship and instrumental spheres and the imperatives thereby placed upon the socialization process. However, unlike the analysis of the institutionalized forms, the deviant type is not analyzed *as* a general type. Limiting himself to one case makes this virtually impossible. Consequently, we have no way of knowing whether or not the factors brought forward by Eisenstadt are the true causes of the German movement. And we have no way of knowing whether these particular empirical conditions can, or should be, understood as a special case of a more general category, or whether they themselves represent the most general formulation possible.

There are other problems. As in the instance of the psychobiological theorists, Eisenstadt fails to provide an explanatory schema that truly differentiates between situations providing soil for growth of institutionalized youth groups and those that give rise to deviant ones. Insofar as I understand him, it seems to me that the only real difference is that the deviant groups are to be found in situations where the tensions between particularistic-ascriptive-collectivity orientations on the one hand, and universalistic-achievement-individual ones on the other, are particularly acute. This condition arose in Germany through the rapidity of her industrialization. Youth were socialized very strongly in the particularistic-ascriptive institutions of the family and the school, the latter of which was viewed as an instrument of the state, "for the training of good soldiers for the state and King." But this is not entirely satisfactory, since some movements have occurred in countries that industrialized quite slowly and gradually, and that do not seem to have such pronounced disjunctions between ascriptive and achievement spheres.

These considerations tend to raise in one's mind the whole problem of conceptualizing the phenomena as "deviant." In order to label anything as "deviant," one must have a relatively clear conception of what is not deviant, of what is healthy. And this in turn tends to confer upon specific forms of society or social organization the merit badge of normality. Obviously there is something wrong with societies in which "deviant" phenomena are found, and one might be inclined to believe that they should be returned to their healthy state. For the action-minded, this might imply a rooting-out or elimination of whatever is held to be deviant. This instance exemplifies what to the minds of many is the conservative bias of functional sociology. Everything comes back eventually to the consensus from which departures must be "deviant" or "dysfunctional."

This is not to say that the functionalist analysis has no value. It has at least two advantages over psychobiological theory. The first is that, in locating the problem of student or youth movements in the interstices of social structure, functional theory makes it possible, in principle, to discriminate between conditions that do and those that do not give rise to movements. This is so despite the theoretically feeble state of the functionalist theory of youth movements. Second, the emphasis on tensions between value systems, and the relationship of these tensions to the socialization process in terms of discontinuities, focus on what is quite obviously a most important component of student movements, and one that it is important to analyze if we wish to understand the nature of such movements. The analysis in earlier chapters is clearly consistent with this. Participants in the movement both perceive and exemplify contradictions in America's value system, although the contradictions might not be explicable in specifically functionalist categories.

Mass-Pluralist Interpretations

It is against this general functionalist perspective that we turn now to the more specifically political mass-pluralist understanding of student movements. Quite a few predominantly liberal scholars identified with this school of political analysis have addressed themselves to the problem posed by the movement, many of them because their own academic existence has been strongly influenced by the movement in action.

Pluralism is essentially a definition of the nature and explanation of the conditions of democracy. Democracy is conceived of as an equilibrium of interest groups operating within a consensus often referred to as "the rules of the game." The equilibrium is a condition under which no group or faction is able to acquire all or the bulk of power. Much of pluralist political analysis is devoted to the question of what conditions are conducive or not conducive to maintaining the equilibrium. Thus, various studies of religious beliefs and attitudes, organizational membership and commitments, class structure, and cultural values are carried out.

Although pluralist political theory is a theory of democracy, it has obvious implications for other types of societies. For instance, to analyze the conditions of democracy is to imply at least something about the conditions of authoritarian regimes. Systematic theoretical expansion of pluralism has occurred through its integration with the conception of mass society. Although this idea can be traced well back into the nineteenth century, it is only with the rise and success of the authoritarian regimes in the first half of the twentieth, particularly

Nazi Germany, that these ideas have been introduced into political sociology and, in particular, brought into conjunction with pluralist conceptions. I will begin by discussing the most systematic integration of pluralist and mass theory, that of William Kornhauser,[19] and then look at some of the treatments of the movement by outstanding representatives of the school.

First of all, pluralist societies are those that are democratic; in Kornhauser's terms, elites are accessible to nonelites (the citizenry in general), but nonelites are not very susceptible to the appeals of mass movements. Mass societies are those which are democratic in form, which is to say that the elites are accessible to nonelites, but the latter are in turn more available for mobilization by mass movements. There are also totalitarian societies, in which the elites are not accessible from below but the people are available (or have been, since the totalitarian government has presumably come to power as a mass movement) for mobilization within a movement. Finally, communal societies are those in which elites are not accessible and nonelites are not available. The empirical models Kornhauser has most clearly in mind are doubtless Germany before (mass) and after (totalitarian) Hitler, the U.S. (pluralist), and any feudal society (communal).

These are only definitions. What important empirical characteristics can be associated with these types? The most important is the presence of "intermediate" groups in pluralist societies: organizations or associations that have some political relevance, but that in checking one another create an equilibrium of a sort. Membership in and commitment to such organizations means, according to Kornhauser, that the individual does not face the power of the state alone, and also that the state cannot usurp to itself total power as long as the associations are

19. William Kornhauser, *The Politics of Mass Society* (Glencoe, Ill.: The Free Press, 1959).

independent of the state. The existence of many such groups also means that many individuals are involved in several, thus spreading out their identification and commitments, a condition not likely to encourage fanaticism or ideological ridigity. Thus, a pragmatic rather than an ideological politics would be promoted. It may also be necessary that the organizations themselves as democratic, a particularly important point in view of the obvious absence of democracy in all sorts of important organizations: corporations, most unions, universities, and so on. And some pluralist theorists have promoted a conception of democracy that requires only that the organizations themselves are, as a class, powerful enough to establish an equilibrium.[20] Taken together, these are hard conditions indeed, and it is extremely doubtful whether any society in the world realistically fulfills them.

It is Kornhauser's contention that authoritarian movements find more fertile ground in mass societies than in pluralist ones. Germany, according to him, was a mass society, and this is the basic reason for Hitler's success. The United States, on the other hand, is a pluralist society, and the typical form taken by movements here and in other pluralist societies is the reform movement. Mass movements differ from reform movements in that they recruit membership from all classes (unlike the labor movement in particular), focus on remote rather than immediate objects (Washington rather than the locality), and are totalistic and uncompromising in their ends or goals, rather than pragmatic and tolerant.

The typical mass-movement supporter is viewed as an "extremist" whose behavior is essentially irrational. Mass-movement members do not accept "the rules of the game," therefore they upset the stability of the institutionalized conflict that constitutes democracy. "Mass

20. See, for instance, Robert Dahl, *Who Governs?* (New Haven, Conn.: Yale University Press, 1963).

man" experiences himself as "an improverished thing dependent on powers outside of himself, unto whom he has projected his living presence."[21] Self-estranged men experience a diffused anxiety and "search for substitute forms of integration." Lacking ego-autonomy, mass man develops an image of himself as being like everyone else. This absence of a sense of personal autonomy often leads him to become, in Eric Hoffer's phrase, a true believer."[22]

In this fashion Kornhauser draws a psychological portrait of "mass man" that is essential to his theory. Mass movements could never get off the ground if there were few such estranged individuals. In a pluralist society,

> the inner cohesion of local groups and cultures provides a firmer basis for self-relatedness, and the diversity of distinctive self-image.[23]

Therefore, pluralist societies are the best bulwark against mass movements that may lead to totalitarianism.

There are a great many difficulties with this theory, both conceptual and empirical. It is not necessary to go into all of this here, but one major point should be made. The idea that mass movements are comprised of such self-alienated and self-estranged men, that their participation is thereby determined by their unconscious and is thereby irrational, is an old idea advanced by many conservative nineteenth-century theorists such as Gustav Le Bon. This idea, as Kornhauser knows well, was intended as a criticism of popular democracy and as a defense of aristocracies. It is, in short, basically a class ideology. This in itself does not, of course, make it empirically untrue. The evidence, however, is at best incomplete. In fact, it has been shown that the reverse is sometimes the case. The isolated (and thereby pre-

21. *Ibid.*, p. 108. The quotation is taken by Kornhauser from Erich Fromm.
22. Eric Hoffer, *The True Believer* (New York: Mentor Books, 1958).
23. Kornhauser, pp. 109-10.

sumably self-estranged), under some conditions at least, tend *not* to become involved in mass movements; on the other hand, there is evidence that at least some movements may emerge from the more organized sectors of society.[24]

Whatever the technical merits of the theory itself, two additional points should be made. First, the theory is to a considerable extent an intellectual celebration of the United States in the postwar period. Indeed, this is true of functionalism generally. But more than this, functionalism and mass-pluralist theory are intellectual systems that project a specifically liberal view of society. Conceptions such as the idea that modern industrial societies have brought about conditions appropriate for an "end of ideology" are direct reflections of standard liberal tenets. Functionalism and mass-pluralist theories may be thought of, in part at least, as systematizations of liberal welfare-state principles, which in a sense "complete" or ameliorate its inherent anomie by providing a moral apologia.[25] In any case, many pluralists hold to the empirical tenet that the U.S. is a pluralist (i.e., democratic)—indeed, the leading pluralist—society. And this often influences the construction of their theories as implicit defenses of the *status quo*.

We can now turn to direct examination of some of the pluralist treatments of the movement. There is now a considerable literature, so that again no attempt to be comprehensive can be made. At the outset I wish to make clear that, despite the introductory remarks above, my discussion of the pluralist treatment of the movement is definitely not intended as a general indictment of the school. Its members have contributed many creative and perceptive analyses to the *corpus* of political sociology. It is perhaps not only unfortunate but reveal-

24. See, for instance, Joseph Gusfield, "Mass Society and Extremist Politics," *American Sociological Review* 38 (February 1962).
25. See Gouldner, for an extensive discussion.

ing as well, that the school should find itself at its weakest in its analysis of the contemporary movements, and of the student movement in particular. One work, in particular, because of the eminence and representativeness of its contributors, may be taken as reasonably representing the pluralist comprehension of the movement. Edited by Daniel Bell and Irving Kristol, both eminent figures, the volume *Confrontation* contains contributions from Nathan Glazer, John Bunzel, S. M. Lipset, Samuel Lubell, Roger Starr, Nathan Tarcov, and Talcott Parsons, as well as Bell and Kristol themselves.[26] Glazer, Lipset, Bell, and Parsons, in particular, are among the intellectual leaders of the functionalist and pluralist schools, and *Confrontation* represents the moderate liberal view of what is going on. The editors themselves believe that the essays provide "a fairly comprehensive picture of the student movement."[27]

I have said that the pluralist understanding of the nature of American society is rather parallel to that held by liberals, or perhaps I should say more specifically, by older liberals, who for the most part were trained and came to academic prominence during the Cold War years. The essence of this view is best seen in its conceptualization of power, and particularly the way power is wielded in American society. It is only a slight exaggeration to say that a basic pluralist assumption holds that all authority exercised in the United States in public life is legitimate authority. It is legitimate because, according to the pluralist's most important empirical assumption, we are a democratic society. The democratic workings of the system, although they sometimes find themselves in

26. *Confrontation: The Student Rebellion and the Universities* (New York: Basic Books, 1968).
27. *Ibid.*, p. xii. For a perspective from the Left wing of liberalism, see Irving Louis Horowitz, *The Struggle is the Message* (Berkeley, Calif.: The Glendessary Press, 1970). For other conservatively liberal views see George Kennan, *Democracy and the Student Left,* (New York: Bantam Books, 1968), and Diana Trilling, "On the Steps of Low Library," *Commentary* 46: 29-55.

trouble, are in all cases sufficient to handle the demands put upon them, and in any case, there is no reason to think that we could get anything much better. There is thus a conservative utopian element in pluralist thought: imperfect though it may be, the United States is the best of all possible societies, since in principle it supposedly permits any organized interest a voice in the political marketplace.

How does this empirical assumption work itself out with respect to conceptions of power posed by the movement? Virtually to a man, pluralist thinkers argue the case for the existence of limited democratic authority in the university. Parsons's emphasis is on the great freedom within the university. First, he argues that the universities are

> an integral part of the generally pluralistic society, with its egalitarian strains and its commitments to equality of opportunity as well as equality of basic citizenship rights, its universalistic legal system and supporting moral sentiments, its modified version of free enterprise and its liberal political system.[28]

Academia, in Parsons view, is itself a highly pluralist system, which means that there are no real or substantial problems of power:

> There are at least four principal entities involved, namely, the trustees, administrations, faculties, and students. They are interrelated in a manner somewhat analogous to the separation of powers in governmental affairs, although the lines are differently drawn. Faculties have a role somewhere between the functions of the judicial and legislative branches of government, participating in both. As the groups most thoroughly committed to academic values, they bear the largest responsibility as judges of the standards of the system and are the most important, though not the sole determiners of the "educational policies" that implement

28. Talcott Parsons, "The Academic System: A Sociologist's View," in Bell and Kristol, p. 174.

these standards. Students and alumni play a role in some respects parallel to those of constituencies in relation to political office-holders. But the "judicial" role of the faculty substantially modifies the "pure democracy" of the constituency type relationship.[29]

This view of students is, however, modified in other passages concerning the basic teacher-student relationship, which is, according to Parsons, fundamental to the university. It is "an extension of 'socialization' begun in the family. . . . Higher education may be considered an extension and culmination of independence training."[30] The student has an "obligation to recognize faculty precedence."[31] As far as student power is concerned,

> it would seem patently silly for students as temporary members of the academic community to have governing power *equal* to that of faculties, to say nothing of a fully democratic pattern of "one member one vote."[32]

Since the universities are pluralistic institutions within a pluralist society, and since the role of students within them is necessarily on the dependent side of a paternalistic relationship, there are no serious problems of power. The pluralistic nature of the system has in effect already solved these, by definition.

Sometimes pluralist theorists completely ignore questions of power in their analyses; in pluralist theory, these are, after all, essentially settled. Others, like Kristol, construct what Herbert Marcuse would call a "mystification" of power:

> University administration in the United States today combines relative powerlessness with near-absolute mindlessness on the subject of education.[33]

29. *Ibid.*, pp. 170-71.
30. *Ibid.*, p. 171.
31. *Ibid.*, p. 172.
32. *Ibid.*, p. 173.
33. Irving Kristol, "A Different Way to Restructure the University," in Bell and Kristol, pp. 147-48.

Who then has power? The trustees? Hardly.

> Though a great many people are under the impression that the boards of trustees are the "real" power structure of the university, this is in fact the one group over which the administration does wield considerable influence. . . .They solemnly rubber-stamp whatever the administration has done or intends to do.[34]

Thus, to speak of the power of the administration or the trustees is really to invent a nonexistent thing. But surely the administration wields some power over students. Very unlikely. According to Kristol, this issue "is hardly worth discussing at a time when the issue being debated is the students' power over the administration."[35]

The faculty? Although the faculty is "the preponderant estate" of the university, it is, like the administration and the students, "deficient in the will to do anything, or the power to do anything, or ideas about what might be done."[36]

Whereas in this passage Kristol simply assumes that no one has any power, he argues elsewhere along with Daniel Bell, in a more positive vein, that our problems have to do with complexity, not power:

> For the liberal. . .the failure to mount effective social programs during these past years was seen as arising out of the inherent complexity of our social problems, the lack of detailed social science knowledge, as to how to "cut" into them, and the shortage of trained administrators.[37]

Thus, he seems to take a "technicist" view; our problems are not so much those of the distribution of power, but of our technical capacity. This is a central tenet of the contemporary liberal view: politics is inappropriate in spheres where technical expertise is available, and this is

34. *Ibid.*
35. *Ibid.*
36. *Ibid.*, p. 145.
37. Bell and Kristol, "Introduction," in Bell and Kristol, p. x.

increasingly just about everywhere. So we witness what Bell some time ago called "the end of ideology."

According to Samuel Lubell,

the demand for "student power" is not the really critical issue for restructuring the universities.[38]

What is the critical issue? According to Lubell it is "the career problems—the drive and the lack of drives—of the record numbers of young people."[39]

The views of the leading pluralist theorists are essentially of a piece. American society is pluralistic and the universities have their place within the consensus. There can, therefore, be no real problems of power. It follows that the movement must be acting in terms of misconceptions and toward goals that are undemocratic (since they move against an already pluralist system) and therefore undesirable. Indeed, this is so. The characterizations of the movement are drawn directly from the mass-pluralist theory of social movements.

These attributions, in terms of both goals and style, are applications of the crowd psychology ideas incorporated into mass-pluralist theory. Goals are held to be "vague, inchoate and diffuse,"[40] a situation that could be expected if there are no objective conditions justifying protest. The idea that the goals of the movement are poorly defined is a common one. Horowitz characterizes the movement as *fin de siècle* radicalism, a situation in which the means rather than the ends come into clear focus and act to displace the ends: "the struggle is the message."[41]

Sometimes this idea is couched in the most negative of terms:

38. Samuel Lubell, "That 'Generation Gap'," in Bell and Kristol, p. 66.
39. *Ibid.*
40. Daniel Bell, "Columbia and the New Left," in Bell and Kristol, p. 96.
41. Horowitz, *The Struggle is the Message,* p. 23.

Very frequently revolutions are the last spasms of the past, and thus are not really revolutions but counter-revolutions, operating in the name of revolutions. A revolution which really either is non-programmatic and has no content, or involves content which is based on the past but provides no guidance for the future, is essentially counter-revolutionary.[42]

And they remind Nathan Glazer

more of the Luddite machine smashers than the Socialist trade unionists who achieved citizenship and power for workers.[43]

There is a germ of truth in these charges, but in general they are inconsistent with the trend of evidence —despite the sensationalism of the media. As I showed earlier, the university presidents in Astin's 1969 study reported a low incidence of violence, even under what were obviously very common conditions of confrontation. And the peak years of campus violence were 1968-70. If confrontation has for the most part, as Morgan's data suggest (see chap. 4), resulted from failures to institute communication or dialogue, and therefore represents an attempt to create such a condition, the pluralists' characterizations would seem to be seriously misplaced.

The point ought to be made that most social movements, particularly in their early stages, are pretty fuzzy about their goals, in the sense of the specific arrangements they would like to institute. This is to say, they lack a blueprint. It is a quite different thing to say that they have no general or abstract goals, or that they spend their time desperately creating them. In earlier phases, the goals of social movements are normally ex-

42. Zbgniew Brzezinski, "Revolution and Counterrevolution (But Not Necessarily about Columbia)," *The New Republic,* June 1, 1968.
43. Nathan Glazer, " 'Student Power' in Berkeley," in Bell and Kristol, p. 21.

pressed abstractly. Students have often found themselves impaled on the horns of a dilemma: when on the one hand they have been cloudy about their objectives they have been told to present a blueprint; when on the other they have pronounced about the proper shape of the future, they have been held to be rigidly ideological. This is a no-win game.

Mass-pluralist theory is even more in evidence in characterizations of the radical's political style. Bell and Kristol write that the activist style is one of "symbolic gesture," of "expressive action," and, "demands resolution on a 'total' level."[44] Also, the style is "irrational," in the sense of committing oneself in action first, then "find[ing] the words to justify the action." "The deed having been done—the acting out of forbidden impulses—the words came next."[45] Bell also maintains that the Columbia insurrectionists experienced a "conversion experience," by which he means a "tearing down of old beliefs and the substitution of a new, stark, 'reality.' "[46] Nothing could better illustrate the blanket application of nineteenth-century crowd psychology as it appears in modern mass-pluralist theory. In fact, Bell even proposes that

> what we had here was a classic illustration of the contagion phenomenon of a mass that Gustav Le Bon described so graphically in Psychologie des Foules in 1895.[47]

Emotionalism, suggestibility (and thus the conversion experience), confrontation—all are together taken to indicate a form of mass irrationality.

Others insist on the same stigmata. Kristol proposes that student activists at Columbia were "a 'mob' in the authentic sociological sense of that term,"[48] and refers to field work in the ghettos or among migrant workers as

44. Bell and Kristol, "Introduction," pp. x and xi.
45. Bell, "Columbia and the New Left," p. 97.
46. *Ibid.*, p. 97.
47. *Ibid.*, pp. 97-98.
48. Kristol, in Bell and Kristol, p. 151.

"off-campus rioting."[49] I have already noted Glazer's reference to students as "Luddites," and Brzezinski's view of the movement as "the guttering last gasp of romanticism." Such images as these exhibit the pluralists' habit of stigmatizing the movement as inherently and essentially violent. The students have simply been "out to wreck the university," and all sorts of discussions proceed on this assumption of the movement's violent orientation. But evidence for this has never been systematically reviewed, nor has its relation to systematic institutional injustice been seriously considered.

Furthermore, the implication that mass movements, because of their style, are not only irrational, but irrational in comparison with presumtively rational routinized institutional procedures, cannot be accepted. The routinized functioning of bureaucratic organizations in particular can be placed in the service of virtually any sort of goal, however irrational. Neither order nor challenge to order is as such rational or irrational.

It is a corollary of such conceptions that there can be no real issues. In the opinion of Edward Shils, another eminent figure of the functionalist-pluralist school,

> Most of the issues on which radicals seek "confrontation" are factitious and not imperatively obtrusive in themselves.[50]

Furthermore, he says,

> Most of the issues that arouse the passions of the radical students are not serious in the sense of being well-grounded in fact or deeply cared about.[51]

One wonders which of the nonissues have failed to become "imperatively obtrusive." Vietnam? Political pris-

49. *Ibid.,* p. 157.
50. *Students in Revolt,* p. 26.
51. *Ibid.,* p. 26.

oners? Racial discrimination by colleges? Poverty? War research on campus? Justice in administrative dealings with students?

These conceptions of the movement have typically led pluralists to predict all sorts of the direst, even disastrous consequences. George Kennan, for example, maintains that the activism of those in the American student movement

> goes well beyond the normal, beyond the healthy, beyond what is safe for society itself. Lacking the balance of a sense of humor, lacking perspective on itself, saturated with scorn for the political system yet devoid of all but the most child-ish ideas as to how that system could be improved, this state of mind takes the form of an embittered *pseudo*-revolutionary nihilism—a nihilism not, for the moment, dangerous in itself, but pernicious in its effect on the cam-pus atmosphere generally, and pregnant with the pos-sibilities for real mischief if not checked and moderated. It serves to confuse the minds of other students less inclined temperamentally to such bitter and antisocial attitudes. And it could become definitely dangerous if it were to be cap-tured by, or to enter into combination with, a political force more mature, more purposeful, better organized and more conspiratorial than itself.[52]

Insofar as the pluralists substitute stigmatization for analysis, they have tended to ignore the actual intentions of protesters. The blanket condemnation, that they want to "wreck the universities," is only the most obvious case in point. Actual study of and communication with pro-testers shows this simply not to be an accurate general characterization of the movement, although sometimes the *rhetoric* might lead one to believe it. But this should be no bar to serious scholarly analysis.

Even more important than such stigmatizing, perhaps, has been the frequent seeming-refusal or inability to comprehend the actual meanings of the varieties of ex-

52. Kennan, pp. 190-91.

perience among radicals. This has been especially evident in the case of experiences associated particularly with the cultural revolution—drugs, sex, religious revelations, and so on—but carries over into more specifically political phenomena as well. These have been typically opposed on various normative and authoritarian grounds, along with the usual dire predictions of the consequences for American and Western civilization. The extent to which this difficulty in comprehending the *meanings* prevalent among radicals has resulted from the behavioristic and positivistic assumptions of mainstream sociology is difficult to say. That it results in part from the theoretical assumptions of pluralist theory and the empirical designation of the United States as the representative pluralist society is difficult to reject.

But why should this be so? The pluralists and functionalists are, and have been for some time, the dominant school of sociological analysis. Part of the answer lies in their theory of social-science knowledge, an enormous subject, but one that nevertheless must at least be mentioned. The liberal theory of knowledge tends to tie social science to a specific kind of social order. This can be seen in Lipset's conception, where social science is equated with a listing of liberal virtues:

> Many intellectuals react to the emphasis on social science and *the concomitant belief in gradualism, expertise and planning,* with a populist stress on the virtues of direct action against evil institutions and practices.[53] (emphasis added)

Social science is thus, in his view, linked to gradualism as a theory of change.[54] This is a position conceivably appropriate for a science of administration or management, but indefensible for social science as such.

---

53. Lipset, in Bell and Kristol, p. 48.
54. Interestingly, Lipset has identified Karl Marx as one of four founders of political sociology. See his "Political Sociology," in *Sociology Today* (New York: Basic Books, 1960).

The weakness of the pluralists' explanation of the movement reflects the concrete assumptions that underlie their liberal view of American society. Since radical movements should not occur in pluralist societies (only reform movements should), and since they cling to their pluralist definition of American society, the pluralists have no way of explaining the student movement within the technical apparatus of their theory. They seem to have two options. They could, on the one hand, entertain the proposition that at least some important aspects of American society are nonpluralistic, or they could, on the other, move outside the technical structure of the theory and apply only the descriptive categories of mass movements. They have opted for the second.

I should add once again that this is not a general indictment of mass-pluralist theory as an intellectual enterprise. The theory has its strengths and weaknesses. I maintain only that, in interpreting the student movement, the pluralists, to a considerable extent, have abdicated a scientific role, and turned their backs on the uses and development of their own theory, for a role as political polemicists. They have not examined the movement seriously in the light of their own theory because of a seeming unwillingness to reexamine their own conceptions of the United States as the leading pluralist society.

Left-Institutional Theories

In contrast to psychobiological, functional, and mass-pluralist theories, Left-institutional theories take as their starting point societal contradictions and the way they engender and exacerbate inequality and exploitation. In both Europe and the United States, but especially the former, Marxism in particular has been revised, interpreted, and sometimes banalized in an effort to adapt to modern conditions a theory developed to explain the emergence and political direction of the industrial labor force created by industrial capitalism in the nineteenth century. The 50s and 60s have seen its adaptation to the liberation movements of Third World peasant societies. Application of Marxism to movements such as those of students, youth, women, or blacks requires important revision of certain basic assumptions, for none of these can *prima facie* be defined as a class. Yet, Marxian theory has been undergoing its most creative time since the period between the great wars, and in some cases students have themselves been active in this resurgence. But do Left-institutional theories[55] provide a good explanation of the movement?

One version holds that the student movement is a modern embodiment of class revolution—students are the contemporary form of the labor movement, and the university is redefined as the "firm" or workplace where student labor is exploited.

> If it is true that knowledge and technical progress are the motors of the new society, as the accumulation of capital was the motor of the preceding (industrial) society, does not the university then occupy the same place as the great capitalist enterprise formerly did? Thus, is not the student movement, in principle at least, of the same importance as the labor movement of the past?[56]

Marx himself insisted that the movement of the working class would proceed not only "an sich" (in itself) but "für sich" (for itself) as well. This means that revolutionary movements can occur only if those constituting the class in which they are rooted have a theoretical understanding of their class position, and proceed actively in

55. As I indicated at the beginning of the chapter, I employ the rather cumbersome term "Left-institutional," to avoid questions centering around what is and what is not "Marxist." Some Left-institutional theories are very "unMarxist" in terms of a narrow interpretation of Marxism, some, as in the case, for instance, of Max Weber, consciously *anti-Marxist* in at least some respects.
56. Alain Touraine, "Naissance d'un Mouvement Etudiant," *Le Monde,* March 7 and 8, 1968.

terms of their own interests as these are revealed and as they are determined by the mechanisms of the capitalist economic system. The main problem obstructing the conception of students as a class is the problem of production. In classic Marxism the workers are, after all, essential, since they are society's producers. But what do students produce? The answer is that they produce knowledge that is essential to the operation of the economy. Knowledge replaces capital as the engine of progress. Students perform essential work, even as they learn. This means, furthermore, that the point of the student revolt is, and must be, in their own interests. Students are the new exploited working class, and are making a revolt essentially in their own interests.

There are a number of serious difficulties with this approach; it need not detain us long. First of all is the fact that students not only are transient, but also upwardly mobile, having professional and career distinctions as organizing principles of their lives. Unlike the working class, they do not live out their lives in a proletarian situation of domination and exploitation. It therefore seems to be unrealistic to attribute to them a class consciousness appropriate to an exploited class. This is even more the case because of the fact that, as I have shown, precisely those students who would seem to be in curriculums most essential to the economy—the applied fields such as engineering, business, and the physical sciences—are the most conservative or nonpolitical. This view further presumes that the power of university administrations is more or less comparable to that of the nineteenth-century entrepreneurs: the firm is replaced by the university as the organizational locus of exploitation. But such a notion borders on the preposterous; clearly, university administrators as a group have no such comparable power.

Furthermore, from the standpoint of the practicalities of the future, the ultimate aim of students within the university is not likely to be revolution. The aim of a revolution is elimination of a ruling class. But although students can perhaps hope to eliminate university management as it now exists, overthrow of the professoriate is not in their *interests,* short of a total revision of the teacher-student relationship. This implies that student ends will come to focus on some type of codetermination, various forms of which already exist in parts of Latin America (co-gobierno), and to a lesser extent in Europe.

A variant of the conception of students as a class is the notion that not students, but youth as a whole, constitute a class. One statement of this position appears in the work of John and Margaret Rowntree.[57] They argue that the contradictions of capitalism have shifted from the private to the public sector. More specifically, defense and education have become adapted to the service of monopoly capital. This is indicated by the fact that defense and education are responsible for the production of one-sixth of our Gross National Product and that both are fast expanding. The societal function of defense and education is to absorb surplus manpower, the majority of which is youth. Students absorb already-produced surplus and in their student role *refrain* from producing still more surplus that would have to be disposed of profitably. However, the increasing productivity of the labor force continues to confound the issue of future disposal of goods. The solutions to this situation are two: (1) to extend the period of schooling for youth, and (2) to train them from specifically unproductive labor. The great increases in university and college enrollments are a consequence of attempts to implement the first solution, increased militarism, which is inter-

---

57. John and Margaret Rowntree, *The Political Economy of Youth* (Ann Arbor, Mich..: Radical Education Project, 1968). See also Herbert Gintis, "The New Working Class and Revolutionary Youth," *Social Revolution* 1 (May/June 1970): 13-44.

preted as organized systematic waste, an attempt to implement the second. But these solutions to increased productivity inevitably involve the exploitation of youth. Students forgo perhaps 50 percent of their earning capacity and experience the highest rates of unemployment in the labor force. Soldiers are exploited on economic grounds as well—conscription constitutes a 38 percent tax in kind. Thus, youth as a class become alienated and begin to form a class with its own distinctive culture and values.

All this is necessary because the United States is an imperialistic nation state; soldiers are essential for holding the profitable territories and education is necessary for those who administer the economy. In fact, the shift of the economy from the public to the private sector is, according to the Rowntrees, the consequence of the needs of the imperialistic system. The question of why we have, or need, an imperalistic system is not broached by the Rowntrees, but can be presumed to lie outside the concerns of their analysis.

The problems inherent in this formulation are as great as those in the students-as-a-class variant. First of all, underlying their entire interpretation is the nature of United States imperialism. The extent to which this system is essential to maintaining the internal economy is debatable, a question not yet resolved—and an enormously complex one that cannot realistically be brought into this discussion. It is enough to note that the youth-/as/a/class position rests to some extent on the degree to which this system is economically essential to American interests.

More directly to the point is the fact that the Rowntrees seem to have produced contradictory formulations. On the one hand, students are held to be where they are and doing what they are doing (as students) because of the necessity of keeping them out of the labor force, which is too productive. On the other hand, they hold that university training is important, even perhaps essential, to maintaining the imperialist system. In their latter role they are surely producers, working productively in the public sector of the system. They thus occupy contradictory roles. Because they work in the sectors central to the maintenance of the imperialist system, youth must be thought of as an exploited class, a major shift away from the exploitation of the working class as a whole in earlier times. The contradiction in this formulation lies in the fact that, if military service and higher education are designed to inhibit production, and if the economy has shifted over to these functions, the economy must then be based on a reduction of production—an odd condition indeed.

Aside from this, there is also the purely factual question of whether the economy has indeed shifted over to the public sector. If, on the authors' calculation, only 16 percent can be found in the public sector, some accounting for the effects and significance of the remaining 84 percent would seem essential to any analysis.

There is the further problem that the students' concerns have not been basically directed to their own interests. The movement began in the South over Negro rights, and has focused on the war, imperialism, and the societal role of the universities. To only a limited extent, in terms of parietal issues and the draft, could youth be interpreted as acting in terms of their own "class" interests. And as we have seen, parietal issues are distinctly secondary in the scale of values of the movement.

Finally, it should be obvious to all that "youth" are in no sense united on anything. In fact, a central political phenomenon of the times—and perhaps one of its tragedies—is the extent to which what Mannheim called "generation units" among youth are violently at odds with each other. Can one simply dismiss as false consciousness the fact that the majority of youth hold conservative and even reactionary positions? In my opinion such a course is simply to reject the need for serious analysis.

A variant of this approach by Horowitz and Friedland attempts to fuse the concepts "generation" and "class."[58] Thus, while there exists a "youth class," the key to understanding it is "students as a social class."[59] Students as a group have most of the characteristics of a revolutionary class, the essential difference being the substitution of a generational base for the poverty base.[60] Horowitz and Friedland claim that, like all social classes, the youth class aims "at the seizure of power, at revolution."[61] This class is led (in 1970) by "100,000 well-organized revolutionaries"[62] with "a potential revolutionary mass base of 40 percent of the student youth" (their interpretation of the Fortune Survey).

The general weakness of the "youth-as-a-class" formulation is reflected in the fact that Horowitz and Friedland actually shift over to a virtually complete emphasis on students, not youth, as the revolutionary class. But the critical strictures mentioned earlier can then be applied to the analysis.

A third approach seems to surmount some of these obstacles. This argument holds that students are not a class, but that they serve essential functions within the capitalist system. Essentially, this view maintains that the most important contradiction of capitalism in modern times is rooted in the system of education.[63] First, it is essential for highly technological capitalism to assure for itself a constant and regular supply of skilled and know-

58. Irving Louis Horowitz and William H. Friedland, *The Knowledge Factory* (Chicago: Aldine, 1970).
59. See chapter 5.
60. *Ibid.*
61. *Ibid.*
62. *Ibid.*
63. It has usually been held by Marxists, and first by Marx himself, that although the *fundamental* contradictions be in the relations of production, at any particular historical period they may appear most obviously in other institutional sectors of society.

ledgeable workers, without which it could not function. Second, it is further necessary to develop various occupational and professional skills that center around conceptions of human or social engineering. And third, there must be a vast army of publicists with literary and social scientific skills to assure a continuing ideological blanket to maintain the "consensus." The contradiction arises in the fact that such social scientific and technical literary skills cannot be acquired without considerable sensitization and development of critical and analytic capacities that unintentionally encourage views of the social order that are anything but sanguine about its justice and legitimacy. As Gorz understands it,

> The problem of big management is to harmonize two contradictory necessities; the necessity of developing human capabilities, imposed by modern processes of production and the political necessity of insuring that this kind of development does not bring in its wake any augmentation of the independence of the individual, provoking him to challenge the present division of social labour and distribution of power.[64]

Another author has distinguished between the need for technicians of production, technicians of consumption, and technicians of consent.[65] The necessity of producing the latter two types, particularly the last —journalists, propagandists, and the like—has the consequence of training the potential power of ideas for *analysis,* as against their sheerly manipulative uses.

64. André Gorz, "Capitalism and the Labor Force," *International Socialist Journal* 10 (Aug. 1965), p. 422. For statements relating to the position described here, see, variously, "Why Sociologists?" by D. Cohn-Bendit, Jean-Pierre Duteuil, Bertrand Gerard, and Bernard Granautler (Nanterre, France, March 1968); "Campaigning on the Campus," by Carl Davidson (Students for a Democratic Society Pamphlet); Gareth Stedman-Jones, "The Meaning of the Student Revolt," in *Student Power,* ed. Cockburn and Blackburn (Middlesex, England: Penguin Books, 1969), pp. 25-28; Kenneth Keniston, "A Second Look at the Uncommitted," *Social Policy* (July/August 1971), pp. 6-19; and various writings of Paul Goodman, Herbert Marcuse, and others.
65. Stedman-Jones, "The Meaning. . . ."

To put this another way: the "production" of such skills is at once necessarily the "production" of one's self as an individual. And this always cradles a potentiality for expansion and extension of one's consciousness beyond narrow technical or job limits, which is to say, generalized to one's entire life-situation. Thus, the basis of protest movements is found in intellectual traditions that not only survive despite attempts to turn everything to the purpose of the state, but that also even actually flourish and develop creatively under at least some conditions of modern life.

This understanding avoids the problems of interpretations that attempt to conceive of students or youth as a class. It clearly fits the facts of the basic origins and continuing base of the movement in social scientific and humanistic ideas. It is in this sense that Lewis Feuer was certainly right when, as opposed to Marxist prophecy, he wrote that in the case of student movements, "consciousness determines existence."

This formulation also avoids the sticky problem of having to conceptualize "class interests" of students in the context of the actual concerns and issues around which the movement has developed. It is entirely compatible with their altruism and relative unconcern over their own "class" interests so characteristic of the movement. It also helps to make sense of the difficulties the movement has had in attempting to reach groups that are not immersed in or familiar with these ideas —students in technically oriented curricula, blue-collar workers, the poor.

Furthermore, this interpretation tends to make us more aware of the difficulty ideas may have of breaking out of their rather narrow and elitist circles. First, there is the reciprocal relationship, mentioned earlier in connection with the earlier phases of the movement, in which ideological hardening follows organizational failures, thus tending to eventuate in further organizational failures. This is perhaps the most fertile condition for the development of an intellectual elitism that could possibly exist. Second, there is the process of homogenization that ideas undergo even if they can penetrate beyond narrow intellectual circles. For example, although it is absolutely central to any discussion of the nature and meaning of contemporary America, the question of imperialism has never, to my knowledge, been seriously broached in any of the public media, especially TV. Discussions of the war were always couched in terms of the old, critical, assumptions: that, like social workers, we were trying to do good, have admittedly made some mistakes, have perhaps proceeded in a muddle-headed way, and so on. Even the publication of the *Pentagon Papers* did not materially change the ideological context of public representation. All such events lend credence to what Marcuse has called "repressive tolerance," by which he means the capacity of a society to absorb radical and revolutionary ideas into the rhetoric of consensus and, in so doing, to transform their fundamental nature, domesticating them and rendering them harmless.

Considering students from the standpoint of their function in acquiring and using knowledge has the consequence of bringing under scrutiny the nature of that knowledge itself, apart from the issues of the political domination and control of the institutions. Clearly this is an important matter; the fact of the strong and persistent relationship between radicalism and protest on the one hand, and curriculum on the other, makes this obvious. Students-as-a-class and youth-as-a-class formulations do not tend to focus our thought in this direction. But the facts relating to the curriculum-activism relationship shown earlier make particular sense in the terms that I have just now been discussing. This is assuredly not merely a matter of the more intelligent being drawn to protest. I have already shown that although there has been some truth to this, at least in earlier years, it applies to conservative as well as radical students. Rather, the strategic point of understanding has to do with the *kind* of knowledge transmitted and acquired, and the ways it does or does not illuminate the condition of men and women in society. It is primarily the social sciences, of course, that create and promulgate such understanding on a systematic basis, along with those sectors of the arts and humanities which have always maintained critical and essentially political views of society—perspectives originating principally in the transformations and uprooting that accompanied industrialization. These critical perspectives remain sources of creative inspiration. In both cases, it is the content or substance of knowledge that is a requisite for perception of societal contradiction—a perception that Marx long ago knew to be essential for the creation and growth of a movement.

In this sense ideas are subversive and may well be an essential condition of the genesis and resurgence of the student movement. However, the relationship is not so simple as it might seem. It is not the case that the universities simply teach radical social science and humanities to students who then become radicals. In the first place, the obviously dominant theoretical versions of social science have been essentially conventionally liberal or conservative interpretations of the social order; Marxist or other radical forms of social science have always maintained at best a struggling minority tradition alongside the professional academic monoliths of functionalism, pluralism, and laissez-faire economics. To this I might add that graduate training in the social sciences has moved progressively in the direction of producing specialized technicians in rather narrow subdisciplinary areas. An emphasis on increasingly technical methodological sophistication has accompanied this trend. The radicalization of students has probably been as much of a reaction against, and a rejection of, prevailing liberal and conservative theory as it has been a simple consequence of propagation of radical ideas. The search for alternatives in theory has, in essence, been a concomitant of rejection of what was already being taught.

Second, the humanistic disciplines contain at their core a conception of man, or at least the principle of debate over some fundamental conception of man, that at some level tends to exercise the intellect and the moral sense of practitioners and students alike. Questions revolving about such ideas as freedom, determinism, and human potential, far from being eliminated, remain critical to conceptions scholars hold about the nature of their disciplines, and perhaps not infrequently, of the meaning of their own activity as well. Some kind of dialectic between the heightening of perception of a received tradition and a renewal of concern over the historic human condition energizes the humanistic disciplines, forcing into view a conception implying not the neutrality of the ivory tower, but action conducted as a moral imperative.

Although the analysis so briefly adumbrated here clearly fits many of the facts of the movement, it is not in itself a completely adequate interpretation. There are several aspects that require critical comment.

First, there is the question of the extent to which the characterization of students as acquirers of socially indispensable knowledge is applicable. In those industrialized societies with a level of technology approximately equal to our own, far fewer students are to be found in the universities. To some extent this results from the more extensive exclusion of professional and technical training from the universities and their incorporation in technical institutes of various sorts—for engineering, education, art, music. But even if all such institutions are included, the proportion of college-age youth in attendance is several times greater in the United States than it is in Great Britain, Germany, France,

Italy, and the smaller European societies. Evidently, university education as a whole cannot be considered indispensable for societal functioning.

There are other reasons that support this proposition. For many years the problem of "underemployment" has plagued employing institutions of all sorts. Obviously, some part of university and college training expands the competence of large numbers beyond the actual technical demands of the available positions. And recent increases in white collar unemployment have added a new problem to the list of those that already plague the economy. Clearly, much of the training that goes on in our institutions of higher learning is unnecessary.

If this is so, the massive enrollments must have other causes. One important source may be the peculiarity of the American status system. It has been observed often that a system combining the moral virtue of striving for upward mobility (which is, of course, a different matter from the actualities of mobility) with a principled reluctance to accept the facts of class differences is not only a contradiction but a condition likely to generate considerable insecurity. In the European societies, especially those with feudal pasts where class distinctions are clearer and more accepted as an organizing principle of life, one's sense of identity is rooted more strongly in one's class. In the U.S. the fluidity of the status system has as one consequence the proliferation of a variety of more formal criteria, of which the college degree is perhaps the foremost. Such certificates function to validate claims for status and the recognition and even deference that accompany it. This is more than saying that college is a way of "getting ahead," for the "getting ahead" in this sense has to do with overcoming specifically status problems—the ambiguities and contradictions of the status system that drive men to seek more tangible vehicles for the lodgement of their claims for recognition. Such status anxieties probably spring from the need of (mainly) middle-class parents to pass on their own nontransmissible credentials to their children. Such status-centered concerns may not, themselves, be entirely irreducible. The rapid development and expansion of the economy itself, especially in those sectors most susceptible to automation, has undoubtedly had the purely functional consequence of adding a welfare function to the academic and other functions performed by academia. Such a functional relationship, of course, requires ideological justifications on other grounds. I will return to this question in chapter 7.

It is also necessary to call into question to some extent the central proposition of this interpretation. It is proposed that protest occurs mainly among those who are being trained as technicians of consumption or of consent, mainly the latter. But we must question whether this is really so. It is by no means obvious that humanities and social science curricula in their entirety are designed to program students for such tasks, or even that they have the consequence of doing so. In the first place, political awareness and activism are heavily concentrated in the specifically nonvocational humanistic and social science departments, schools, and colleges. As we have seen, the effect of vocationalism—including vocationalism in socially and politically oriented fields—is to make political activism rather unlikely, or less likely than in nonhumanistic or social-science-oriented but nonvocational fields. This suggests that the experience of discovering oneself to be programmed in such a fashion—through unfortunate exposure to liberating ideas—may not be so central or decisive an element as the theory considers it to be. It is quite possible, even probable, that those who become activated politically are, for the most part, precisely those who have never had such occupational destinations. This is especially true of those in the arts and humanities.

Related to this is the fact that the social or political

need for technicians of consent seems to be highly variable. The number of social scientists in the United States
is proportionately far greater than in any other industrialized society. In the U.S., large numbers of students
in these fields have always ended up essentially per-
petuating more people like themselves—mainly through
teaching jobs at all levels, but particularly in higher education. And surely much of the social research turned
out serves no apparent political function other than
keeping people busy at various innocuous enterprises.
Furthermore, there is the question of the proportion of
social science research that is usable (to say nothing of
actually used) for purposes of political or economic
domination (as in market research). In addition, I must
add that its real potential for control has always been
greatly exaggerated, in part because social scientists in
search of research funds have often pushed their pro-
jects on the grounds of the possible usefulness of the
findings, this in hopes of loosening the purse strings of
potential sponsors. But we simply do not know this
much, and what is known is formulated and understood
very inexactly and imperfectly.

In view of these considerations it would not be correct,
in my opinion, to overestimate the general political effect of the social sciences. Their effect has not been
monolithic in a conservative direction. At the same time
I would insist that the enterprise of social science research as a whole has been deflected away from defining
problems in critical or radical (and in the root sense of
the word, more fundamental) terms. This surely has
been true, and is a powerful indictment, especially since
the social sciences, and sociology in particular, have
made such a great issue of being objective and
"value-free."

We should finally note that the situation of the
humanities confounds the theory to an even greater degree. While we must admit substantial political and

economic influence on the recent growth of the social sciences, this can hardly apply to the humanities. They have never been considered worthy of much financial support, either by the government or private enterprise (in Europe, we should note, the situation is slightly different), and their growth is a result almost entirely of other factors. Students who study in these fields end up in the most varied occupational and political contexts. On the whole, they have never been considered very useful to either government or business (one clear exception is that many end up in mass communications and other industries like book publishing, fields that have always placed a higher value on their services). The humanities, to an even greater extent than is true of the social sciences, are a group of self-perpetuating, self-reproducing enterprises that survive, in part at least, on bases other than the production of technicians of consumption or consent. On balance, a considerable segment of the social science-humanities enterprise cannot, in terms of the actualities of its academic and professional situation, be understood as merely a creation of the corporate capitalist system.

7
THE THEORY OF THE STUDENT MOVEMENT

In this analysis I have attempted to apply the core-periphery paradigm to the several facets of the student movement by elaborating it in ways that seemed appropriate for each. In this chapter, after briefly reviewing the foregoing, I will try to integrate these materials into a coherent theoretical conception, emphasizing the more critical aspects revealed in the analysis.

Generating Core and Periphery in the Social Origins and Mobilizing Conditions of the Student Movement: A Review

The status of humanist families so important in the origins of the movement is located structurally in spheres generally remote from the industrial-commercial and governmental core: occupationally in universities, especially those with liberal-humanist traditions and in various professions professing a humanitarian ethic, such as the liberal ministry; politically, in milieux ideologically well to the Left. The constellation of Left-wing politics and humanist cultural values, anchored in an economically relatively secure occupation relatively remote from economic and political instrumentalism, has been the principal seedbed of student radicalism. In this context the role of the mothers as socializing influences has evidently been particularly important. The mothers, as will be recalled, were themselves found to be involved in occupational milieux and civic enterprises that were generally consonant with humanistic values and practices, and inculcated in their offspring high standards of both achievement and personal morality.[1] The home experience of activists-to-be was one of a high level of democratic participation in family affairs.

The importance of all these elements is indicated by the fact that essentially nonpolitical counter-culturalists have also come from upper-middle-class backgrounds politically somewhat to the Left, but implanted occupationally more centrally with the core, and especially in those occupations created by the newer technologies, occupations essentially bereft of occupation, professional, or political traditions. This entire pattern has thus been important as the germinating ground of student activism, and has been imparted to and acquired by youth as a general life orientation.

The complementary and interlocking nature of preparatory social experience and conditions within the academic setting can be understood partly from the angle of vision of the family. Youth prepared in the ways described in chapter 2 have generally been headed for high-quality higher education. Emphasis on the great importance of intellectual activity, and on achievement as well, in conjunction with their generally affluent situation, has resulted in their over-selection by those high-

1. See chap. 2.

quality institutions to which they have aspired—generally the great private and public universities, or the well-endowed, highly selective liberal arts colleges.

The relation of specific characteristics of these institutions to student protest—size, quality, and bureaucratization—was also brought within the core-periphery paradigm, in terms of the concepts of structural coordination and value ethos. It has been the co-ordinated-humanistic institutions that have demonstrated the capacity to sustain protest (although the per student rates have been highest at the uncoordinated-humanistic type) and that have generated the greatest violence. I argued that this resulted from the contradiction between institutional ethos and the structural coordination present in such settings.

Following this, an analogous set of relationships between protest and educational experiences was shown, in which certain features of the social sciences and humanities were held to underlie the ideological basis of dissent and protest. This theme was developed further in chapter 6, where it was seen that, although interpretations defining students or youth as a class were untenable, it still seemed reasonable to consider students from the standpoint of their being acquirers, bearers, and purveyors of knowledge. This was so despite some weaknesses in the view maintaining that the function of the university was, in effect, to turn out technicians of production, consumption, and consent.

The escalating process of confrontation described in chapter 5 was also interpreted within the format of the paradigm. The most intense protest on the largest scale, and especially protest accompanied by violence, not only occurred at coordinated-humanistic institutions, but occurred over issues specifically involving the manifestation of aspects of great national issues over which local administrations have had effective potential control but from which students have been excluded. Concretely, this has meant that not only extensive protest but the greatest violence as well have been associated, on the one hand, with military or war-related business recruiting on the campus, draft-connected issues, and war-related research; and on the other, with matters relating to the race question.

These fundamental relationships have constituted a condition under which an extensive proliferation of protest over all sorts of local matters has occurred. Managerial defense of coordinated relationships, in particular, has set in motion struggles ultimately centering on "student power," for the confrontations themselves, even those that have exacted a price, typically revealed the political weakness of students. If anything, the tokenism that creates a new office for special "communications" with those high up, which places a student or two on the board of trustees or in the academic Senate, or which even relinquishes to students a voice in student judiciary affairs, has merely underscored their lack of power.

Students as Intellectuals and the Knowledge Sector

Upon a moment's reflection, the reader will doubtless realize that most of the critical points elaborated in this analysis have had something to do with the nature and uses of social knowledge. This is true of virtually everything I have presented having to do with the relation of protest to the organizational structure of the institutions, the claims of rationality made by administrators and faculty, the utilization of academic brainpower for presumptively amoral purposes, and so on and so forth. But it holds as well for those patterns of moral belief—a form of knowledge—so critical to the emergence of the movement, and for the significance of occupational and political anchorages of movement creators and participants. It may be well worth while to give some serious attention to the question of the role of knowledge in student radicalism.

The reader will recall that my earlier discussion of certain treatments of this problem revealed certain difficulties. I argued that it would be incorrect to consider the entire educational enterprise as in some sense necessary for the functioning of society or even the economy. This was in part so because the enormous enrollments in the U.S. are not paralleled in the industrialized societies of Europe, and because there is a surplus of technical and professional competence. In this connection it was argued that the educational system in part reflected status concerns growing out of the ambiguities of our stratification system. I also argued that the fields of study from which activists have come are precisely those that have a less definitive relationship to specific technical and professional demands in the occupational world. This is to say that students' occupational expectations often cannot be realistically linked to specific job possibilities and careers. However, it is of importance to distinguish between those fields that combine a substantive concentration on social and political subjects with a strong vocational orientation, such as education, journalism, business, and social welfare, where protest has on the whole been relatively weak, and the "pure" or more theoretically oriented fields, such as sociology, political science, and philosophy. Awakening of political consciousness has occurred much more commonly in these latter spheres, where substantive concern with man and society is essentially divorced from clear-cut training for and tracking into the occupational system. The higher levels of activism have sprung from contexts in which both conditions—absence of vocationalism and substantive preoccupation with man-society questions—have been present.

Clearly, we cannot treat the educational establishment as an undifferentiated unit. Its effects are highly selective, predisposing different types of students to move in different political directions. The theory of students as trainees, while revealing an important aspect of the system, must be modified and supplemented by other considerations. I would hold that, far from being economically and politically essential, and consequently programmed for service on the fronts of economic and political manipulation, activists have become such precisely because, as students, they find themselves in spheres essentially peripheral to the central needs of the core institutions. It remains, then, to clarify the relationship between student radicalism and knowledge itself. In order to do this it will be useful to consider activist students as bearers of a specific type of intellectualism.

To reiterate once again (and asking the forbearance of the reader), politically active students as a whole were shown to be considerably more knowledgeable, creative, and supportive of intellectual values than students as a whole; were reared mostly in settings where traditional humanistic intellectual values were strongly held; and became politically active in institutions where relatively great numbers of such intellectuals were concentrated. This pattern, however, makes no particular sense in and of itself, but requires an interpretation that, I think, should address three issues. First, there is the matter of the anti-intellectualism mentioned earlier; second, the analytical question of just how the *thesis* of intellectualism is to be framed, and thereby limited; and third, the historico-cultural question of the sources and continuing intellectual bases for radical politics.

Characterizations of anti-intellectualism in the American student movement seem to have taken two forms, and they present quite distinct (and to some extent, even contradictory) images. First, there have been the numerous categorizations resulting from behavioral observations and experiences on the part of observers, critics, and sometimes targets of protest themselves. These usually involve either or both of the following: (1) an attribution of a presumed nonreflective or nonintellectual state underlying the protest in question, or even more broadly (and by extension) all student protest; and (2) a judgment that, even if the protest can be credited as manifesting serious intellectual and reflective activity, it is of a weak or undeveloped sort, and fails to incorporate an adequate comprehension of the university, democratic politics, and the nature of American society.

Both of these arguments have been touched on earlier (in chapters 4 and 6) and found wanting. Attribution of an inherent irrationality to disruptive or violent protest in the absence of either systematic evidence or a clear conception of what in fact it means to be "irrational" is indefensible. There is nothing inherently irrational or anti-intellectual about disruptive or violent activity; indeed, in many contexts it may be entirely rational (depending, of course, on our definition), in both instrumental and consequential senses. Furthermore, the presumptively superior rationality of administrative forms, procedures, and ideologies, often promoted as "reasonable means," cannot be merely assumed, but must, in many instances, be subjected to serious challenge.

A somewhat better case can perhaps be made for the second type of characterization, that the intellectual substance of radicals' conceptions of American society (and its component institutions and practices) or of the presumed consequences of movement protest (mainly the conservative reaction), or both, is inadequate. Even this argument, however, presumes that there is some other, superior knowledge against which the conceptions of movement ideologues or intellectuals can be measured and judged. This is an extremely difficult question, if only because of the highly opaque and uncertain state of social science knowledge concerning these matters. Left-wing (New Left, Old Left, or other) conceptions of American society, although often dismissed as irresponsible ideology, constitute at least a reasonable, if not proved or conclusive, set of propositions, focusing on such major issues as the distribution of wealth and income, the power of corporations, the extent of elite and upper-class rule, the link between expansive American capitalism and foreign policy, the role of corruption in American political life, and at least the partial participation of American higher education in much of this. The point is that these are matters in dispute, and there is therefore no "objective" body of knowledge in terms of which the theories of Left can be proved false.

There is an additional point that perhaps should be aired here. Compared with many other student movements (the German and French, in particular) the American movement revealed itself as somewhat less developed theoretically (and ideologically), a weakness recognized by many movement participants themselves. This has probably been a reflection of at least three factors. First, the diverse sources of the American Left generally, in terms of issues and cleavages, the proliferation of racial and ethnic groups, as well as regional and other bases of divisiveness, has made the development of anything like a unified tradition of radical thought almost impossible. Second, the ascendance of a positivist theory of knowledge—mainly in the form of pragmatism—emphasizing the piecemeal nature of experience, has undoubtedly inhibited the development of social thought of a generalizing sort, applicable at the societal level. Third, and perhaps most important, the movement's very *raisòn d'être* was a rejection of indigenous American radicalism, particularly the "Old Left," hence the ransacking of Third World ideologies in search of an intellectual ground.

All this should by no means be understood as an endorsement of movement practice generally. Indeed, in the later years, one would have to agree that remnants of the movement indulged themselves in the kind of extreme leftism condemned by Lenin as an "infantile disorder." But however severe a qualification this fact imposes on my characterization of the movement's rationality, it is a judgment of practice, not of general intellectual orientations, and I will shortly consider it under this rubric.

The second interpretive mode requires an analysis of the thesis of movement intellectualism and how it must be limited theoretically. Initially, it must be noted that most intellectuals have not only not become politicized, but are not on the far Left, although the political center of gravity among them today is that of a somewhat liberal disposition, a consequence in large part of the intellectual component of the role itself.

This question can be refined by reformulating my earlier statement as follows: (1) some kinds of intellectuals (those whose disciplinary materials involve analysis of social phenomena), (2) who are found in certain kinds of knowledge settings (mainly those of a nonapplied or nonvocational character), tend to be more responsive than others to societal contradictions. This is, of course, anything but surprising. Those intellectuals whose occupational life preoccupies them with the materials and means of social and cultural analysis would be expected to be the ones most responsive to contradictions in the social order. But why is it that, among intellectuals generally, and student intellectuals in particular, the specifically vocationally oriented have been so much less likely to become political activists? Formulated in terms of the core-periphery paradigm, the answer seems clear: in terms of both structural location and value ethos they find themselves well within the core institutions.

The vocational-nonvocational, and socially oriented-nonsocially oriented dimensions of educational experience may be thought of in terms of the way these axes place students relative to the instrumentally oriented core institutions—economy and state. Corporations and state in general have greater demand for technical specialists in the "applied" sciences than for specialists in the related "pure" disciplines or for vocationalists in the social sciences and humanities. They are surely least interested of all in nonvocationalists in the social sciences and, particularly, the humanities.

The relation of these different situations within the knowledge sector to the institutions and values of the core is a crucial question. Within the "pure" category the value of "knowledge for knowledge's sake" is much more strongly held. The values of the core, on the other hand, *inherently* penetrate the applied sector, being of a practical and technical sort. Applied fields, by definition, aim primarily not at understanding, but at some form of technical manipulation of a problem situation. This is not to say that theoretical principles are not either desirable or often even necessary, only that in and of themselves they are of secondary importance. There is, of course, great variation in this relationship. The social worker trained to do case work, for example, may or may not study, say, the principles of social stratification; the job one actually acquires probably will not require such understanding.[2]

Just as in the larger society, the bases of potential opposition in particular institutional contexts are those where the core values penetrate least effectively, thus permitting counter-core values to continue to flourish.

2. In fact, it may often be the case that efficient functioning in terms of specific job definition depends to some extent on an actual masking of such realities in terms of situational or psychological definitions of reality. A systematic theoretical grasp of poverty and the way it is perpetuated may suggest to such workers that their efforts are only minimally ameliorative, and lead them to attempt to break out of bureaucratic constraints and routines. An engineer, on the other hand, cannot design a bridge without knowledge of certain principles of physics. In fact, the extent to which an area of applied knowledge requires theoretical understanding is one important index of the degree to which it is professionalized. We might say that the context of problem definition for applied fields is inherently nontheoretical, although theoretical understanding may be required to deal with society generally. Until rather recently this relationship has been a fairly haphazard one. Only in recent decades—since World War II—has the locus of control shifted to immediate and relatively direct links between universities on the one hand, and corporations and state on the other, through extensive proliferation of grants, consultations, and relationships of other sorts.

246 • THE CLOUDED VISION

Within educational institutions it is in those curricula furthest removed from the tracks leading quite directly to occupational involvement within the core that political activism has been most powerfully generated. Specifically vocational tracks that are accompanied by relatively clear-cut expectations of employment in or close to the core institutions have provided the least fertile milieux for deviant ideas and action. Conversely, the nonvocational programs having the most diffuse and indefinite occupational expectations have been the ones with the highest potential for arousing radical political activity. Vocationalism means, in part, the presence of a close structural relation through tracking. And the values that permeate vocational settings, whether in nonsocially oriented or socially oriented disciplines, tend to be those of the institutions that are the social and occupational destinations of those within the track, rather than autonomously derived from other sources and traditions.

The third aspect of the significance of intellectualism has to do with cultural and historical roots. In addition to its obvious relation to the remarks just above, what I have to say on this point has to some extent been prefigured in earlier discussions, particularly those in which I set forth my critical views of "students as a class" formulations, and those having to do with the apparent differences between the family origins of political activists and "counter-culturalists."

The historical origins of one major modern intellectual type are to be found in the breakdown of the patron system of the feudal period, the ascendance of the bourgeosie, and the creation of a literate public. In France, after the turn of the century, free intellectuals like Saint-Simon, Comte, and Proudhon grappled with the problem of the society of the future, while at the same time, as Cesar Graña has shown so well, men of letters like Baudelaire, Stendhal, and Flaubert were creating the prototype of the modern alienated intellectual, rooted in contempt for the bourgeoisie and the civilization they were in the process of creating, and despising what they regarded as a democratic rabble while yet dependent on them for sale and appreciation of their works.[3] Elsewhere as well, of course, there were intellectuals whose world view and self-assigned social role centered on principled opposition to bourgeois values. Much earlier in England the titanic figure of John Donne inaugurated much of the same moral and intellectual configuration and later, romantics like Byron and Shelley would express such sensibilities outside of a religious context. In Germany the Romantic tradition, and in the U.S. figures such as Emerson, Thoreau, and above all, Walt Whitman (in whose case, of course, the anti-democratic element was absent) stand in much the same relation to what Karl Polanyi called the "great transformation."

All such instances have one thing in common: the social dislocation of the intellect from a secure economic and psychological condition. Much of intellectual life in the nineteenth century paralleled the dislocations suffered by rural peasantry as the market principle expanded. Coming into being everywhere, in Karl Mannheim's characterization, was a *"freischwebende Intelligenz,"* or loose stratum (although the term *stratum* probably designates a highly structured or organized entity) of unattached thinkers,[4] typically with loyalties to nothing (church, state, university, social movements, etc.) so much as abstract principles and sometimes to themselves as the intellectual elite of the future. Some joined or formed movements, including the array of socialist

3. Cesar Graña, *Modernity and Its Discontents* (New York: Harper Torchbooks, 1964). In this connection, see also S. N. Eisenstadt, "Generational Conflict and Intellectual Antinomianism," in Philip G. Altback and Robert S. Laufer, *The New Pilgrims* (New York: David McKay Co., 1972), pp. 139-54.
4. Karl Mannheim, *Ideology and Utopia,* trans. Louis Wirth and Edward Shils, (New York: Harcourt Brace, 1936).

groups, but even this was not typical, particularly for men of letters, although there were important national differences on this score. More frequent was the emergence of the cult of genius rooted in the charismatic circle of fellow travelers eking out a bohemian existence.

In every industrial society, then, there has been a continuous growth of this stratum, although in recent times, of course, the terms of existence of its members have tended to become more comfortable and secure. Academia, publishing, and other professions have absorbed many on both permanent and temporary bases (Marx, for instance, made his living for a time as a journalist). Under differing conditions such intellectuals have sometimes been directly involved in the labor and other movements, especially in Great Britain, perhaps most rarely in the U.S. But whatever the occupation or source of income, the hallmark of such men and women is their alienation from bourgeois society and an organization of their life and work in opposition to it. It is in this sense that such "traditional" intellectuals are alienated.

Quite distinct from this is the necessity of core institutions of all complex societies, and particularly modern scientific ones, to create what Gramsci called "organic" intellectuals. Organic intellectuals are the products of the specialization of the modern state and economy; they are to be distinguished from the "traditional" intellectuals; thus, they are typically experts. They are, moreover,

> the "officers" of the ruling class for the exercise of the subordinate functions of social hegemony and the political government.[5]

Beyond this,

5. Antonio Gramsci, *The Modern Prince and Other Writings* (New York: International Publishers, 1957), p. 125.

One of the most important characteristics of every class which develops toward power is its struggle to assimilate and conquer "ideologically" the traditional intellectuals. Assimilations and conquests are the more rapid and effective the more the given social class puts forward simultaneously its own organic intellectuals.[6]

Although one might question the proposition put forth in the last sentence above, Gramsci's basic distinction is most useful for purposes here. Traditional intellectuals, although in various ways and degrees "assimilated" or "conquered," remain a clearly identifiable and important stratum in all modern societies, a stratum with an acute sense of its own tradition and consciousness of mission. Furthermore, although many, today probably the great majority of such traditional intellectuals are in some sense experts, in the sense of being specialists in some field of discipline, they are nevertheless bearers of a sense of the ideological meaning of their work, a meaning that tends to induce in them a sense of unity with others opposing bourgeois society. To employ Richard Hofstader's distinction, their *intelligence* tends *not* to define their world, but rather, assumes its significance in terms of their larger morally rooted ideological *intellectualism.*[7]

The structural and historical dimensions of the roots of student radicalism are thus seen to lie in a tradition that has been activated under specific conditions, conditions that I have analyzed in this study and will very shortly summarize and state in general analytical form.

All this seems to be at considerable variance with the classic Marxist position that radical movements could emerge only when the work force was highly integrated into the economy. But it is a matter of historical fact that

6. *Ibid.,* p. 123.
7. Richard Hofstadter, *Anti-intellectualism in American Life* (New York: Random House, 1962).

the radical and revolutionary movements of the proletariat have appeared mainly during the transition from feudal to industrial society, and not during their later, developed period. That is to say, they have appeared during periods prior to national industrial and political integration. (This is so important a fact that it has been converted by some intellectuals into a virtual philosophy of history, a designation for which all "end of ideology" formulations, in particular, surely qualify.) To say that large sectors of the working classes of industrial societies have acquired a basic security through collective action is not, of course, to suggest that these societies are approaching equality. It is only to say that in acquiring a seeming guarantee of basic economic security, they have become incorporated in the general consensus. Their politics is one of only moderate opposition and of generally working within the rules of the game. The organized working class has a central position in the corporate economy and its actions reflect its position of security, not its lack of equality. In fact, in terms of equality, it is clear that the bulk of organized labor see themselves primarily as superior to blacks and other minorities, as enjoying great security relative to the unemployed, as vastly richer than the impoverished peoples of the world, and even better off economically than many of their status "superiors" in white-collar occupations.

The main point is that the characterization of the student movement presented herein seems at least partly consistent with the facts of labor-movement history. The student movement has developed out of spheres of cultural experience and social organization as yet peripheral to, yet threatened by, incorporation within the dominant institutions. These spheres stand in a relation to the core that is in this respect—although not in all respects, of course—parallel to that of a proletariat in the making.

Ideology, Structural Incorporation,
and Vulnerability

Analytically, it is fruitful to think of the core-periphery distinction as having three components: ideology, structural incorporation, and vulnerability. The effects of each are quite distinct, with different strata and groups finding themselves in differing situations with respect to them. By *ideology*, I mean the availability of anti-capitalist or anti-industrial ideas, insofar as these are shared by a group, class or stratum; by *structural incorporation*, those arrangements whereby men are bound to roles essential to and dominated by organizational or political elites, or, by extension, the extent to which they find themselves incorporated within career "tracks" tending to lead them to such involvement, as, for example, in the case of students of engineering; and by *vulnerability*, the extent to which meaningful sanctions can be visited upon a group or individual. General factors in vulnerability are of two sorts: (1) objective susceptibility to withdrawal of or limitations of various resources, mainly income, jobs, status, personal freedom, and opportunities of various sorts (e.g., education); and (2) aspects of one's personal situation in which either the salience of the sanction (as in the difference between a man with ten children and one who is single in losing his job) or its personal *significance* (as in instances of college dropouts, who just don't care) varies.

Different groups and strata, as well as subunits of these, find themselves in quite distinct situations relative to these three dimensions. Workers in large-scale industry are fully incorporated structurally, highly vulnerable to both company and union authorities, and (in most cases) ideologically enveloped within a union ideology generally favorable to capitalist enterprise and society. Although there are some general commonalities, the situation of students is a highly varying one, especially in terms of curriculum and type of institutional authority. Those in vocational tracks are structurally incorporated to a greater degree than those in nonvocational ones. Those in the social sciences and humanities are routinely subject to ideas having to do with man and society, ideas accessible to others to only a limited degree. Those in loosely run, permissive, high-quality liberal arts colleges are less vulnerable than those in institutions more oriented to discipline.

It seems to be the case that the three factors operate independently to increase predisposition to political activism. I noted earlier that the *per student* rates of participation in smaller liberal arts colleges were the highest, among all types. It is precisely at such places that the reinforcing effort of these three factors is the highest. Some of these institutions have virtually nothing but nonvocational students of social sciences and humanities. Furthermore, the primary group atmospheres of such places tend to encourage diffusion across disciplinary and organizational lines to a degree that is practically impossible in massive vocationally oriented, highly bureaucratized public institutions. At such places, students, and thus ideas as well, tend to remain encapsulated within disciplinary or college environments.

The actions of other groups are comprehensible on the same grounds. Faculty members in social sciences and humanities tend to be more liberal (and sometimes even radical) than those in either vocational disciplines oriented to man and society, or those in nonsocially oriented disciplines. Yet, while the ideology is rather widely held, their actions have been limited, due to their relatively high degree of structural incorporation and vulnerability. The situation among students in developed socialist societies such as the Soviet Union can also be characterized in this fashion. Obviously, political control of students there is tighter, partly because practically all students are on State grants and alternative careers can be made highly punitive. The levels of both vulnerability and structural incorporation are much higher. Thus, although alienation from and disenchantment with the system may be fairly widespread among youth, effective protest is minimal.

This analysis of the dimensions of the core-periphery paradigm is also consistent with the theory of social movements advanced by Oberschall. The reader will recall that his explanation of social movements rests on two distinctions, the first between vertically integrated as distinct from structurally segmented collectives, the second between internally communally unified and communally fragmented collectivities. Social movements were shown to be facilitated under conditions of structural segmentation and communal unity,[8] and more likely to emerge when social control is loosened[9] (this latter being one of the more hoary observations regarding social movements).

To modify Oberschall's formulation slightly, it may be said that the conditions for generation of social movements are both cultural and organizational. Oberschall's emphasis seems to be on the former, but specific cultural factors are clearly significant, as can be seen in the case of the student movements. The *culture* of the democratic-humanist family is the root of both the principle of political activism as a value, and the specific politics of the Left. Its organizational, or interactional, structure encourages Left politics because of its democratic form.

Within the academic setting the same principles apply. From an organizational standpoint "looseness" in applying organizational authority was an important condition facilitating development of the movement. At least as important, if not more so, has been the specific nature of certain variants of the academic subculture.

Ideology, structural incorporation, and vulnerability manifest themselves in cultural and organizational terms.

8. Obershall, chap. 4.
9. *Ibid.*, pp. 137ff.

The subculture of the democratic-humanist family on the one hand, and that of the social science-humanities cluster on the other, are clearly conducive to emergence of a leftist ideology, whereas this is emphatically not true of other *milieux*. Students in vocational tracks, in particular, are incorporated structurally in a most powerful fashion, in contrast with those whose studies have no occupational direction. Students generally, for several reasons, are somewhat less vulnerable than most other groups, especially employed workers with families or members of the military. For the most part, life options remain open to them because of their youth. For most of them, to have become students in the first place implies a basic economic security that they can usually fall back on. Furthermore, the vulnerability of students in the better, more permissive institutions is perhaps somewhat less than is the case for those who study elsewhere. The exceptionally high social-economic status of the families of activists generally (with some qualification for the members of the Young Americans for Freedom) was a not-inconsequential condition of low vulnerability.

In conclusion it is necessary to note that, despite the confluence of such a set of propitious cultural and organizational conditions, there would have been no student movement in the United States in the 60s had there been no great moral issues around which organization was possible. Racial oppression, poverty, and the war in Southeast Asia were the issue-generating conditions that created moral contradictions to which the movement addressed itself, under a concatenation of specific cultural and organizational conditions.

A Note on Parallels

At this point, one might note the parallel between the student movement and some other contemporary insurgencies. The student movement, the counter culture, and the women's and black liberation movements, all have a common situation with respect to their receptivity to core values.

Women in general find themselves more remote from the core in terms of both organizational participation and values. They have much lower rates of economic and political participation then men. And when they work at the professional level, it is most often in "women's" occupations such as social work and primary school teaching. Women have been demonstrated to hold values that are more consistently "deviant" from the standpoint of the core; for example, they tend to reject competition as a norm more strongly than do men, and they have been more consistently anti-war in their attitude than men.

The blacks who participated most directly in the urban revolts of the late 60s were mostly young unemployed males who were and still are at the extreme periphery of economic life. Young blacks constitute the furthest fringe of the contemporary urban *subproletariat,* with local unemployment rates reaching fantastic levels of 30, 40, and 50 percent. They are needed for only the dirtiest and most occasional jobs; thus, their integration into economic life and corresponding subjection to the values of the core are virtually nonexistent.

In various ways youth in general are also peripheral. Most obviously, they ordinarily do not work, so the values and discipline normally inculcated and reinforced at the place of work are foreign to them. Furthermore, they stand at various stages of the socialization process; indoctrination with core values is a process only partially accomplished.

Women, young black workers, youth, those in the humane and literary professions, have in common with students in nonvocationally oriented milieux a social location at the periphery of society. More detailed analysis, not possible here, might well reveal that in the dimensions of ideology, structural incorporation, and vulnerability, the militant sectors of each occupy objective situations parallel to those of activist students.

American Society and the Student Movement

The focus in this study has fallen primarily on the proximate conditions and milieux underlying the mobilization of the movement. This, however, does not constitute a complete analysis. For this, it would be necessary to analyze the larger historical drift of American society and to explain the quantitative and qualitative growth of the (1) democratic-humanist family, (2) the massive changes in the functioning of higher education, and (3) the transformations of the state. This is obviously not a task that can seriously be undertaken here. However, it is appropriate to note that these three trends are all, at root, to a very large extent consequences of the technological transformations up until now endemic to capitalist industrial society (and, indeed, to socialist ones as well). The stability of all industrial societies, but of capitalist ones especially, is based on growth.

Two aspects of the functioning of capitalist societies, institutional inequality, and the tendency to create an underclass of unemployed, rejected, incapacitated, aged, and productively useless, are implicated in the problem of growth. Both inequality and the underclass are generated by the normal functioning of the uncontrolled market. Of course, there is no such thing as a completely free or uncontrolled market system anywhere in the world. The market as a master determining principle or mechanism has always been virtually unknown in all pre-industrial societies, but all industrial societies have introduced an array of measures that in a variety of ways and in different degree ameliorate its destructive effects.

The meaning of inequality in developed industrial societies is very different from that in pre-industrial ones. For one thing, in the latter there are normally powerful cultural legitimations, usually religious, that serve to justify and maintain inequality. In industrial societies, the legitimation of inequality is much weaker, due to the internal character of industrialism and ancillary factors attending it. The specific nature of inequality in industrial societies is manifest most importantly in the class system, which is determined primarily by the occupational structure.

One of the central strains of capitalist, indeed of all industrial societies, centers on the dissociation of productive and consumption spheres. Production is organized hierarchically in structures of increasing scale, increasingly rationalized and bureaucratized. On the consumption side more and more goods and services are produced, goods and services that can be distributed —typically, through the market process—in grossly unequal fashion. As long as production and control of the means of production and distribution remain the province of a small elite, inequality will remain the fundamental institutionalized social condition of industrial society.

In creating increasing abundance, however, industrialism tends to undermine the correspondence of position between productive and consumption spheres. The growth of output encourages aspirations for a better life materially and for social advance as well. Thus, there exists a growing dynamic centering around expectations for continuing improvement in life conditions. However, from a relative standpoint, income and wealth have not proved redistributable, for access to the apparatuses of both economic and political domination remains securely in the hands of the economic elite. Since this is the case, relative shares of income and wealth remain almost constant for vertically ordered strata.[10]

The strains attending inequality are ameliorated to a considerable extent by the continuing expansion of the productive capacity of the system. This assures some degree of absolute improvement for most, even though the *relative* shares of income and wealth remain unchanged. However, growth implies continual technological transformation, restructuring of the occupational system, the destruction and creation of jobs, and thus the threat and reality of chronic technological unemployment. The latter is exacerbated with particularly great intensity wherever productive functions are automated. In this way growth routinely tends to perpetuate an underclass, which, in the absence of compensating factors, must somehow subsist outside the apparatus of production.

All industrial societies, of course, handle the problem of the under-class through governmental intervention in the economy in two generalized ways: (1) with fiscal or monetary policies, including state investments in both public and private sectors, up to extensive state planning; and (2) direct or indirect payments to individuals or families. In some Northern European countries these measures have been developed to the point of virtual abolition of the underclass. These policies, however, have little impact on inequality, except to restrict somewhat the incomes and wealth of those at the very top, and to place a floor beneath which no one is allowed to fall. In the future, if dwindling resources dictate a no-growth economy, increasing pressures to redistribute will undoubtedly be felt and class conflict may assume more intense forms.

It has been argued that a major turning point in the development of capitalist societies occurs when expan-

10. See, for example, Gabriel Kolko, *Wealth and Power in America* (New York: Frederick A. Praeger, 1962).

sion of the production of goods increases at a faster rate than does the employment of labor power. In Martin Sklar's view, this process actually reverses the older accumulation of capital defining earlier capitalist development; he therefore calls it "disaccumulation."[11] Disaccumulation is important socially and politically because, in Sklar's estimation, it has as a consequence the freeing of labor from the kind of iron determination of activity that characterized the stages of primary accumulation and industrial consolidation.

Release from dull routine and the realm of necessity, however, predisposes individuals to acquire expectations of life possibilities never before envisioned—possibilities, however, that to a considerable extent must go unrealized because the system cannot relinquish its basic principles of competition and growth, and the consequent ones of objectification of human qualities and institutionalized inequality.

Now, for the most part it is fair to say that conceptions of personal freedom in American society have generally been tied to status and mobility considerations, and the latter, particularly during the period of great and growing abundance following World War II, have been interpreted in basically materialistic terms. This is to say that to a considerable, perhaps overwhelming degree, the value system of consumerism has served to contain and canalize the thrust for greater personal freedom accompanying disaccumulation. Over the past several decades the consumer ethic has replaced the Protestant Ethic as the dominant societal value system, especially among the middle classes. This is economically appropriate, of course, for thrift and penury make little sense under conditions of abundance. In terms of restructur-

11. Martin Sklar, "On the Proletarian Revolution and the End of Political Economic Society", *Rad. America* 3, no. 3. See also Robert B. Carson, "Youthful Labor Surplus in Disaccumulationist Capitalism," *Soc. Rev.* 2, 3 (May/June 1972).

ing of the class system, it has meant the rapid quantitative expansion of the upper middle class at the expense of all lower strata. It must be said at this point, of course, that to speak of abundance is not to presume that it characterizes all strata. Indeed, if this were so there would scarcely be any problems to write about. When I refer to abundance, I have in mind that period of capitalist development wherein, first, real possibilities of discretionary disposal of wealth or income became available on a relatively large scale to strata below the upper class (which in all societies probably constitutes less than one percent of the population), and second, in which chances of realizing a "comfortable" life style became a possibility for a broadly defined middle class.

To return to the brief consideration of the three movement-related aspects of societal drift mentioned at the outset of this section, the expansion of the middle classes generally, and especially the upper-middle classes, is mainly a result of technological—including organizational—transformations. Particularly in higher occupational strata, this has meant a greater degree of autonomy, or at least potential autonomy, for the bearers of knowledge, for while knowledge itself is not power, as Socrates believed, it is still one kind of power base, and its social application as work may be facilitated by, if it does not actually require, varying degrees of autonomy.

The expansion of higher education, of course, is in good part due to a number of demands for skills and knowledge, which have increased with the altering of the occupational order. But as I argued earlier, the massive enrollments cannot be fully explained on this basis. Much of the growth must have other causes and I would suggest that the pressures chronically generated on the labor market by technological displacement of workers account for a good deal of it.

To some extent the expansion of the university system

has been due to its fulfilling this function, and the surplus seems to appear mostly in areas peripheral to the educational functions essential to maintenance of the core institutions. Between 1950 and 1965 the rate of expansion of the social sciences and humanities was much greater than for all the other academic programs. This is so despite the jump in engineering, the natural sciences, and education following Sputnik. While the increase in the number of undergraduate degrees during this period was one of 24 percent, the comparable figure for the social sciences and humanities was 60 percent. The same pattern holds for graduate degrees.[12] To some quantitatively unspecifiable degree, higher education has served to ameliorate pressures in the labor market.

It is of more than ancillary interest to note that this development is more or less coextensive with the rise of the general education movement, which, whatever the intrinsic merits of its practice or ideology, is from an economic and occupational standpoint a way of employing regularly the increasing number of those trained in English, history, sociology, political science, art, and so on. These, and other disciplines falling within the social sciences-humanities rubric, are practically everywhere organized within departments having mainly educational service functions.

The important point here, if this analysis is correct, is that the process of disaccumulation has had the effect of rapidly expanding that sector of higher education structurally uncoordinated with the needs and imperatives of the core institutions. The connection of this with all that has preceded is obvious.

It may be noted in passing that such "featherbedding" is a function performed in some degree by all social institutions. Welfare transfers for the stigmatized poor at the bottom have their parallels in the welfare arrange-

12. The sources for this are *The Statistical Abstracts of the U.S.* for 1951 and 1967, pp. 124 and 140 respectively.

ments of corporations for their middle and higher ex-
ecutives, in less-than-busy or ritualized government
bureaucrats, and in the well-known "inefficiency" of the
military. In these terms labor-union featherbedding is
only one among many societal arrangements that
ameliorate the social destructiveness of the market under
the imperative of growth. The same function performed
by the colleges and universities may perhaps be appro-
priately designated as mere "supplemental featherbedding."

The burgeoning of the state to supermonolithic proportions has, in some ways, been a consequence of the
same process. This is so especially in its increasing mar-
riage to militarism, mainly following World War II. Mills
was in all probability wrong about the causes of that
military ascendency he so caustically described,[13] but as
to its presence there can be no question. Apart from the
economic value of its colonial and imperial support functions, the military establishment is in a strict sense
unproductive.[14] In fact, it makes more sense to think of
the military as an institution organized for the systematic
production of waste, waste on a prodigious scale, rational only from the standpoint of a social imperative of
waste-making. Numerous experts unaffiliated with the
Pentagon—and some who have been—have charged
that, even from a specifically military standpoint, it is irrational, if only because of its enormous overkill capacity, an important cost-benefit consideration.

Certainly the growth in scale and expansion of power
of the state lies at the root of that "military ascendency"
and "crackpot realism" denounced so brilliantly by Mills
twenty years ago. The amoral character of the state—in
perpetrating foreign wars and in its internal dealings

13. C. Wright Mills, *The Power Elite* (New York: Oxford University Press,
  1956).
14. In contrast, for example, to China, where the army regularly performs
  productive labor.

with its own citizenry—is the fount of those contradictions of values, or better, denial of any values save power itself, in the absence of which the student movement is practically inconceivable.

Thus, although the movement in the 70s is at a low point, at least some of the conditions that brought it into being remain essentially unaltered. Or so, at least, it seems. There seems to be no reason in particular to expect either quiet or turmoil among students in the immediate future. Whatever happens will depend on the specific configuration of historical forces. The one great lesson that should have been learned by students is that while a movement encapsulated within academic milieux may have some effect in meliorating or modifying specific policies or initiating minor structural reforms, it cannot itself be the agency of radical social change.

The Zengakuren, the Japanese student movement, stands as an object lesson for the future of any student movement. Probably the largest organized student movement in the history of the world, the Zengakuren has failed to induce radical change in Japanese society, or to institutionalize itself in the Japanese political system. Any student movement, in order to become a *continuing* political force, must break out of purely student, academic, or even youthful context. This is something the movements in the capitalist democracies have, in general, been unable to do thus far, although arguments for their having common interests with all sorts of other groups and strata abound. In the absence of a strong Left, the formula for such a political extension remains unknown, but the ultimate objective of the student movement can only be to bring such a condition into being.

It is reasonably clear why the student movement has failed to transcend its more or less strictly middle-class student intellectual circles. As I argued earlier, the principal factor has probably involved general cultural differences relative to the working classes generally, but more specifically, with regard to working-class youth. While those in the colleges have used their privileges and knowledge, as often as not, to evade the draft, working-class youth, not having comparable resources or *inclinations,* have borne the brunt of the war. The politicization of this stratum explictly *against* college youth (despite considerable disaffection rooted in the workplace) has certainly been rooted in the patriotic sensibility—artfully nurtured by politicians such as Nixon and Agnew—that those sacrifices demand a collective sacralization. Dissenters from such a symbolic confirmation become disgusting deviants, or even traitors.

Despite such obstacles, the future may yet see something approximating what Rudi Dutschke has called the long march through the institutions. Some of the seeds of such a continuing movement have been sown—in the radical caucuses of professional societies, for example —and the students must be credited with preparing some of this soil. What is at issue is whether the "long march" will be contained at the periphery as a kind of continuing rancorous but ineffectual cacophony of voices, loud enough, perhaps, but never seriously penetrating the core of corporation and state. This is a real possibility and it only underscores the need of continuing political work—work that will have to be conducted in ways well above the levels of the recent past if it is to be effective. If the student movement has done nothing else in its few short years, it has helped to show by both actions and omissions that such a politics must be at once visionary, pragmatic, and theoretical. A transformed America of the future may yet look back and acknowledge that the student generation of the 60s played a significant role in helping start the world's most developed and powerful industrial monolith on the road to guaranteeing a good life for everyone.

BIBLIOGRAPHY

Books and Monographs

Abel, Theodore. *The Nazi Movement.* New York: Prentice-Hall 1938.

Adelson, Alan. *SDS: A Profile.* New York: Scribner's, 1972.

Adorno, Theodore W., *et al. The Authoritarian Personality.* New York: John Wiley and Sons, Inc., 1964.

Almond, Gabriel and Verba, Sidney. *The Civic Culture: Political Attitudes and Democracy in Five Nations* Boston, Mass.: Little, Brown and Company, 1965.

Altbach, Philip G. *Student Politics And Higher Education in the United States: A Select Bibliography.* (St. Louis, Mo. and Cambridge, Mass.: United Ministries In Higher Education And Center For International Affairs, Harvard University, 1968.

Aries, Philippe. *Centuries of Childhood.* Translated by Robert Baldick. New York: Random House Vintage Books, 1965.

Barron, Frank. *Creativity And Psychological Health.* Princeton, N.J.: Van Nostrand, 1963.

Bell, Daniel. *The Coming of Post-Industrial Society.* New York: Basic Books, 1973.

―――. *Confrontation: The Student Rebellion and the Universities.* New York: Basic Books, 1968.

―――. *The End Of Ideology.* rev. ed. New York: The Free Press of Glencoe, 1962.

Berger, Peter L. and Neuhaus, Richard J. *Movement and Revolution.* New York: Doubleday, Anchor Books, 1970.

Bottomore, T. B. *Critics of Society.* (New York: Pantheon Books, 1968.

Bourges, Herve. *The French Student Revolt.* New York: Hill and Wang, Inc., 1968.

Braungart, Richard. *Family Status, Socialization and Student Politics.* Ph.D. dissertation, Penn State University, 1969.

Brinton, Crane. *The Anatomy of Revolution.* New York: Vintage Books, 1965.

Buchanan, Garth and Brackett, Joan. *Survey Results of the Survey for The President's Commission on Campus Unrest.* Washington, D.C.: The Urban Institute, 1970.

Cameron, William B. *Modern Social Movements.* New York: Random House, Inc., 1966.

Cohen, Mitchell and Hale, Dennis. eds. *The New Student Left.* Boston, Mass.: Beacon Press, 1966.

Coser, Lewis. *The Functions of Social Conflict.* Glencoe, Ill.: The Free Press, 1956.

Cowan, Paul and Egleson, Nick. *State Secrets: Police Surveillance in America.* New York: Holt, Rinehart and Winston, 1974.

Cox Commission Report. *Crisis at Columbia.* New York: Random House, 1968.

Crick, Bernard, and Robson, William A. *Protest and Discontent.* Middlesex, England: Penguin Books, 1920.

Dahl, Robert. *Who Governs?* New Haven, Conn.: Yale University Press, 1963.

Dahrendorf, Ralf. *Class and Class Conflict in Industrial Society.* Stanford, Calif.: Stanford University Press, 1959.

Denisoff, R. Serge, and Peterson, Richard. *The Sound of Social Change.* Chicago, Ill.: Rand McNally and Co., 1972.

Doress, Irvin. *A Study of a Sampling of Boston Student Activists.* Ph.D. Dissertation. Boston, Mass.: Boston University, 1968. Reported in Charles Hampden-Turner, *Radical Man.* Cambridge, Mass.: Shenkman, 1970.

Draper, Hal. *Berkeley, Calif. The New Student Revolt.* New York: Grove Press, 1965.

Durkheim, Emile. *Suicide: A Study in Sociology.* Translated by George Simpson. Glencoe, Ill.: The Free Press, 1951.

Eddy, Edward D. *The College Influence on Student Character.* Menasha, Wis.: George Banta Company, Inc., 1959.

Eisenstadt, S. N. *From Generation to Generation.* Glencoe, Ill.: The Free Press, 1956.

Erikson, Erik H. *Identity, Youth and Crisis.* New York: Norton and Company, 1968.

———, ed. *The Challenge of Youth.* Garden City, N.Y.: Doubleday Anchor Books, 1965.

Esler, Anthony. *Bombs, Beards, and Barricades.* New York: Stein and Day Publishers, 1971.

Etzioni, Amitai. *The Active Society.* New York, N.Y.: The Free Press, 1968.

Evans, M. Stanton. *Revolt on the Campus.* Chicago, Ill.: H. Regnery Company, 1961.

Feuer, Lewis. *The Conflict of Generations.* New York, N.Y.: Basic Books, 1959.

Flacks, Richard. *Youth and Social Change.* Boston, Mass.: Markham, 1971.

Foster, Julian, and Long, Durward. *Protest: Student Activism in America.* New York, N.Y.: Morrow and Company, 1970.

Gillespie, J. and Allport, G. *Youth's Outlook on the Future.* Garden City, N.Y.: Doubleday and Company, Inc. 1955.

Goldsen, Rose. *Report on the Cornell Student Body.* Ithaca, N.Y.: Social Science Reserve Center, June 1951.

———, Rosenberg, Morris, Williams, Robin, and Suchman, Edward. *What College Students Think.* Princeton, N.J.: D. Van Nostrand Company, Inc. 1960.

Gorz, Andre. *A Strategy for Labor: A Radical Proposal.* Translated by Martin Nicolaus and Victoria Ortiz. Boston: Beacon Press, 1967.

Gouldner, Alvin. *The Coming Crisis of Western Sociology.* New York: Basic Books, 1970.

Greenstein, Fred I. *Children and Politics.* New Haven, Conn.: Yale University Press, 1965.

Gusfield, Joseph R. *Symbolic Crusade.* Urbana, Ill.: University of Illinois Press, 1966.

Havermann, E. and West, P. S. *They Went to College.* New York: Harcourt, Brace and Company, 1952.

Heberle, Rudolf. *Social Movements.* New York: Appleton-Century-Crofts, Inc., 1951.

Hoffer, Eric. *The True Believer.* New York: Menton Books, 1958.

Hofstadter, Richard and Metzger, Walter P. *The Development of*

Academic Freedom in the United States. New York: Columbia University Press, 1955.

Horowitz, Irving Louis. *The Struggle is the Message.* Berkeley, Calif.: The Glendessary Press, 1970.

——— and Friedland, William H. *The Knowledge Factory.* Chicago, Ill.: Aldine Publ. Co., 1970.

Hyman, Herbert H. *Political Socialization.* Glencoe, Ill.: The Free Press, 1959.

Jacob, Philip. *Changing Values in College.* New York: Harper & Brothers, Publishers, 1957.

Jacobs, Harold, ed., *Weatherman.* Berkeley, Calif.: Ramparts Press, 1970.

Jacobs, Paul and Landau, Saul. *The New Radicals.* New York: Vintage Books, 1966.

Jencks, Christopher and Riesman, David. *The Academic Revolution.* Garden City, N.Y.: Doubleday and Company, Inc., 1968.

Katz, Joseph. *The Student Activist: Rights, Needs, and Powers of Undergraduates.* Stanford, Calif.: Institute for the Study of Human Problems, 1967.

Keniston, Kenneth. *The Uncommitted.* New York: Harcourt, Brace and World Inc., 1965.

———. *The Young Radicals.* New York: Harcourt, Brace and World Inc., 1968.

Kennan, George. *Democracy and the Student Left.* New York: Banton Books, 1968.

Kerpelman, Larry C. *Student Activism and Ideology in Higher Educational Institutions.* Washington, D.C.: Bureau of Research, Office of Research, U.S. Department of Health, Education and Welfare, March, 1970.

Kerr, Clark. *The Users of the University.* Cambridge, Mass.: Harvard University Press, 1963.

King, C. W. *Social Movements in The United States.* New York: Random House, Inc., 1964.

Kolko, Gabriel. *Wealth and Power in America.* New York: Frederick A. Praeger, 1962.

Kornhauser, William. *The Politics of Mass Society.* Glencoe, Ill.: The Free Press, 1969.

Lazarsfeld, P. F., *et al. The People's Choice.* New York: Columbia University Press, 1948.

Lens, Sidney. *Radicalism in America.* New York: Alfred A. Knopf, Inc., 1965.

Levy, Marion. *The Structure of Society.* Princeton, N.J.: Princeton University Press, 1953.

Liberale, Marc and Seligson, Tom, eds. *The High School Revolutionaries.* New York: Random House, Vintage Books, 1970.

Lipset, Seymour M. and Wolin, Sheldon S. *The Berkeley Student Revolt.* Garden City, N.Y.: Doubleday and Company, Inc., 1965.

Luce, Phillip A. *The New Left.* New York: David McKay Company, Inc., 1966.

Mannheim, Karl. *Essays on Sociology and Social Psychology.* London, England: Routledge and Kegan Paul, Ltd., 1966.

Marcuse, Herbert. *An Essay on Liberation.* Boston: Beacon Press, 1969.

———. *One Dimensional Man.* Boston, Mass.: Beacon Press, 1966.

Marx, Karl and Engels, Friedrich, *Manifesto of the Communist Party.* New York: International Publishers, 1932.

Mendel, Gerard. *La Crise de générations.* Paris: Payot, 1969.

Merton, Robert. *Social Theory and Social Structure.* Glencoe, Ill.: The Free Press, 1957.

Miller, Michael and Gilmore, Susan, eds. *Revolution at Berkeley.* New York: Dell Publishing Company, 1965.

Mills, C. Wright. *New Men of Power.* New York: Harcourt, Brace and World Company, 1948.

———. *The Power Elite.* New York: Oxford University Press, 1956.

Musgrove, F. *Youth and Social Order.* London: Routledge and Kegan Paul, Ltd., 1964.

Myrdal, Gunnar. *An American Dilemma.* New York: Harper and Row, 1944.

Newcomb, Theodore. *Personality and Social Change: Attitude Formation in a Student Community.* New York: Holt, Rinehart and Winston, 1943.

———, et al. *Persistence and Change: Bennington College and Its Students after Twenty-Five Years.* New York: John Wiley and Sons, Inc., 1967.

Newfield, Jack. *A Prophetic Minority.* New York: New American

Library 1966.

Oberscholl, Anthony. *Social Conflict and Social Movements.* Englewood Cliffs, N.J.: Prentice Hall, Inc., 1973.

O'Brien, James P. *The Development of the New Left in the United States, 1960-65.* Ph.D. Dissertation, Department of History, University of Wisconsin, 1971.

Oglesby, Carl. *The New Left Reader.* New York: Grove Press, Inc., 1969.

Parkin, Frank. *Middle-Class Radicalism.* New York: Praeger, 1968.

Parsons, Talcott. *The Social System.* Glencoe, Ill.: The Free Press, 1951.

Paulus, George. *A Multivariate Analysis Study of Student Activist Leaders, Student Government Leaders, and Non-Activists.* Ph.D. Dissertation, Michigan State University, 1966.

Peterson, Richard E. *On a Typology of College Students.* Princeton, N.J.: Educational Testing Service, 1965.

———. *The Scope of Organized Student Protest in 1967-1968.* Princeton, N.J.: Educational Testing Service, 1968.

Piaget, Jean, *The Moral Judgment of the Child.* London, England: Routledge and Kegan Paul, Ltd., 1932.

Pinckney, Alphonso. *The Committed: White Activists in the Civil Rights Movement.* Storrs, Conn.: University of Connecticut Press, 1968.

President's Commission on Campus Unrest. *Report of the President's Commission on Campus Unrest.* Washington, D.C.: Government Printing Office, 1970.

Proudfoot, Merill. *Diary of a Sit-In.* Chapel Hill, N.C.: University of North Carolina Press, 1962.

Reich, William. *The Greening of America.* New York: Random House, 1970.

Reisman, David. *Constraint and Variety in American Education.* New York: Doubleday Anchor Books, 1956.

Roszak, Theodore. *The Making of a Counter Culture.* New York: Doubleday Anchor, 1969.

———. *Source: An Anthology of Contemporary Materials Useful for Preserving Sanity While Braving the Great Technological Wilderness.* New York: Harper & Row, 1972.

Roundtree, John E. and Roundtree, Margaret. *The Political Economy of Youth.* Ann Arbor, Mich.: Radical Education Project, 1966.

Rush, Gary B. and Denisoff, R. Serge. *Social and Political Movements.* New York: Appleton-Century-Crofts, 1971.

Sack, Allen. *General Support for Radical Student Politics.* M.A. thesis, Department of Sociology, Penn State University, 1970.

Sanford, Nevitt, ed. *The American College.* New York: John Wiley and Sons, Inc., 1962.

Schumpeter, Joseph. *Capitalism, Socialism and Democracy.* 3d ed. New York: Harper & Row, 1950.

Sears, R. R., Maccoby, E., Levin, H. *Patterns of Child Rearing.* Evanston, Ill.: Row, Peterson and Company, 1957.

Sherif, Carolyn, and Sherif, Muzafer. *Attitude, Ego-Involvement and Change.* New York: John Wiley and Sons, Inc., 1967.

Slater, Philip. *The Pursuit of Loneliness.* Boston, Mass.: Beacon Press, 1970.

Smelser, Neil J. *Theory of Collective Behavior.* New York: The Free Press of Glencoe, 1963.

Students for a Democratic Society, *The Port Huron Statement.* New York: Students for a Democratic Society, 1964.

Teodori, Massimo. *The New Left: A Documentary History.* Indianapolis, Ind.: Bobbs-Merrill, 1969.

Toch, Hans. *The Social Psychology of Social Movements.* New York: The Bobbs-Merrill Company, Inc., 1965.

Turner-Hampton, Charles. *Radical Man.* Cambridge, Mass.: Shenkman Publishing Company, 1970.

von Hoffman, Nicholas. *We Are the People Our Parents Warned Us Against.* Chicago: Quadrangle Books, 1968.

Wallerstein, Immanuel. *University in Turmoil: The Politics of Change.* New York: Atheneum Books, 1969.

Waskow, Arthur. *From Race Riot to Sit-in, 1919 and the 1960's.* Garden City, N.Y.: Doubleday & Co., 1966.

Weber, Max. *The Protestant Ethic and the Spirit of Capitalism.* Translated by Talcott Parsons. New York: Scribner Publishing Company, 1929.

Williamson, E. G. and Cowan, John L. *The American Student's Freedom of Expression.* Minneapolis, Minn.: The University of Minnesota Press, 1966.

Wolff, Robert. *The Ideal of the University.* Boston, Mass.: Beacon Press, 1969.

Yankelovich, Daniel. *The Changing Values on Campus: Political and Personal Attitudes of Today's College Students.* New

York: Washington Square Press, 1972.

Young Americans for Freedom. *Young Americans for Freedom and You.* Washington, D.C.: Young Americans for Freedom, Inc., n. d.

Zinn, Howard, *SNCC: The New Abolitionists.* Boston, Mass.: Beacon Press, 1967.

Articles and Periodicals

Adelwon, J. "What Generation Gap?" *New York Times Magazine* (January 18, 1971).

Adler, Renata. "Radicalism and the Skipped Generation." *Atlantic Monthly* 225 (February 1970).

Altbach, Philip G. "The International Student Movement." *Comparative Educational Review* 8 (October 1964).

————. "Students As Rebels." *Progressive* (May 1969).

Anthony, Richard and Semas, Phil. "The Many Voices of the New Left." *The New Republic* 158 (June 29, 1968).

Astin, Alexander. "Determinants of Student Activism," in Durwand Long and Julian Foster, *Protest!* New York: William Morrow and Co., Inc., 1970.

————. "Personal and Environmental Determinants of Student Activism." *Measurement and Evaluation in Guidance* 1 (Fall 1968).

———— and Bayer, Alan E. "Antecedents and Consequences of Disruptive Campus Protest." *Measurement and Evaluation in Guidance* 4 (April 1971).

Baird, Leonard L. "Who Protests: A Study of Student Activists." In *Protest: Student Activism in America.* New York: William Morrow and Co., Inc., 1970.

Bakke, E. Wight. "Roots and Soil of Student Activism." In S. M. Lipset, ed., *Student Politics.* New York: Basic Books, Inc., 1967.

Bay, Christian. "Political and Apolitical Students: Facts in Search of Theory." *Journal of Social Issues* 23 (July 1967).

Bayer, Allen E. and Astin, Alexander, "Violence and Disruption in the U.S. Campus, 1968-69." *The Edu. Record* 50 (Fall 1969).

————. "Campus Unrest 1970-71: Was It Really All That

Quiet?" *The Edu. Record* 52 (Fall 1971).

Bell, Daniel. "Columbia and the New Left." *The Public Interest* 13 (Fall 1968).

————. "Columbia and the New Left." In *Confrontation: The Student Rebellion and the University.* New York: Basic Books, 1968.

Bengtson, Vern L. "The Generation Gap: A Review and Typology of Social-Psychological Perspectives." In Philip Altback, and Robert Laufer, *Youth and Society* 2, no. 1 (September 1970).

Berger, Peter L. "Between System and Horde." In *Movement and Revolution.* New York: Doubleday, Anchor Books, 1970.

Blau, Peter and Slaughter, Ellen. "Institutional Conditions and Student Demonstrations." Mimeo, Department of Sociology, Columbia University, Fall 1970.

Block, Jeanne H., Haan, Norma, and Smith, M. Brewster. "Activism and Apathy in Contemporary Adolescence." In James F. Adams, *Understanding Adolescence.* Boston, Mass.: Allyn and Bacon, Inc., 1968.

————. "Socialization Correlates of Student Activism." *Journal of Social Issues* 25 (1969).

Blum, Richard. "Epilogue": Students and Drugs." In Richard Blum and Associates, *Students and Drugs: Drugs II.* San Francisco, Calif.: Jossey-Bass, 1969.

Bronfenbrenner, Urie. "The Changing American Child." In E. P. Hollander, and R. G. Hunt, eds. *Current Perspectives in Social Psychology,* 2d ed. New York: Oxford University Press, 1967.

————. "Socialization and Social Class Through Time and Space." *Readings in Social Psychology* New York: Holt, Rinehart and Co., 1958.

Brooks, Peter. "French Student Power." *The New Republic* (June 1, 1968).

Brzezinski, Zbgniew. "Revolution and Counterrevolution (But Not Necessarily About Columbia)." *The New Republic* (June 1, 1968).

Burgess and Hofstetter. "The Student Movement: Ideology and Reality." *Midwest Journal of Political Science* (November 1971).

Chesler, Mark and Schmuck, Richard. "Student Reactions to the Cuban Missile Crisis and Public Dissent." *Public Opinion Quarterly* 2, no. 38 (Fall 1964).

Carson, Robert B. "Youthful Labor Surplus in Disaccumulationist Capitalism." *Soc. Revolution* 2, no. 3 (May/June 1972).

Clark, Burton and Trow, Martin. "College Subcultures." In Leonard Broom, and Phillip Selznick, *Sociology*. 4th ed. New York: Harper and Row, Publishers, 1968.

Clark, Kenneth B. "The Civil Rights Movement: Momentum and Organization." *Daedalus* 98 (Winter 1966).

Clarke, James W. and Egan, Joseph. "Social and Political Dimensions of Campus Protest Activity." *Journal of Politics* 34, no. 2 (May 1971).

Clausen, John A. "Perspectives on Childhood Socialization." In J. A. Clausen, ed., *Socialization and Society*. Boston, Mass.: Little, Brown and Company, 1968.

Cohn-Bendit, Daniel; Duteuil, Jean-Pierre; Gerard, Bertrand; and Granautler, Bernard, "Why Sociologists?" *Nanterre* (March, 1968).

Craig, A. "Egyptian Students." *Middle East Journal* 7 (Summer 1953).

Crozier, Michel. "French Students: A Letter from Nanterre-La Folie." *The Public Interest* 13 (Fall 1968).

Davidson, Carl. "Campaigning on the Campus." SDS Pamphlet, undated.

Donald, David. "Abolitionism." In *Protest, Reform and Revolt*, edited by Joseph Gusfield. New York: John Wiley & Sons, Inc., 1970.

Donner, Frank. "The Theory and Practice of American Political Intelligence." *The New York Review* (April 22, 1971).

Draper, Hal. "The Student Movement of the Thirties: A Political History." In R. J. Simon, ed., *As We Saw the Thirties*. Urbana, Ill.: University of Illinois Press, 1967.

Drucker, A. J. and Remmers, H. H. "Citizenship Attitudes of Purdue Seniors College Graduates and High School Pupils." *J. of Educ. Psychology* 42, no. 4 (1951).

Duberman, Martin. "On Misunderstanding Student Rebels." *Atlantic Monthly* 222 (November 1968), and *Discussion* 222 (December 1963).

Dunlap, Riley. "Radical and Conservative Student Activists: A Comparison of Family Background." *Pacific Sociological Review* 13 (Summer 1970).

Easton, David and Dennis, Jack. "The Child's Image of Government." *The Annals* 361 (September 1965).

———— and Hess, R. D. "The Child's Political World." *Midwest Journal of Political Science* 6 (August 1962).

Edelstein, Alex S. "Since Bennington: Evidence of Change in Student Political Behavior." *Public Opinion Quarterly* 26 (1962).

Eisenstadt, Schmuel N. "Generational Conflict and Intellectual Antinomianism." In Philip G. Altbach and Robert S. Laufer, *The New Pilgrims: Youth Protest in Transition*. New York: David McKay Company, Inc., 1972.

Endleman, Robert. "Oedipal Elements in Student Rebellions." *Psychoanalytic Review* 57 (1970).

Erskine, Hazel. "The Polls: Is the War a Mistake?" *Public Opinion Quarterly* 34 (Spring 1970).

Etzioni, Amitai. "Confessions of a Professor Caught in a Revolution." *The New York Times Magazine* (September 15, 1968).

————. "Mobilization As a Macrosociological Conception." *British Journal of Sociology* 19 (September 1968).

Fishman, Jacob R. and Solomon, Frederick. "Youth and Social Action: An Introduction." *Journal of Social Issues* 20 (July 1964).

Flacks, Richard. "On the New Working Class and Strategies for Social Change." In Philip G. Altbach, and Robert S. Laufer, *The New Pilgrims: Youth Protest in Transition*. New York: David McKay Company, Inc., 1972.

————. "Some Social and Cultural Meanings of Student Revolt: Some Informal Comparative Observations." *Social Problems* 17 (Winter 1970).

————. "Student Activists: Result, Not Revolt." *Psychology Today* 11, no. 1 (October 1967).

————. "The Liberated Generation: Exploration of the Roots of Student Protest." *Journal of Social Issues* 23 (July 1967).

———— and Mankoff, Milton. "Revolt in Santa Barbara and Why They Burned the Bank." *The Nation* 210 (March 23, 1970).

Gales, Kathleen E. "A Campus Revolution." *British Journal of Sociology* 17 (March 1965).

Gergen, Mary and Gergen, Kenneth. "How the War Affects the Campuses." *Change* 3 (January/February 1971).

Geschwender, James A. "Explorations in the Theory of Social Movements and Revolutions." *Social Forces* 48 (December 1968).

Gintis, Herbert. "The New Working Class and Revolutionary Youth." *Socialist Revolution* 1 (May/June 1970).

Glazer, Nathan. "The Jewish Role in Student Activism." *Fortune* 79 (January 1969).

————. " 'Student Power' in Berkeley." In Daniel Bell and Irving Kristol, eds., *Confrontation*. New York: Basic Books, 1968.

Goodman, Paul. "For a Real Experience in Education: Why Our Colleges Are Crippled, How They Might Be Revived." *Harper's* 223 (November 1962), and *Discussion* 226 (January 1963).

Gorz, André. "Capitalism and the Labor Force." *International Socialist Journal* 10 (August 1965).

Gramont, Sanche. "Two Who Bridge the Generational Gap." *The New York Times Magazine* (September 29, 1968).

Greene, Arnold. "The Middle-Class Male Child and Neurosis." in N. W. Bell, and E. P. Vogel, *A Modern Introduction to the Family*. Glencoe, Ill.: The Free Press, 1960.

Greenstein, Fred I. "Personality and Political Socialization: The Theories of Authoritarian and Democratic Character." *The Annals* 261 (September 1965).

Greenstein, Robert. "The Student Revolt in West Germany." *The New Republic* 158 (June 8, 1968).

Gusfield, Joseph R. "Beyond Berkeley: High Noon on Campus." *Trans-Action* 2 (March/April 1965).

————. "Intellectual Character and American Universities." *Journal of General Education* 14 (January 1963).

————. "Mass Society and Extremist Politics." *American Sociological Review* 38 (February 1962).

Haan, Norma; Smith, M. Brewster, and Block, Jeanne. "Moral Reasoning of Young Adults: Political-Social Behavior, Family Background, and Personality Correlates." *Journal of Pers. and Soc. Psych.* 10, no. 3 (1968).

Halle, Louis. "The Student Drive to Destruction." *New Republic* 159 (1969).

Hobbs, A. H. "The SDS Trip: From Vision to Ego Shriek." *The Intercollegiate Review* 5 (Spring 1969).

Hodgkinson, Harold. "Student Protest: An Institutional and National Profile." *Teacher's College Record* 71 (May 1970).

Holtzman, W. H. "Attitudes of College Men Toward Non-Segregation in Texas Schools." *Public Opinion Quarterly* 20 (1965).

Holzner, Burkart. "Institutional Change, Social Stratification and the Direction of Youth Movements." *Journal of Educational Sociology* 36 (October 1962).

Howe, Irving. "The New 'Confrontation Politics' Is a Dangerous Game." *The New York Times Magazine* (October 20, 1968).

Jencks, Christopher. "Is It All Dr. Spock's Fault?" *The New York Times Magazine* (March 3, 1968).

———. "Limits of the New Left." *The New Republic* 157 (October 21, 1967).

Kahn, Roger. "The Collapse of SDS." *Esquire* 454, no. 4 (October 1969).

——— and Bowers, William J. "The Social Context of the Rank-and-File Student Activists: A Test of Four Hypotheses." *Sociology of Education* 43, no. 1 (Winter 1970).

Katz, Joseph and Sanford, Nevitt. "Causes of the Student Revolution." *Saturday Review* 48 (December 18, 1965).

Kauffman, Joseph F. "Youth and the Peace Corps." In Erik H. Erikson, ed., *Youth: Change and Challenge*. New York: Basic Books, Inc., 1963.

Keniston, Kenneth. "Alienation and the Decline of Utopia." In H. M. Ruitenbeek, ed., *Varieties of Modern Theory*. New York: E. P. Dutton and Company, 1963.

———. "A Second Look at the Uncommitted." in *Social Policy* (July/August 1971).

——— and Lerner, Michael, "Campus Characteristics and Campus Unrest." *The American Academy of Political and Social Sciences* (May 1971).

———. "The Faces in the Lecture Room." In Robert S. Morison, ed., *The Contemporary University: U.S.A.* Boston, Mass.: Houghton Mifflin Company, 1966.

————. "The Sources of Student Dissent." *Journal of Social Issues* 23 (July 1967).

————. "You Have to Grow Up in Scarsdale to Know How Bad Things Really Are." *The New York Times Magazine* (April 27, 1969).

Kerr, Clark. "Sections from the Uses of the University." S. M. Lipset, and Sheldon S. Wolin, eds., *The Berkeley Student Revolt*. Garden City, N. Y.: Doubleday Anchor Books, 1965.

————. "The Frantic Race to Remain Contemporary." In Robert S. Morison, ed., *The Contemporary University: USA*. Boston, Mass.: Houghton Mifflin Co., 1966.

Keys, Donald F. "The American Peace Movement." In E. G. McNeil, ed., *The Nature of Human Conflict*. Englewood Cliffs, N.J.: Prentice-Hall, Inc., 1965.

Kirk, Russell. "The University In Revolution." In Gary Weaver and James Weaver, eds., *The University and Revolution*. Englewood Cliffs, N.J.: Prentice Hall 1969.

Kohn, Melvin L. "Social Class and the Exercise of Parental Authority." *American Sociological Review* 24 (June 1959).

————. "Social Class and Parent-Child Relationships: An Interpretation." *American Journal of Sociology* 68 (January 1963).

Kristol, Irving. "A Different Way To Restructure the University." In Daniel Bell and Irving Kristol, eds., *Confrontation*. New York: Basic Books, 1968.

Lane, Robert E. "Fathers and Sons: Foundations of Political Belief." *American Sociological Review* (August 1959).

Lippitt, Ronald. "An Experimental Study of Authoritarian and Democratic Group Atmospheres: Studies in Topological and Vector Psychology," *University of Iowa Studies in Child Welfare* 16, 3 (Iowa City, Iowa, 1940).

Lipset, Seymour M. "American Student Activism." In P. G. Altbach, ed., *Student Politics and Higher Education in the United States: A Select Bibliography*. St. Louis, Mo. and Cambridge, Mass.: United Ministries in Higher Education and Center for International Affairs, Harvard University, 1968.

————. "Students and Politics in Comparative Perspective." *Daedalus* 97 (Winter 1968).

————. "Youth and Politics." In Robert Merton and Robert Nesbit, eds., *Contemporary Social Problems.* New York: Macmillan & Co., The Free Press, 1970.

————. "The Activists: A Profile." In Daniel Bell and Irving Kristol, eds., *Confrontation.* New York: Basic Books, 1969.

————. "Political Sociology." In *Sociology Today.* New York: Basic Books, 1960.

———— and Altbach, Philip. "Student Politics and Higher Education in the United States." In S. M. Lipset, *Student Politics.* New York: Basic Books, 1967.

———— and Ladd, Everett Carll, Jr. "The Political Future of Activist Generations." In Philip G. Altbach, and Robert S. Laufer, *The New Pilgrims: Youth Protest in Transition.* New York: David McKay Company, Inc., 1972.

Long, Durward and Foster, Julian. "Dynamics of Institutional Response." In Durward Long and Julian Foster, *Protest: Student Activism in America.* New York: William Morrow Company, 1970.

————. "Levels of Protest." In Durward Long, and Julian Foster, *Protest: Student Activism in America.* New York: William Morrow Company, 1970.

Lubell, Samuel. "That Generation Gap." *The Public Interest* (Fall 1968). Reprinted in Daniel Bell, *Confrontation: The Student Rebellion and the Universities.*

Lynd, Staughton and Yancy, Roberta. "Southern Negro Students: The College and the Movement." *Dissent* 11 (Winter 1964).

Mankoff, Milton and Flacks, Richard. "The Changing Social Base of the American Student Movement: Its Meaning and Implications." *The Annals of the American Academy of Political and Social Science* 395 (May 1971).

Matza, David. "Subterranean Traditions of Youth." *The Annals* 338 (November 1961).

Mauss, Armand L. "The Lost Promise of Reconciliation: New Left vs Old Left." *The Journal of Social Issues* 27, no. 1 (1971).

Middleton, Russell and Putney, Snell. "Student Rebellion Against Parental Political Beliefs." *Social Forces* 41 (May 1963).

Mills, C. Wright. "Letter to the New Left." *New Left Review* (September/October 1960).

———. "On the New Left." *Studies on the Left* 11 (1961).

———. "The New Left." In I. L. Horowitz, ed., *Power, Politics and People.* New York: Ballantine Books, Inc., 1963.

Morgan, William R. "Faculty Mediation in Campus Conflict." In Durward Long and Julian Foster, eds., *Protest.* New York: William Morrow and Company, Inc., 1970.

McCormick, Thelma H. "The Motivation of Radicals." In R. H. Turner, and L. M. Killian, *Collective Behavior.* Englewood Cliffs, N.J.: Prentice-Hall, Inc., 1957.

McEvoy, J. and Miller, A., " 'On Strike—Shut It Down': The Crisis at San Francisco State College." *Transaction* 6 (March 1969).

McIntyre, William R. "Students' Movement." *Editorial Research Reports* 11 (December 1957).

Nasatir, David. "A Note on Contextual Effects and the Political Orientation of University Students." *American Sociological Review* 23 (April 1968).

Newfield, Jack. "SDS: From Port Huron to La Chinoise." *Evergreen* (December 1969).

Nogee, P. and Levin, M. B. "Some Determinants of Political Attitudes Among College Voters." *Public Opinion Quarterly* 22 (Winter 1958).

O'Brien, James P. "The Development of the New Left." In P. G. Altbach, and R. S. Laufer, eds., *The New Pilgrims.* New York: David McKay Company, Inc., 1973.

———. "The New Left's Early Years." *Radical America* 11 (May/June 1968).

Orum, Anthony and Orum, Amy. "The Class and Status Bases of Negro Student Protest." *Social Science* 2, no. 49 (December 1968).

Pace, Robert. "What Kind of Citizens Do College Students Become?" *Journal of General Education* 3 (April 1949).

Parsons, Talcott. "The Academic System: A Sociologist's View." In Daniel Bell and Irving Kristol, eds., *Confrontation.* New York: Basic Books, 1968.

Peterson, Richard E. "The Student Left in American Higher Education." *Daedalus* 97 (Winter 1968).

Petras, James. "Politics of Democracy: The Free Speech Movement." *Phi Delta Kappan* 46 (March 1965).

—— and Shute, Michael. "Berkeley; '65," *Partisan Review* 32 (Spring 1965).

Piercy, Marge. "The Grand Coolie Dam." In Robin Morgan, ed., *Sisterhood Is Powerful*. New York: Vintage Books, 1970.

Pinard, Maurice. "Mass Society and Political Movements: A New Formulation." *American Journal of Sociology* 73 (May 1968).

Plimpton, Calvin. "The Amherst College Statement." *New Republic* (May 17, 1969).

Rader, Dotson. "More About Columbia." *New Republic* (June 8, 1968).

Raskin, A. H. "Yesterday's Berkeley Rebel Says: 'I'm Just Here To Study.'" *The New York Times Magazine* (January 30, 1966).

Rudd, Mark. "Symbols of the Revolution." In Jerry L. Avorn, *Up Against the Wall: A History of the Columbia Crisis*. New York: Atheneum Books, 1968.

Rush, Gary B. "Status Consistency and Right-Wing Extremism." *American Sociological Review* 32 (February 1967).

Sampson, Edward E. "Student Activism and the Decade of Protest." *Journal of Social Issues* 23 (July 1967).

Schiff, Lawrence F. "Dynamic Young Fogies—Rebels on the Right." *Transaction* 4 (November 1966).

Scott, Joseph and El-Assal, Mohammed. "Multiversity, University Size, University Quality and Student Protest." *American Social Review* 43, no. 5 (October 1969).

Selvin, Hannan and Hagstrom, Warren O. "Determinants of Support for Civil Liberties." In S. M. Lipset and S. S. Wolin, eds., *The Berkeley Student Revolt*. Garden City, N.J.: Doubleday and Company, Inc., 1965.

——. "The Obedient Rebels: A Study of College Conversation to Conservatism." *Journal of Social Issues* 20, no. 4 (October 1964).

Sigel, Roberta. "Assumptions about the Learning of Political Values." *The Annals* 361 (September 1965).

Sklar, Martin. "On the Proletarian Revolution and the end of Political Economic Society. *Rad. Am.* 3, no. 3 (May/June 1970).

Smelser, Neil J. "Personality and Explanation of Political

Phenomena at the Social-System Level." *Journal of Social Issues* 24 (November 1968).

Soares, Glaucio. "The Active Few: Student Ideology and Participation." In S. M. Lipset, ed., *Student Politics*. New York: Basic Books, Inc., 1967.

Solomon, Fredric and Fishman, Jacob. "Perspectives on the Student Sit-In Movement." *American Journal of Ortho-Psychiatry* 33 (October 1963).

————. "Youth and Peace: A Psychological Study of Student Peace Demonstrators in Washington, D.C." *Journal of Social Issues* 23, no. 3 (1967).

Somers, Robert H. "The Mainsprings of the Rebellion: A Survey of Berkeley Students in November 1964." In S. M. Lipset, and S. S. Wolin, eds., *The Berkeley Student Revolt*. Garden City, N.Y.: Doubleday and Company, Inc., 1965.

Spiegel, John. "Campus Conflict and Professional Ego." *Transaction* 6 (Oct. 1969).

Stedman-Jones, Gareth. "The Meaning of the Student Revolt." In *Student Power*. Middlesex, England: Penguin Books Ltd., 1969.

Steinberg, David. "Black Power on Black Campuses." *Commonwealth* 88 (April 19, 1968).

Taber, Robert A. "From Protest to Radicalism: An Appraisal of the Student Movement." In *The New Left: An Anthology*. Boston, Mass.: Beacon Press, 1966.

Touraine, Alain. "Naissance d'un mouvement etudiant." *Le Monde* (March 7-8, 1968).

Trent, James W. and Craise, Judith L., "Commitment and Conformity in the American College." *Journal of Social Issues* 23, no. 3 (1967).

Trilling, Diana, "On the Steps of Low Liberty," *Commentary* 46 (Nov. 1968).

Trimberger, Ellen Kay. "Columbia: The Dynamics of Student Revolution." In Howard S. Becker, *Campus Power Struggle*. New York: Aldine Publishing Company, 1970.

————. "Why a Rebellion at Columbia Was Inevitable." *Transaction* 5 (Summer 1968).

Watts, William and Whittaker, David. "Free Speech Advocates at Berkeley." *Journal of Applied Behavioral Science* 2 (January 1966).

Watts, W. A. and Whittaker, D. "Some Socio-Psychological Differences between Highly-Committed Members of the Free Speech Movement and the Student Population at Berkeley." *Journal of Applied Behavioral Science* 11 (April-May-June 1966).

Watts, William A.; Lynch, Steve; and Whittaker, David. "Alienation and Activism in Today's College-Age Youth." *Journal of Couns. Psychology* 16 no. 1 (1969).

Weber, Max. "Bureaucracy." In Hans Gerth and C. Wright Mills, eds., *From Max Weber: Essays in Sociology*. New York: Oxford University Press, 1946.

Webster, H.; Freeman, M.; and Heist, P. "Personality Changes in College Students." *The American College*. New York: John Wiley & Sons, Inc., N. Sanford, 1962.

Westby, David L. and Braungart, Richard G. "The Alienation of Generations and Status Politics: Alternative Explanations of Student Political Activism." In Roberta Sigel, ed., *Learning About Politics: Studies in Political Socialization*. New York: Random House, Inc., 1970.

————. "Class and Politics in the Family Backgrounds of Student Political Activists." *American Sociological Review* 31 (October 1966).

————. "Into Utopia: The History of the Future as Written by Student Political Activists, Left and Right." In Durward Long, and Julian Foster, eds., *Students in Revolt*. New York: William Morrow and Company, 1970.

Wylie, Laurence. "Youth in France and the United States." In Erik H. Erikson, ed., *Youth: Change and Challenge*. New York: Basic Books, Inc., 1963.

Zolo, Daniel. "Student Power, Italian Style." *The New Republic* 158 (April 27, 1968).

NAME INDEX

Abel, Theodore, 31n
Adorno, Theodore, 78
Agnew, Spiro, 264
Almond, Gabriel, 107n
Altback, Philip, 37n, 106, 106n, 118n, 199n, 247n
Arendt, Hanna, 105
Aries, Phillippe, 195
Astin, Alexander, 94, 96, 106, 107, 108, 112, 119, 130, 135n, 137, 150, 215
Avorn, Jerry L., 148n

Baird, Leonard L., 63, 65
Bakke, E. Wight, 194
Barron, Frank, 63, 65, 73
Baudelaire, 246
Bayer, Alan E., 94, 96, 106, 107, 130, 137, 150
Becker, Howard S., 138n
Bell, Daniel, 46n, 47n, 142-43, 149, 210, 211n, 212n, 213, 214n, 215n, 216, 219n
Bell, N. W., 53n
Berger, Peter, 79
Blackburn, Robin, 227n
Blau, Peter, 93, 95, 100, 106, 109
Block, Jeanne, 51, 59n, 67, 69(Tables 2 and 3), 71-72
Blum, Richard, 80n
Bowers, William J., 42n, 94-95, 96, 123n
Brackett, Joan, 94n
Braungart, Richard G., 41, 42, 44 (Table 1), 45, 51, 55, 57, 60, 64n, 81n, 115, 116(Table 6), 120n, 196
Bronfenbrenner, Urie, 53
Brzezinski, Zbigniew, 215n
Buchanan, Garth, 94n
Bunzel, John, 210
Byron, Lord, 247

Carmichael, Stokeley, 160
Carson, Robert B., 259n
Centers, Richard, 193
Chesler, Mark, 71n, 77
Clarke, James W., 174, 175
Cockburn, Alexander, 227n
Cohan, John, 98n
Cohn-Bendit, Daniel, 227n
Coleman, James, 107n
Comte, August, 246
Conrad, Joseph, 194
Coser, Lewis, 185
Coudry, James, 84n
Cowan, Paul, 181n

285

SUBJECT INDEX